MW01196733

# MIND YOUR BRAIN

OPTIMIZING YOUR LIFE AND HEALTH
USING ESSENTIAL OILS

# MIND YOUR BRAIN

OPTIMIZING YOUR LIFE AND HEALTH USING ESSENTIAL OILS

## ELIZABETH ERICKSON

pegasus
MEDIA

**MIND YOUR BRAIN:**
**OPTIMIZING YOUR LIFE AND HEALTH USING ESSENTIAL OILS**

Copyright © 2017 by Elizabeth Erickson

All rights reserved. No portion of this book, except for the use of brief quotations in a book review, scholarly journal, or educational setting, may be reproduced, stored in a retrieval system, or transmitted in any form or by any means—electronic, mechanical, photocopying, recording, or otherwise—without written permission of the publisher. For information contact Pegasus Media.

ISBN: 978-0-9995692-0-7

Pegasus Media LLC
1408 N. Riverfront Blvd., Suite 164
Dallas, Texas 75206
www.PegasusMedia.us
(682) 463-9693

Editors: Paul Risse and Amanda Workman
Brand Designer: Audrey Elise
Cover Design: Chris Alexander
Photography: JerSean Golatt

Printed in the United States of America.

Library of Congress Cataloging-in-Publication Data is available.

These statements have not been evaluated by the Food and Drug Administration. This product or any discussed herein, including all contents of this book, are not intended to diagnose, treat, cure, or prevent any disease. This is for educational use only and you should consult a licensed healthcare professional before starting or changing any supplement, dietary, or exercise program, especially if you are pregnant or have any preexisting injuries, medical, or psychological conditions.

## To My Family

(both biological and otherwise...
you know who you are).

**Thank you for wading through deep water with me and being patient in my process. I couldn't have done this, or a lot of other life, without you.**

**Cheers to a new way of living and loving.**

**-Liz**

# TABLE OF CONTENTS

# INTRODUCTION

I've known for a long time I was passionate about understanding the mind and how it works. I was raised by a mom who was a psych nurse just out of college and my dad was a philosophy student. So, you can imagine that growing up in their home with five other equally precocious siblings, there was a great appreciation for the mind and a natural curiosity for how it worked. When I began pursuing my undergraduate degree in Journalism, I did it based on my skills, but I knew deep down that I was supposed to help build solutions for people to overcome trauma. I didn't know exactly how to do that, but I was ready for just about any adventure that was to come. Or, so I thought.

While in my junior year of college, I began to have panic attacks. I distinctly remember it started early one morning before a photography class. I felt strange sensations in my arms and legs, like pins and needles. I had no grid for what was happening to my body: shallow breathing, racing thoughts, cold sweats, and limpness all over. Soon, I realized I was having a panic attack. They didn't stop that morning. In fact, they began to increase in intensity and frequency.

Shortly after I graduated college, I began to have feelings of depression as I learned my "new normal". I was running my own company, undergoing major life transition moving abroad and then back to Dallas, and figuring out what to do with my life. I didn't know that my gut, which had begun acting up a year or so prior, was directly involved in perpetuating the emotions that themselves needed support and balancing.

As I attempted to sort out my life, my feelings didn't seem to improve. One day, I arrived at my parents' home and my mom handed me a couple of bottles of essential oil she had just been introduced to: peppermint and lavender. My eyes rolled and I believe I told her aloud cynically that this would last "about six months before the fad wears off and you abandon yet another product." To me, it was like anything else she had brought home and used for a brief time before forgetting about it.

I didn't pay the bottles of oil much thought at all until a few months later when my older sister, who is typically the greater cynic than I, began chasing people around the house asking if they had certain ailments before rubbing peppermint essential oil on them. It was then I realized there was something there. Typically, I was the one who was the "early adopter" so if my sister could get on board, surely there was something to these essential oils! I needed to get on really fast or I'd miss out. I tried two bottles of oil, a blend for balancing emotions and a blend for digestion. The emotional blend I used one time in the middle of a panic attack and it stopped immediately! Needless to say, I was convinced. The same was true of the digestive blend—I saw equally powerful effects on my body as I found immediate relief to bloating and indigestion when applied topically.

My collection of essential oils grew steadily as I experimented with different things. I began noticing changes in my body and emotions and soon the panic attacks stopped altogether. During this same time, I made some slight dietary changes and also began seeing a counselor and pursuing the inner healing I desperately needed. I believe it is because of my multi-pronged approach that I received the healing. I can't point to any particular thing that was a silver bullet.

Each tool in my healing toolbox was beneficial and each played a part in restoring my spirit, soul, and body to wholeness. It's because of my own path that I have a value and appreciation for everyone's unique healing journey. Formulas are great so long as they adapt to the needs of the individual.

After experiencing essential oils, I knew first-hand that they worked powerfully, but I wasn't satisfied with the cliché answers as to why. So, I began to do more research. I read, attended classes, listened to countless experienced individuals, and kept experimenting on my own.

Not long after discovering essential oils, I began my graduate studies at the University of Texas at Dallas in Applied Cognition and Neuroscience. I loved every single moment of my grad school experience. I loved that I could learn not just the psychological theories of the mind, but I could be in the thick of discovering the "how and why" behind the structure and function of the brain. It didn't take me long after entering graduate school to begin asking questions to my professors and the researchers around me. I'd ask them about their experience with essential oils, what they were finding in the research, and how essential oils might be able to benefit and be developed for treatments for the mind and the brain. It also didn't take me very long after asking to realize that they had *no idea* what I was talking about. Most of them either dis-missed it as "snake oil" or they wanted to see the quantitative research. Very few had any experience with essential oils at all. I began to see a clear disconnect between the essential oil and naturally-minded community that was having amazing breakthroughs, and the medical community full of researchers, doctors, and brilliant scientists who were also finding solutions for people, but were still missing keys which could revolutionize how they treated patients. I was in the midst of both communities and I loved them equally. So, I made it my mission to do my own research and help bridge the gap between the natural health community and the allopathic (Western) model of medicine. That's where this book was born.

So, who is *Mind Your Brain* for? Well, if you are holding this book, there's a high percentage chance that you fall into one of those two people groups. Either you're someone open to or interested in natural medicine and wellness, or you're in the medical or scientific community and you're interested in some quantitative data and research. Whomever you are, I'm glad you are here!

With that said, I'm aware that some of you reading this book are interested in data and others in stories. I'm not a believer in the "left brained is all analytical and right brained is all creative" mantra. That is a nice idea, but it's pop psychology and is a bit too simplistic. However, I recognize that there are those who approach topics from an analytical viewpoint and others are more comfortable with abstract ideas and even the "supernatural" or unexplainable phenomena. Strangely, I'm in the camp with both of you. I am highly analytical (hence why there is so much data in this book because I wasn't content to take someone else's word about essential oils), but I'm also one who chooses to jump head first into new ideas and experiment because great things come from taking risks on new ideas.

If you consider yourself more analytical, or if you are more comfortable with the abstract and therefore probably will be skimming this book and jumping straight to the back of the chapters for the summaries, (Yes, I know how some of you are), I want you to please approach this book as both an orthodoxy *and* an orthopraxy. Orthodoxy is often used in religion to describe the concept of "correct belief". It encompasses the doctrine or creeds that house the religion. In contrast, orthopraxy means "correct practice," and the emphasis is on right belief, practices, and rituals regarding the faith.

I would venture to guess that those who are analytical would approach this book as your "orthodoxy" or bible that proves the data. Others will see this as a vehicle for their "orthopraxy," informing their practice of essential oils. This is designed to be a *"both/and"* book. Use the data and feel free to venture out. Don't get bound by all of the questions that haven't been answered by the "doctrine" or data. Remember there are practical applications and rituals you can implement from the data. But for those who have been experimenting and practicing orthopraxy in their healing journeys thus far, here is some doctrine to give you a foundation. You'll find a lot of "both/and" information in this book. In fact, orthodoxy versus orthopraxy aren't at war with each other any more than structure is at war with function. One builds upon another and unless we value both for their uniqueness and contribution, we won't be able to live out the vibrancy in our healing as much as we could if we embraced the tension of the both/and.

I'd like to say that this book is for anyone and everyone, and yes that's true, but this book is designed to be a bridge. This is meant as a resource for you to come and discover knowledge and apply it in your own sphere, wherever that may be. *Mind Your Brain* is designed to bring quantifiable data from the research community together with crystallized knowledge in an accessible form to explain how and why essential oils work to affect the structure and function of the brain and mind as well as give a framework for the process of inner healing.

This book isn't just for you. My goal is that you read and absorb the information and then translate it to the people and communities around you in ways that make sense to them. If you are a doctor, show it to your patients. If you're a researcher, find new solutions. If you're an educator, make this practical to teach others. Please do not consume this book and do nothing with it. Your personal health education is wonderful and necessary, but I want this to benefit more than just you and I. So, take the information and share it how you will.

As soon as graduate school started, the first week of neuroanatomy, my professor (a clinical researcher in her own right) stood at the head of the class and made a strong pronouncement.

"If you're feeling intimidated as we embark on studying the brain, don't be," she said firmly. "Researchers have found that the brain is as unknown as the universe. We know about as much about the brain right now as we do about the galaxies."

I breathed a sigh of relief then and I still do today. I'd encourage you to take a deep breath too. We don't know it all. It should come as a relief. I also say that to caution you. If you're looking for a "one stop shop" guide to inform you about the brain or how to cure or treat a specific condition, this is not the place. And I don't know that you're going to find it anywhere else either. The brain (and our bodies) is hugely complex and we're continually learning.

At the end of each chapter, you can find a chapter summary entitled, "In Other Words..." if you don't want to embark on the whole chapter, but would rather hit the highlights. The appendices also have research studies and more information to further your personal study. With that said, I encourage you not just to skip ahead. You are free to read this book non-linearly (i.e. jump around at your leisure) if you need and come back to the headier parts later for indepth study. There's freedom to do what works for you. My suggestion is to take the time to read through the book with the intention of gaining an understanding and appreciation for the structure and function of your brain. If you do, then when you approach the "orthopraxy" of applying essential oils and natural substances, you'll be primed and ready with a framework to guide you.

# The Principle of "Yes, And..."

Recently, I started taking an improv class with a friend. We thought it would just be a fun activity, but I soon began to realize it was nothing short of therapy for me. It's pretty much adult playtime. In just the first week of my improv class, I learned a key that has proved to be life-changing. The instructor said simply: "There are no wrong answers here." Allow me explain what that means.

When you start a scene in improv, the pair (or group) of people are given the same prompt. It can be one word, like "balloon". Each person then thinks of something related to that prompt word and that is how they begin their scene. No words are exchanged between the members of the scene before you begin, so you have no idea what your partner(s) is thinking when the scene commences. From the cue of "balloon", I might start the scene thinking of a child's birthday party and my partner, a hot air balloon. When the scene starts, you and your partner(s) just go. One person starts with a line and the other person merely responds to that line and initiates a new piece of information. You tag team in this fashion, constructing a scene completely from your collective imagination using nothing but a single-word prompt. It could make for a messy scene if you were to approach it in doubt or are worried about whether you're going to "get it wrong". But there is no "wrong answer" here. You're simply listening to the last thing the person said and choosing to say, "yes, and..." and build with new information. There are no wrong turns because you're constructing the reality as you go. It's freeing, isn't it?

That's the approach I want you to take with your healing journey. There are *no* wrong answers here. If you remove fear, then all you're left with are potential variables and they're all weighted pretty equally—they're all weighted on your ability to choose. Take the data that you currently have about your wellness, choose to say "yes, and..." and add a new piece of the puzzle. You can't mess this up. And I guarantee you, if you will take this approach, life is going to look a lot more fun and free.

**Chapter One**

# ECOSYSTEMS: PNEUMA + PSYCHE + SOMA

My grandfather was a farmer his entire life. "Grandpa Cain," we'd call him. As a child, I remember, standing at the edge of the timber next to him and together we'd look upon his vast fields. In my innocence, it seemed like they went on for days. Even as young girl, I recall asking him every visit about the process he underwent for the particular crop that year. Every few years he would rotate crops and would explain to me why. "This year the soil needed more nitrogen," he'd say in his gentle and matter of fact way. In a couple years, it needed more phosphorus. I learned the constituents of the soil were key. If you continually planted one crop, the soil would be blanched and cause chlorosis. The result was an inability to grow anything for a few years. Your options were then to introduce nutrients into the soil from fertilizer or you'd have to let the land rest before you could plant something else. If you rotated the crops, you could avoid stripping the soil of the nutrients.

In just a few words, my sweet, soft-spoken Grandpa Cain would tell about the conditions that year: how much rainfall had come; how the sunlight was affecting the plants; whether or not there had been a blight. Some years, the crop was food to eat, distribute, and sell, and some years it was plants for healing the body.

As we approach talking about the brain and the mind, I want us to discuss from the context of an ecosystem. The essential oils that we're using to benefit our minds and brains are formed in an ecosystem. Some plants are for food and some plants are for healing, but all plants grow in a complex environment. The soil conditions affect the plants, as does the weather and interactions from other living creatures like animals, plants, and humans. It doesn't matter if it's a seed in a greenhouse, a field ready for reaping, or a giant redwood in the forest, every plant lives in a biodynamic environment. There are any number of things that could affect the plant on any given day, in any given year, of its life cycle. Similarly, what affects the plant one day may be different from the variables that affect it the next day. There might be cloud cover that protects the plant from getting scorched by the sun. Another day, the plant needs the sunlight in order to nurture the development of chlorophyll. Sometimes the soil composition needs altering and another day the roots have to go deeper in order to sustain life by gaining access to the deep water source. Plants can be affected by drought and at other times be susceptible to root rot from too much moisture.

The beautiful thing about a plant's life is that it's highly dynamic, resilient, and responds to its environment. There's a beauty in the universe in how it adapts and how it finds strength in its resiliency. We humans are created in the same way. We're adaptable. We're resilient. We're much stronger than we think we are.

Like a plant, we live in a biodynamic environment. Many things affect us—positive things like: nutrients that we feed our bodies, healthy relationships that cause us to flourish, natural resources like sunlight and water, and plants. But, negative things can affect our biosphere and ecosystem as well: stress, trauma, broken relationships, lack of nurture and care. Each variable affects the makeup of who we are. Often the expression of what we see has to do with the environment we're rooted in. Just like a plant can have a good yield one year and a negative yield the next year, the plant's expression, yield, or function is directly correlated to the conditions it was in that particular year. The greater the negative input, the greater the negative expression. The more positive the input, the more positive the expression. The same is true as we approach talking about the mind and the brain.

## Pneuma, Psyche, Soma

The study of the mind, began in the late nineteenth century. The movement is credited to one of the early fathers of the discipline: Wilhelm Wundt, a German philosopher, professor, and physician who worked in Leipzig, Germany between 1832 and 1920. "**Psychology**," as he called it, was distinctly different than **philosophy** or **physiology**, in that it studied mental processes. Wundt's main methodology was that of introspection, which in his case, consisted of carefully trained observers who conducted systematic analysis on their own sensations and reported them as objectively as possible. This technique is largely considered subjective by modern-day psychologists.

In a similar vein of research, Carl Jung and Sigmund Freud, strongly influenced the field of psychology by introducing their processes of psychoanalysis. Many of their theories involved unobservable conditions such as "id," "ego," or "superego"—things in the **subconscious mind** versus the **conscious mind**. These concepts have strongly influenced, not only psychological theory, but popular culture and remain as terms in our common, everyday language.

During the first half of the twentieth century, the theory of "**Behaviorism**" was a leading perspective regarding the mind in the United States. The approach was championed by B. F. Skinner and other psychologists. For many years, the only inferences they made about the expressions of the mind were those that could be observed through behavior. The group of Behaviorists argued that researchers could not objectively study mental processes and they rejected the concept of introspection entirely. Though the psychological community has not adopted all of the theories from the Behaviorist movement, their practices have greatly influenced modern cognitive science.

While Behaviorism was taking rise in the United States, the theory of Gestalt psychology was growing in popularity in Europe. **Gestalt** (pronounced "gehshtahlt") psychology contends that humans have the basic desire and tendency to organize details into a whole that can be readily processed. This is where we derive the phrase, "the sum is greater than the parts." These scientists valued the unity of multiple psychological phenomena.

The emergence of modern **cognitive psychology** arose in the late 1950s, and with it came a specific interest in studying not just the subconscious/introspection, but also the mind. Instead of just examining behavior, scientists began to observe key aspects of cognition including linguistics, memory, and the development of the mind. As technology has improved, more and more theories are either being disproved or quantified. Thus, the field of psychology is now paired with neuroscience and often known as "cognitive psychology." It covers many facets of research as we move into an age of unprecedented discovery.

When studying the mind and the brain in the 21st century, there are multiple streams: **neurology** (the study of the physical nervous system), **psychology** (the science of behavior and the mind), and **cognitive neuroscience** (the study of the biological processes and aspects that underlie cognition). My particular area of study is applied cognition and neuroscience. Therefore, I am interested not only in the theoretical (as is often the case in traditional psychology), or in the strictly medical (as in neurology), but rather a quasi-combination that examines how the structure of the brain and nervous system supports and affects the cognitive processes such as memory, attention, emotional regulation, and cognition.

There are a lot of conditions that affect the mind and the brain. Some of these things are unrecognizable or defy our conscious mind; they may live in our spirits or below the part of our brain that gives language to our conscious or rational thoughts. Alternatively, some things that affect our behavior can be structural issues. Once again, using the analogy of a plant, the soil conditions might not be right or the seed of the plant had a genetic mutation. We'll talk more about this later.

Sometimes, that which affects our behavior—the things we show to the outside world or ourselves—may actually need some retraining. When growing a little sapling, often farmers will attach the sapling to a rod in order to correct the behavior so that the growth pattern of the plant will be straight, tall, and strong. If you don't attach a weak plant to something, it will only grow so large. In fact, it will actually stop growing without assistance in order to preserve itself from perishing. Once the plant can support itself, the support is removed and the plant can continue to grow correctly in the direction it's been encouraged in. We too, have a natural bent that has to be corrected or need extra support if we're going to grow to our full potential. The connections in understanding the ecosystem of plant life, including the plants where we get our essential oils, and those we use regarding the brain and the mind are too many to number. As we talk about the brain and the mind, I ask you to remember that you live in an ecosystem.

It's true of human nature that anytime we begin to make changes and initially don't see progress, we want to abandon the venture and move on to something else that feels more productive. In your healing journeys, like mine, you probably have experienced this a time or two, where you wanted to make a change to your physical or emotional ecosystem and felt discouraged. Maybe you wanted to lose weight or alleviate a specific condition or behavior. Without seeing the progress you expect, it's easy to feel the urge to give up. Maybe you feel like the little plant who has been beaten down year after year and you're struggling just to find refreshment or bask in the sunlight. Maybe you feel like you've been choked with not much fight left in you. Maybe you can't get the nutrients you need and it's like you're missing just one key ingredient in order to be healthy again. I hear you. It can become really tiring waiting and working to achieve vitality. My goal in this book is to remind you that there is hope that change CAN and WILL happen.

At the outset, I want to lay framework that is going to give context to how we're going to talk about "minding our brains." Many people come to me wanting answers to specific conditions. It is wonderful to search out specific answers for the things that ail or pain us, but if we miss the nature of our biodynamic selves, it would be no better than a farmer who only manipulates one variable and prays the plant will thrive. Likewise, with our bodies and minds, if we just manipulate one variable or apply an essential oil or particular therapy method without examining the entire ecosystem, it's likely we won't get the full benefit available to us. It would be selling ourselves short of full healing being manifested in our lives, if we fail to look at our lives holistically.

We're going to talk a lot from the structure and function of the brain and mind, but before we even get there, let's talk about the context of a theoretical model named "Pneuma, Psyche, Soma". *Pneuma*, *Psyche*, *Soma*, are the Greek words for spirit, soul, and body. This model argues that you are a spirit, you have a soul, and you live in a body and are designed to flow in that order: spirit, soul, and body. However, for most people, instead of the expressions of their function flowing in that order like a stream, they live the reverse out of their body's sensations and perceptions, which then forms cognitive structures in their soul based on the input, and the human spirit is regarded little, if at all.

Our human spirit is the primary place we are designed to live. The soul (mind, will, and emotions) are to be yielded to the spirit. The body works under the direction of the spirit and soul. Sadly, however, this is not how most of us were trained. In our Western culture (primarily), because the spirit has been so disconnected from the realities of our souls and bodies, the functions of the soul and body (i.e. cognitions, memories, emotions, and the behaviors that follow through the body) are the only considerations.

Many people are comfortable with nurturing their bodies. They'll change nutritional habits, exercise, take supplements, and use essential oils. These things all affect the body, and to a certain extent, the soul of the person, but many people don't actually recognize that our human spirit is the foundation from which all of this stems. If we're only addressing the body and issues in the mind without addressing the conditions of our spirit, there's only so much healing that will be had.

This spirit, soul, body model might be a paradigm shift for you. If so, let me assure you that this is not a new model. In fact, it's one that has been seen throughout history and still appears in sects of modern society. However, by and large, there was a fragmentation between the concept of "spirit", "soul," and "body" being integrated in the post-Reformation age, at the time of Descartes around the 17th century.

## A Brief History of the Model

To the Greek philosophers, the concept of the human brain followed that of ancient Egyptian thought. The great debate between Plato and his pupil Aristotle was where the brain (or its functions) sat in the cosmos. Plato contended in his dialogue, *Timaeus*, that the "soul" of a person was placed there by the gods and existed in the gut, and the brain was at the apex of the spiritual anatomy. Aristotle disagreed. He became the world's first biologist, dissecting everything from sea urchins to elephants in an attempt to quantify his view of the soul. His philosophy conjectured that the soul was the form of living things and it encompassed everything that creature did to stay alive. He placed the physical heart at the center of the model of a "rational soul" since he correlated the amount of heat produced by the blood as the indicator of intelligence—the warmer the creature, the more intelligence it possessed.

Multiple other philosophers challenged and modified opinions including Galen, a young doctor who traveled from Turkey to Alexandria in 150 A.D. He was a doctor to gladiators, but couldn't bring himself to examine human cadavers. He formulated his theories on emotion by synthesizing the theories of Plato and Aristotle with the medical knowledge of Hippocrates and his personal observations. Galen believed that food and breath once consumed transformed into flesh and spirit with a soul-like power that carried purification to the body. Through his theories, Galen believed he had found more than a way to heal people; he had developed the philosophy of a soul.

According to Zimmer, "He [Galen] declared he had found the physical underpinnings of Plato's trio of souls—the vegetative soul of the liver, responsible for pleasure and desires, the vital soul of the heart, which produced passions and courage, and the rational soul of the head."[1]

Over the next century or so, as technology improved, the theoretical models morphed. The greater the technology to research the human figure, the more information was gathered and new theories developed. Much of the Western view of the brain and its relation to the soul and spirit was birthed out of the Greek philosophers' contentions, as can be evidenced by much of the Renaissance movement. It wasn't until the 17th century that a monumental shift happened, forcing a new way of thinking. It was a young man by the name of René Descartes, a French philosopher and mathematician, who historians believe ushered in the thinking of our modern age in relation to faith and science.

"In his reaction to the religious wars and the resulting turmoil that spread across Europe for most of his adult life, Descartes formulated the concepts of rationalism and the necessity of visible proof that were to become the founding principles of modern science. In that era, emotions seemed a thing of magic, fleeting and undefinable in the framework of the science of the day. In Descartes's orderly division of the world into rational and irrational—provable and unprovable—

emotions and their relationship to health and disease clearly fell into the latter domain. And there they remained until scientific tools powerful enough to challenge the categorization could rescue them."[2]

It was Descartes, who not only conjectured about the brain, body and soul, but also the natural world, who began to theorize about the matter of the universe. (Note: we derive the mathematical graph of "Cartesian coordinates" from Descartes). Between 1629 and 1633, Descartes wrote his book, *The World*, in which he anchored his work in the metaphysical world. He then began to base his Catholic faith in the tenants of science, researching and publishing a short book, *Discourse on Method* in 1637.

Descartes believed that the entire universe depended on the idea of soul for its survival. He summed up this reality in his famous motto, *Cogito, ergo sum*, or "I think, therefore I am." He felt strongly that the foundation of a perfect soul [God] was the basis for the function of reality seen in the visible world.

"From those words [*Cogito, ergo sum*] flowed a security that would bring him back to the natural world, and even the most suspicious priest would be carried along by the waves. Any idea as clear and distinct as the Cogito must also be true. Descartes's mind existed beyond a doubt, and it could imagine perfection. Perfection could not be imagined without its existing, he argued, because a cause could not be any less than its effect. Therefore, God exists. And by God's very nature, He would not create an elaborate deception for Descartes. 'He has not permitted any falsity to exist in my opinion which He as not likewise given me the faculty of correcting,' he wrote. God had created the universe and the laws that governed it, and He had stamped those laws on our minds. Here was a divine guarantee that if a person followed Descartes's methods of clear ideas, he could learn how nature worked."[3]

Yet, his work—like that of Galileo—was persecuted strongly by both the Catholic and Protestant churches. Dutch universities taught his philosophy, but removed the metaphysical supports, and therefore, the theories did not hold up to religious views. Riots began and the Dutch theologians viewed Descartes's philosophies as an attack on the view of the Trinity and their understanding of the nature of the soul itself.

It was in this period that the breach between faith and science occurred. The institution of the Church largely rejected the new discoveries of science, holding on to their doctrines. Descartes and other philosophers and scientists began to separate their theories from the realm of faith. Thus, the age of rationalism was born that gave way for our age of modern medicine wherein "if it can't be quantified, it must not be valid."

Why am I emphasizing a "spirit, soul, body" model for a book about the brain? Frankly, because I recognize the importance of replanting the spirit at the center of our understanding. As you will see in later portions of this book (and maybe have experienced in your personal journey of healing), many times the physical input we use in/on our bodies or the substances we use to alter our minds can have profound impact beyond our conscious mind. What is the explanation for spontaneous, "miraculous" healing except that there is another dimension to our person that is unseen and does not fit in our society's current view of a dualistic mind-body connection?

One of the first times that I encountered an emotional-trauma release using essential oils, I was in a room full of strangers. I was observing a doctor well-versed in essential oils on stage leading the group through a simple trauma release I now use with clients and teach readily. Very simply, the essential oil is applied to a trauma point on the forehead, the right hand is then placed over the forehead and the left hand over the chest, and a simple phrase is repeated three times to integrate the trauma release between the spirit, soul, and body. I believe we were, as a group, releasing fear—a simple emotion that many people (if not all) can have trapped in their spirits, souls, or bodies. The group repeated the phrase three times and then suddenly a man spoke up loudly from across the room. He was in awe. He had a shoulder that had been locked for years and he suffered limited mobility. As we dealt with the trauma behind the trapped emotion of fear, the man's shoulder completely unlocked and he could move it normally. No one was addressing the shoulder. He didn't even touch or think about his shoulder. He was dealing with fear and the emotion had been trapped either in his spirit or soul and then manifested in his body because it had nowhere else to go. The trapped emotion, manifesting in his body, was suddenly released when he came out of agreement with fear and chose to take on the opposite. This phenomenon is not unusual and it's not "magic" or some kind of religious activity that requires some incredible level of faith to experience. On the contrary, I think that as we dive into the pages to come, you're going to see clearly how the integration of spirit, soul, and body is designed to work in unison and there are some very clear tenants in science that explain the "how and why" something like this can and does happen.

We're not going to go much into the spirit in this book as we will primarily be focused on the structure of the central nervous system and the functions of the soul (i.e. mind, will, and emotions). However, as we're setting the framework, I want to note that the spirit does have functions similar to that of the soul. There is much data and research on how the human spirit has emotions, can remember things unknown to the conscious mind, and can even make decisions by the will, separate from the mind in the soul. When we speak later about the nature of epigenetics and quantum physics, I will approach it mainly from the context of soul, but understand that the spirit is just as powerful and plays a part in these phenomena. Failing to address the spirit and only working with the soul and the body will result in a fragmented healing long-term. The soul and body are vitally important and great healing can come through altering them, but true wholeness comes when you also address the human spirit inside of you. The beautiful thing about essential oils is that they can and do affect the spirit, soul, and body. As you approach healing the soul and body, the human spirit can be affected as well.

Researcher Arthur Burk, has done extensive work building models and evidence about the human spirit. He argues that there is evidence for the human spirit being the fundamental element existing during the time in utero when the baby's spirit is present and responsive at conception though the heartbeat isn't detectable until around twelve weeks. He argues that the soul does not start functioning until shortly before or after birth, when the myelination of the nerve sheaths (telomeres) takes place. The spirit existed first and was designed to have a nine month "head start" on the soul.

Burk describes an experiment done by another researcher on an unrelated matter that sheds light on his hypothesis on the human spirit's viability prior to birth. A medical doctor a few decades ago underwent a series of experiments (albeit highly unethical) on pregnant mothers. While performing an ultrasound on their developing babies, the doctor spoke quietly, softly, and at the same tempo so as to "lull" the baby into a relaxed state. Then, when he knew the baby was still, he proceeded to tell the mother that the baby had died. The child inside, time and time again in various mothers, began kicking and moving rapidly in an effort to alert the mother that they were indeed alive and well. Based on simple developmental neurobiology, the baby should not have the ability to understand language to that degree until potentially months out of the womb. The only feasible explanation is that the spirit understood even though the conscious mind was not developed to the same extent.

# Soil

A few months ago, a friend gifted me a small succulent she'd acquired on a farm in West Texas. It was a symbolic gesture given to represent a portion of my life as a symbol of hope for what was to come. She gave me the plant and I graciously thanked her and then soon realized I was terrified of the succulent that sat before me. I was terrified almost to the point of tears.

Rational? Not at all. Fear rarely is.

*What if I kill it?*, I thought. *What does it mean that I haven't even been able to keep an air plant alive? And those are supposed to be indestructible. Not to mention this is a significant plant—what am I to <u>do</u>?*

It took me some time to figure out why I was so afraid of owning this succulent. I feared I didn't, or wouldn't, know how to nurture the thing. Every other plant I'd ever had I neglected (on accident) and they each died. I didn't know the proper care and feeding, or I apathetically didn't care to know how. It was a constant battle of too much water; not enough water; too much sunlight; not enough sunlight; the wrong kind of soil; the pot wasn't right to grow the roots. You name the variable; I'd done it all.

One day, it dawned on me that for years, I had been treating plants the same the way I had treated myself: too much of one thing (i.e. work, spending time with people) or not enough of another (i.e. rest, sleep, food, etc.). For years, my life had been a constant binge and purge of busyness then "rest", which never really felt like rest because my internal soil probably wasn't right.

I realized that I was terrified because I didn't know if I knew how to nurture the thing, much less how to nurture myself. Theoretically I did, but I also didn't know practically. I knew the right variables needed to grow it, but like what I'd done to plants I'd also done to myself... I would give it the good stuff, but I didn't give it *consistently*. It was feast or famine.

**What changed for me, and when the fear left, is when I recognized that I was failing to nurture the plant (and myself) because of two things: trust and worth. You can have one without the other, but you won't have vibrancy if you don't combine both. I didn't trust that I had what it took to keep the plant alive and I didn't trust that it was worthy of receiving. I decided that wasn't how I wanted to be anymore. I decided it for the plant, but what was manifesting in my plant also began a breakthrough in my life. A deep knowledge rooted:**

**I'm worthy of receiving love and I trust that what is needed will be provided.**

As that revelation rooted, a profound confidence was gained. The evidence to me that fear was gone was about a month ago. Instead of the ugly plastic container that housed my precious symbolic succulent (complete with a dingy cardboard box underneath to collect the runoff), I commissioned a friend to make me custom pots. Yes, pots. I didn't want one for just this succulent, but I wanted to make room for more to come. I was going to run headfirst into nurturing these plants as a symbol of nurturing my own spirit, soul, and body.

**You, too, are like a plant. You're a beautiful, miraculous thing that has been planted in a field by a very good Farmer. A good Farmer only plants good seed. For many people, the healing in their lives is blocked because they don't fundamentally understand that they are good seed that has been made into a good plant and is worthy of love. We look at ourselves and we judge ourselves as being something that isn't worth living and loving in the first place.**

**I'm here to tell you that you ARE worth it! You are worth receiving healing and vitality and abundance! You are worth receiving love! A good Farmer only plants good seed. And you can trust that what you need will be provided.**

I remember the great care my grandfather would take. When he first bought his land as a young man, just about the time he and my grandmother were newlyweds, he planted seedlings into the ground. By the time I was a little child running through the timber, it was an entire forest of beautiful spruce trees. It would make sense then why spruce essential oil is one of my favorites and one to which my body responds deeply. My grandfather didn't plant those seeds in the ground because he expected to have a bad crop. He believed it would flourish and he nurtured it as it grew.

**Likewise, when we talk about altering the structure and function of our spirits, souls, and bodies, the intentionality that you put into it is key. You have to know fundamentally that you are worth it and that the seeds that you will be planting in the soil of your spirit, soul, and body are good seeds going into good soil. The functional expression or outgrowth of that is something beautiful that you get to offer the**

**world and it's unique to you. Nobody else can offer what it is that you're bringing to the world! I'm here as a guide to help you understand how to unblock the things that have kept you from expressing your uniqueness to the world. Whether it's structural or functional issues—whether your soil hasn't received the right nutrients or you just need a fresh drink of proverbial water, I'm here to give you practical tools that will help you in your journey.**

Oh, and by the way, this journey isn't actually about you or me. It's about all of us unlocking our lives so we can unlock creation together by offering the world the expressions of who we really are—unfettered by trauma or stress, fully functioning in our identities. We are to be rooted and grounded knowing that we are good seed planted in good soil and the expression of our lives, individually and collectively, is something powerful the universe needs.

# IN OTHER WORDS...
## (A SUMMARY OF CHAPTER 1)

Just like a plant lives in a highly dynamic environment, humans also live in an ecosystem. We are adaptable, resilient, and much stronger than we know.

Like plants, many things affect us including positive input (i.e. nutrients, healthy relationships, and natural resources). Negative things can also affect us including stress, trauma, broken relationships, lack of nurture and care. Each variable affects the makeup of who we are. The greater the negative input, the greater the negative expression. The more positive the input, the more positive the expression. The same is true as we approach talking about the mind and the brain.

If we just try to fix one variable or apply an essential oil or particular therapy method without examining the entire ecosystem of our brains and bodies, it's likely we won't get the full benefit available to us if we fail to look at our lives holistically.

We are working from a theoretical model named "Pneuma, Psyche, Soma", the Greek words for spirit, soul, and body. You are a spirit, you have a soul, and you live in a body and are designed to flow in that order.

In order to have a vibrant life, the "soil" of your spirit, soul, and body must contain two key elements: trust and worth. You can have one without the other, but you won't have vibrancy if you don't combine both.

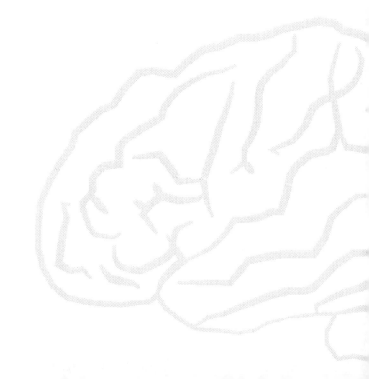

# Glossary of Introductory Terms

*behaviorism:* A theoretical perspective that focuses only on objective, observable reactions. Behaviorism emphasizes the environmental stimuli that determine behavior.

*cognition:* Mental activities involving the acquisition, storage, transformation, and use of knowledge.

*cognitive neuroscience:* The field that examines how cognitive processes can be explained by the structure and function of the brain.

*cognitive psychology:* (1) a synonym for cognition. (2) The cognitive approach to psychology; a theoretical approach that emphasizes people's knowledge and their mental processes.

*conscious mind:* of or relating to any process or content of the mind which the individual is aware of at the present moment. May be an awareness of the external world, as well as thoughts and emotions about one's internal world.

*consciousness:* an awareness of the external world, as well as thoughts and emotions about one's internal world.

**Gestalt psychology:** the theoretical approach which emphasizes that humans have basic tendencies to organize what they see, and that the whole is greater than the sum of the parts.

**neurology:** the branch of medicine dealing with disorders of the nervous system.

**philosophy:** a particular system of philosophical that studies of the fundamental nature of knowledge, reality, and existence, especially when considered as an academic discipline.

**physiology:** the branch of biology that deals with the normal functions of living organisms and their parts

**pneuma:** Greek, literally "that which is breathed or blown." Translated into English as "spirit".

**psyche:** Greek, literally "breath, life, soul." Translated into English as the human soul or mind.

**psychology:** the science of behavior and mind, embracing all aspects of conscious and unconscious experience as well as thought.

**soma:** Greek, literally "body."

**subconscious** (or **unconscious**) **mind:** of or relating to any process or content of the mind of which the individual is not aware at a particular moment in time; in general usage, any part of the mind outside the awareness of the individual.

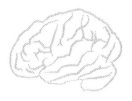

**Chapter Two**

# THE BASICS OF ESSENTIAL OILS

I have been an avid essential oil user and researcher for years. My goal here is to offer some basic information and tools about essential oils so that as we talk further about the brain, you are able to make connections and understand the research.

It's vital to note here at the outset that essential oils should not be approached just like a medicine. Thanks in large part to the modern era of scientific knowledge and the desire for the quantification of data (which I agree with in general), many people approach the topic of essential oil usage in the same way that they would a prescription or a "cure". Many researchers, when studying essential oils in clinical settings, try to isolate one or two molecular compounds to account for specific effects on the body. However, they forget that essential oils are dynamic and work in a dynamic environment.[4] Lest we reduce the power of an essential oil to one or two compounds, let's reframe our view here at the start.

Kurt Schnaubelt said, "Subordinating aromatherapy to what can be proven scientifically is either folly or execution of a hostile agenda. The role of science in aromatherapy is clear: it can help us understand some of the more complex mechanisms in which oils can be used to treat symptoms of diseases, but science is *not* equipped to explain the miracles of life to which the interaction with essential oils and plants opens a glimpse."[5]

Personally, I respect and need the scientific process—not just in my research, but it's often how I approach life: seeking to quantify and prove. This chapter will give you the basic structure to understand the science behind the essential oils we're discussing in this book. I hope it will also give you a framework for your own research. In later chapters, greater explanations of the "miracles" of life that cannot be as easily quantified will be discussed.

A last note as we discuss essential oils: many use the term "aromatherapy" in regards to essential oils. Though this term is applicable and is used in this text, I do not ascribe to the belief that essential oils should be used exclusively aromatically. Rather, when this text uses the term **aromatherapy**, it is considered a catchall for the multiple uses of the compounds in an essential oil which we will soon examine.

## What are Essential Oils?

What are essential oils, you may ask? In short, they are the lifeblood of plants. In fact, some argue they're called "essential" because they are essential to the vital processes of living plants, while others insist "essential" comes from the fact the material is distilled from the raw plant matter.

The International Organization for Standardization defines an essential oil as a "product obtained from natural raw material, either by distillation with water and steam, or from the epicarp of citrus fruits by mechanical processing, or by dry distillation. The essential oil is subsequently separated from the aqueous phase by physical means."[6]

From trees to shrubs, flowers to grasses, many plants have essential oils in them, but not all plants produce significant amounts of essential oils. In fact, there is only a subset that do and among those not all have been studied for human usage.

Plants produce essential oils in small cellular "factories". All life forms use the same four building blocks of life: proteins, carbohydrates, nucleic acids, and lipids and these are known as the **primary metabolites**. The oils produced are considered **secondary metabolites** because the plant manufactures them by converting raw materials. The plant "factories" are literally spending energy to manufacture the secondary metabolites from glucose. If you remember from school, glucose converted from sunlight in the process of photosynthesis is how the plant is constructed and serves as its main energy source.

So why do plants spend valuable resources and time to create essential oils? The short answer is that because plants are immobile, essential oils become their primary way of defending themselves. They divert valuable resources away from photosynthesis to create secondary metabolites in order to protect the plant and preserve longevity.

Essential oils serve the plant in a variety of ways including: participation in the metabolism and nourishment of the plant; regulation of plant functions including acting like various hormones and ligands; aiding in the regulation of homeostasis; offering protection to the plant by fighting off viruses, bacteria, parasites, and fungi; initiating the internal healing process when wounded; helping to shield the plant from intense sunlight, excessive heat, and dehydration.[7]

In short, essential oils in a plant serve the plant in four main ways:

1. **They bring nourishment**
2. **They help reduce inflammation and combat infection**
3. **They help provide and balance hormones (ligands)**
4. **They help repair damage at the cellular level**

**Because the molecular structure of essential oils is so minuscule, essential oils provide many of the same functions in humans as they do in plants. Essential oils can help to bring nourishment and participate in metabolic processes in our bodies, they promote homeostasis and restore equilibrium, they reduce inflammation and combat infection, they provide hormonal balancing and regulating effects, and they repair cellular damage in the DNA.**

Each essential oil contains hundreds of chemical compounds that provide benefits to our bodies. In fact, there are so many compounds that not one essential oil has had all of the molecular compounds identified and analyzed.

Essential oils are extracted from the plant either by a specialized distillation process of the raw plant matter, or for some plants (like citrus fruits), by cold pressing from the rind. The essential oils extracted are volatile, meaning they vaporize quickly and easily and evaporate when left alone. Essential oils are water-insoluble oily liquids that are usually colorless and are different than lipid oils in both their molecular structure and volatility. Lipid oils (also called "fatty oil," "vegetable oil," "carrier oil," or "neutral oil"—they're generally the kinds of oil you cook with) are pressed from seeds and are not essential to the plants that create them.

They are often used in combination with essential oils to act as a diluting agent or increase the reach of the essential oil by serving as a base.

**In general, there are three main ways to use essential oils:**

### 1. Aromatically through direct inhalation or passive diffusion.

Volatile essential oils when inhaled reach the body through the lungs and bloodstream or through the nose and subsequently the brain (more on that in the next chapter).

Direct inhalation usually means taking a drop or two of essential oil in the palm of your hand, stirring clockwise with your finger and cupping your hand to your nose and inhaling.

Passive diffusion of essential oils into the air through a special diffuser is a great way to get oils over a period of a few hours. Often the diffuser uses water to suspend the oil and then through ultrasonic waves, the diffuser disperses the molecules into the air over time. Some people utilize clothing or jewelry to act as a diffuser.

### 2. Topically

Topical use of essential oils often occurs by rubbing the essential oil on the skin either *neat* (without dilution) or diluted with a fatty, vegetable oil (like coconut or olive oil).

### 3. Internally

Internal use of essential oils could entail consuming orally an essential oil deemed safe (as in "Generally Regarded As Safe" (GRAS) standards by the U.S. Food and Drug Administration) by putting it in water, food, or other drink, in a capsule diluted with a vegetable oil, or directly under the tongue. Internal use also could be oil being put (especially in a gel capsule) in any orifice of the body except the eyes or ears.

There is talk of various schools of thought as to the "correct" way to use essential oils. Debates exist between the French, British, and German "models" as well as schools of thought from Chinese, Islamic, and Ayurvedic traditions of aromatherapy and essential oil use. In general, for the purposes of this text, we will be ignoring all of the nuances and stick to the three possible uses (aromatically, topically, and internally) based upon the research, common sense, and common usage.

It is because the **molecules** of essential oils are so small (generally less than 300amu [atomic mass units]) and because of the intelligent structure of the living oils that they work quickly—sometimes within seconds and usually within a couple of minutes in our bodies. They are rapidly absorbed into the body, especially by breathing them in through direct inhalation or applying them topically.

Though essential oils can have similar chemical components to some medications, they are completely different. Essential oils are living and can't be outsmarted by bacteria and viruses like many synthetic compounds. As we will discuss in a later chapter, essential oils are able to cross the **blood-brain barrier**—the highly selective barrier that separates the circulating blood from the brain and the fluid in the central nervous system. Most medications cannot cross that barrier, but molecules of essential oils are so small and fat-soluble they easily can. As a result, not only are essential oils powerful for your body, but there are many that help with mental and emotional conditions.

# The Basics of the Process

Essential oils and their mixtures of fragrant compounds can be isolated from plants by the process of **steam distillation**. In this procedure, steam is driven through the plant material and then condensed, with the subsequent oil and water phases separating out. Often the oil is slightly modified by the steam distillation process, so that it does not exactly reflect what is found in the plant. In some cases, (such as chamazulene produced from matricine in German chamomile), steam distillation actually produces substantial quantities of a new chemical.

Other processes are also used to produce essential oils and these include solvent extract using hexane or liquid or super-critical carbon dioxide, enfleurage (oil extraction of delicate essential oils in flowers) and cold press (as in the case of citrus fruits like orange and lemon oils from the peel).

Although you might not be able to tell it from looking at a bottle of essential oil, or even the oil itself with the naked eye, there is a huge difference between "real" naturally occurring essential oil and that which has been made synthetically by a lab or a natural oil that has been adulterated. **Adulteration** is an important issue and many sophisticated techniques have been developed to imitate and extend essential oils. In some cases, trade in the synthetic oil has completely supplanted the natural product. One survey found a large variability between the biological activities of different samples of oils and groups of oils under the same general name, for example, lavender, eucalyptus or chamomile.[8] This reflected on the blending, rectification and adulteration that occurs with some commercial oils.

**It's important to note that adulterated essential oils won't display the same pharmacological or aesthetic qualities of the natural, pure essential oils.**

So how do you know if an essential oil is pure and natural? There are several testing methods that give an indication. The most common technique employed in identifying the chemical characterization of essential oils is **gas chromatography** coupled with **mass spectrometry (GC-MS)**. Because essential oil constituents are relatively small in molecular size, they are all volatile and can be separated according to boiling points. The GC process takes place in a long thin column (approximately 30m) that looks like a coiled wire and is pre-packed with a porous stationary phase that is either polar (slightly charged) or apolar. The essential oil is diluted into a solvent and injected into a heated injection chamber (approximately 300 °C) so all components of the essential oil are evaporated and delivered by a benign (non-reactive) gas (i.e., nitrogen or helium) to the start of the column, which is usually at a lower temperature (approximately 60 °C) so that the components of the essential oil precipitate onto the column.[9]

In gas chromatography, separation is performed by heating the column in an oven. This is most commonly done by employing a programmed temperature ramp, from a lower to a higher temperature. Occasionally, isothermal (constant temperature) programs are used. Separation of components occur when the temperature is rais-ed to each of the component's individual boiling points. At this point, the component vaporizes and is carried by the non-reactive gas to the detector. The most common detector used in gas chromatography is a mass spectrometer. In a GC-MS chromatogram, the retention time of components generally reflects their sizes and the presence of functional groups.

In mass spectrometry, the separated component is fragmented by electron impact ionization, which produces a spectrum of ions that are separated according to mass, with heavier components exerting a greater inertial resistance to a magnetic field than lighter components, which creates a spectrum that shows the sizes and abundance of various ions. This spectrum is like the fingerprint of each component in the essential oil. Because the mass spectrum can be replicated reliably, a spectral library is kept and each new test can be compared across a spectral library. Using other pieces of information, such as retention time, a fairly reliable match can be made, with minor exceptions.

Also, the **chirality** and **stereochemistry** of components are highly important and can be a good indicator of purity because the spatial orientation of the connective parts of the molecule can significantly influence the chemical behavior and activity of the compound. As we will soon see, molecules with the same molecular formula and the same bonds between atoms, but different spatial arrangements of these atoms, are called stereoisomers. Generally, a pair of stereoisomers are distinguished as separate entities in routine chemical analysis, such as in gas chromatography (GC) or nuclear magnetic resonance spectroscopy (NMR).

Many essential oils on the public market have unfortunately been adulterated with synthetic materials and can be harmful if used. Besides the expensive and elaborate testing methods, as a consumer and essential oil user, the easiest way to tell if an oil has been adulterated (other than doing further research into safe and reliable brands) is simply by the price point. It's common to find essential oils at retail prices at well below their production cost. This is especially common in essential oils like rosemary, lavender and peppermint which can be sold for rates so low that logic indicates it is only possible by extending the oil with less expensive materials.

# Notes on Purity

**The safety of an essential oil is difficult to predict from merely examining its chemical composition. In general, pure, unadulterated essential oils are very safe for use.**

When examining safety, researchers like to isolate the compounds in essential oils for specific study. However, this approach doesn't give the full picture because naturally occurring combinations rarely demonstrate the same biological activity as the individual separated components. Often, a constituent based approach[10] is used to examine possible reactions (i.e. citrus oils containing the coumarin group are often cited as a cause of the photosensitivity or phototoxicity).

There are some precautions for certain essential oils or for their use on specific conditions (including age or medical issues). For more specifics on the safe use of oils there are a variety of reference guides readily available on the market to consult and several are listed in the "Resources" section of the appendices.

# The Differences Between Herbs and Essential Oils

As a child, I was raised regularly walking up and down the health food store aisles and was given capsules of dried Echinacea at the first signs of the onset of illness. It wasn't until I was a young adult that I discovered essential oils. At first, I wondered how it was different than the herbs I grew up taking and soon realized there was a world of difference. Though essential oils and

***herbs*** both begin from plant material, they vary vastly though both are valuable.

In general, three big differences exist between herbs and essential oils. Firstly, herbs are dried plant material, whereas essential oils still contain active compounds preserved through the distillation process. Herbs can take days, weeks, or months to build up in the body, whereas essential oils enter the body and go to work within a matter of minutes and also leave the body quickly. Both herbs and essential oils take a large volume of raw material to be packaged down for use, but the concentration and potency of essential oils, in general, is much greater than that of herbs.

As we later approach more specific data on essential oils, I want to make a note that some of the research referenced by third parties has been done on extracts of the specific constituents of the plant material and not necessarily on the essential oil itself. I am aware that, in not every circumstance, can the results of the research on extracted plant material be considered to be the same potency or even contain similar properties to the essential oil. However, I agree with the conclusion reached by Kurt Schnaubelt who summarizes the dilemma this way:

> "Research into the pharmacological properties of medicinal plants often concentrates on components found in the alcohol (or water) extract. A recurrent issue in aromatherapy is the attribution of those results to the essential oil of the same plant. This is problematic, as many of the extracted molecules are different from those found in the essential oil. Frankincense essential oil is a salient example. The properties of boswellic acid, isolated from Frankincense resin by extraction, are often attributed to Frankincense essential oil,

even though there is no boswellic acid in the essential oil.

Critics have discredited such claims as aromatherapy exuberance. From a pharmacological standpoint, there is no reason to expect the properties of the extracted, large water-soluble molecules to be identical to those found in the essential oil. Except that occasionally there is the odd observation that essential oils reflect the properties of extracts of the same plant, even though the active components of the extract are not present.

An evolutionary perspective might shed some light on this. As plants have evolved to master their challenges, their secondary metabolites, water soluble and lipophilic, all work toward the same goal. It is conceivable that lipophilic components of the plant ultimately have similar effects as the polar ones. While there is no boswellic acid in Frankincense essential oil, it is not impossible that components of the essential oil do have identical or similar properties as boswellic acid."[11]

## Are Essential Oils Nootropics?

Increasing interest is arising from people wanting to alter their brain states. A common class of "drug" (whether natural or synthetic) is **nootropics** (or "smart drugs"): substances that can enhance learning, memory, and recall without other effects on the central nervous system. The term "nootropic" stems from the Greek roots meaning literally, "acting on the mind."

Though we will be looking at how essential oils work specifically on cognitive functions in later chapters, I wanted to take a moment to clarify the terminology here as to whether or not essential oils can be classed as nootropics.

There are certain classes of adaptogens which have already been classified as known nootropics, but according to Dr. Corneliu E. Giurgea, who coined the term nootropics, a substance must fulfill five criteria:

1. The substance should enhance the brain in some way.
2. The substance should improve cognitive performance under stress (such as electrical shock or oxygen deprivation).
3. The substance should have protective properties that guard the brain against harmful substances.
4. The substance should "increase the efficacy of neuronal firing control mechanisms in cortical and subcortical regions of the brain."
5. The substance should be non-toxic and have no harmful side effects.

Though there is no formal definition or regulation of exactly what constitutes a nootropic, in general, as evidenced by the research, I think it's safe to say that most (if not all) essential oils that have been shown to work on neural activity can be considered "smart drugs" or nootropics.

# The Basic Chemistry of Essential Oils

### (But first... a brief story to calm your nerves)

So, before we dive in to take a deeper look at some of the basic chemistry that comprises an essential oil, let me tell you a brief story. When I was in junior high, I once had a debate with my chemistry teacher in class. I was the precocious child who raised her hand when the teacher asked if anyone knew what "organic" meant. As a frequent purveyor of health food stores with my parents growing up, I, of course, knew the correct answer and thus began speaking.

"Organic means you grow the food without pesticides!" I proclaimed with confidence.

My teacher smiled and responded, "Yes, but I'm looking for the answer that organic matter is based on carbon."

So, basically, I was right *and* wrong.

Do you remember learning about the periodic table of elements? Most of them are irrelevant to our everyday life and only 27 elements are necessary for human life. Among them, are the "CHOSN" elements: Carbon, Hydrogen, Oxygen, Sulfur, and Nitrogen. Each of them sitting near the top of the table and each of them light in molecular weight.

All living things are some combination of carbon. Interestingly enough, humans, plants, animals, and even microbes can share similar biological processes at a cellular level. As we talk about the chemistry of essential oils, my goal here is to break it down in a way that we all can understand it and how it's applicable to the chemistry and biology of our brains and bodies. So, as we talk about isomers, sesquiterpenes, and other chemistry-related words, just remember it's not much more than those "CHOSN" molecules sitting at the top of the periodic table of elements.

## Types of Molecules in Essential Oils

Essential oils are complex natural mixtures that can vary quite vastly in their chemical compositions. A typical essential oil can contain, on average, between 20 and 50 various **constituents** (or components, used interchangeably) at different concentrations. Some essential oils may contain over 100 various constituents and others (like *Lavandula angustifolia*) has over 200 components, some of which have not yet been identified. Often an essential oil will contain two or three major components at fairly high concentrations (20 to 70 percent) with other components existing in trace amounts.

Even within a species of a plant, the chemical composition can vary dramatically, and these varieties in essential oils are known as **chemotypes**. The same plant species (for example, the mint family) can produce quite different oils in terms of their chemistry, pharmacology and toxicology. Chemotypes often occur where a geographical or geological difference influences diversification of biosynthetic pathways in the plant. Chemotypes can arise as a result from diverging evolutionary pathways, or from environmental cues, such as soil type, altitude, or weather. When chemotypes occur in a species, often there are published standards that are generally specific and regularly updated.

In general, the constituents of essential oils can be classified into two major groups: the **terpenoids** and the **phenylpropanoids** (aromatic compounds). Within these two main groups, the structural features that make it possible to classify compounds into families are called **functional groups**. A functional group is a group of atoms within a molecule that has a characteristic chemical behavior.

# Terpenoids

In regards to essential oils, the terpenoids are, by far, the most important group of natural products. Terpenoids is the group of molecules originating from the terpenoid biosynthetic pathway and is responsible for all types of chemical signals in plants. (Note: some use the term "terpene" for the group, but that is considered to be antiquated vocabulary as terpene is now reserved for the monoterpenoid hydrocarbons.)

More than 35,000 different terpenoids are known. Some are open-chain molecules, and others contain rings; some are hydrocarbons, and others contain oxygen. Hydrocarbon terpenoids, in particular, are known as *terpenes,* and all contain double bonds.

Within the terpenoid group, the basic building block of essential oil chemistry is an *isoprene unit*. It consists of a 5-carbon molecule with two-double bonds. From this, many more complicated molecules can be formed. As more complicated molecules begin to form, isoprene units can be added together in various ways. The molecules may have the same starting blocks, but how the blocks are assembled and arranged will determine what essential oil is expressed.

When two isoprene units are put together, it forms a terpene (or terpenoid). The naming of terpenes is based on how many multiples of 10 carbons (two isoprene units) have been bonded. Hence, molecules with 10 carbons are called *monoterpenes*; those with 15 are called *sesqui-terpenes* (sesqui- means one and a half) and so on. Only mono- and sesquiterpenes are found in essential oils. Higher terpenoids are too large and hence not volatile in steam. Diterpenes occur in resins as resin acids and triterpenes are found as saponins. Not even all mono- and sesquiterpenes are volatile in steam.

Not only do the number of isoprene molecules play a part in what constituent is expressed in the essential oil, the arrangement of the molecules is also a factor. Depending on how the isoprene units form, and if other items are added, the corresponding compound can be vastly different. In the case of the monoterpenes geraniol, alpha-pinene, and menthol, they are all considered compounds made by two isoprene units (thus they are monoterpenes), but their arrangements account for their uniqueness.

With geraniol (as is commonly found in geranium essential oil), the two isoprene units are stuck together in a "head-to-tail" connection. In the case of alpha-pinene (a constituent commonly found in frankincense essential oil), the two isoprene units are sandwiched side-by-side. Contrasting, is menthol (commonly found in peppermint essential oil), the two isoprene units are built entirely differently.

Essential oil components can be classified according to their functional groups. The most common compounds in essential oils are **hydrocarbons, alcohols, aldehydes, ketones, phenols, oxides** and **esters**. These functional groups play a large part in determining the pharmacology and toxicology of the essential oil component. For example, ketones are more active and toxic than alcohols; alcohols and phenols are more potent as antimicrobial agents, with phenols being more irritant.

Another distinctive expression of the molecular structure of essential oil is how they are ex-pressed in mirror form. Essential oil components often exhibit optical isomerism (where the two isomers are mirror images of each other). For example, (+)-carvone isolated from caraway oil has a caraway-like odor and (–)-carvone isolated from spearmint oil has a spearmint-like odor.

# Phenylpropanoids

**Phenylpropanoids**, known as "**aromatic compounds**," are derived from phenylpropane and occur less frequently than the terpenes. The biosynthetic pathways for terpenes and phenylpropanic derivatives generally are separated in plants but may coexist in some, with one major pathway as a dominant. Aromatic compounds comprise: Aldehydes, alcohols, phenols, methoxy derivatives, and methylene dioxy compounds.

The principal plant sources for these compounds are anise, cinnamon, clove, fennel, nutmeg, parsley, sassafras, star anise, tarragon, and some botanical families (Apiaceae, Lamiaceae, Myrtaceae, Rutaceae).

## Why Is This Important?

After *all* of that, you might be asking why we're talking about the chemistry of essential oils in a book on the brain? Surely, it's not *that* important. But, in fact, it is! Understanding the building blocks that comprise the essential oils helps guide us in determining how an oil can and should be used. An architect can build a much taller (and stronger) skyscraper by using steel instead of bricks made of clay. Are steel and bricks both materials for making a building? Yes, but *what* you can make with them and how the building can be used is dependent on which material you utilize.

As a child, I grew up sandwiched between three brothers—one, eight years older than I, and two several years younger. Being around brothers all the time meant I was subject to all of their "boy" activities: shooting guns, experimenting with fire, baseball, and, of course, playing Legos. My younger brothers and I inherited quite a collection accrued by my older brother Jonathan. He often played on his own, since he was sandwiched by sisters. Lucky for us, my younger brothers and I had two giant tubs filled with thousands of Lego building blocks ready for hours of entertainment. The three of us all had the same materials to build with, but what we created were very different. The materials were the same, but the structure of each piece and what you could do with it varied depending on the imagination of the creator. While our middle brother, Nathaniel, made a spaceship, Joshua built a boat and I created a house. We all used the same building blocks that not only became different things, but served different purposes. Fundamentally, a spaceship is used to fly, a boat is used to sail, and a house is used as a place to live. However, even though those creations were designed to serve a certain purpose, they also could have crossover uses. If our "Legoman" needed shelter, all three creations— spaceship, boat, and house—could be used for that purpose. A house is the ideal place for shelter, but that doesn't mean that the others might not contain the right materials to be used in a similar way.

Just like our Lego creations, essential oils are made of building blocks. Knowing how the essential oil is made is important *so that* we understand how it can work. The amazing thing about essential oils is that, unlike static Lego blocks, they are constantly adapting and changing. Even better than Legos, the building blocks of essential oils often have crossover properties. Even though a certain oil might have "better" building blocks for a particular condition doesn't mean that you can only use that essential oil. Most essential oils, (just like our Lego spaceship, boat, and house), can all serve similar useful purposes even if it wasn't the original or highest intention.

You can't "build" the essential oil—nature has already taken care of that part. But, having a healthy appreciation for the building blocks of essential oils as well as the building blocks of our brains (as we'll discuss in the next chapter) gives us a better understanding for how to match the blocks so that we can appreciate and support it all—spaceships, boats, *and* houses.

**Fig. 2.1**

# THE MORE YOU KNOW

The most important types of aromatic molecules encountered in essential oil bearing plants and their most important properties for aromatherapy.

SOURCE: MEDICAL AROMATHERAPY BY KURT SCHNAUBELT

| MOLECULES | PROPERTIES | ESSENTIAL OIL |
|---|---|---|
| Terpenes | stimulant, antiviral, potentially irritant | most cirtus and needle oils |
| Alcohols | tonifying, energizing, antibacterial, antiviral, antifungal, germicidal | *Eucalyptus radiata*, marjoram, rosemary, peppermint, geranium, cypress |
| Phenols | bactericidal, strongly stimulant, potentially irritant | thyme, oregano |
| Aldehydes | sedative, antiviral, anti-inflammative | *Lemon verbena*, melissa, *Eucalyptus citriodora* |
| Esters | active on the central nervous system | lavender, clary sage, orange, petitgrain, Roman chamomile |
| Ketones | mucolytic, cell regenerative, potentially neurotoxic | *Rosemary verbenone*, sage, hyssop |
| Oxides | expectorant | *Eucalyptus globulus*, bay laurel, hyssop, *Rosemary cineol* |
| Sesquiterpenes | anti-inflammative, anti-allergic | German chamomile |
| Sesquiterpene alcohols | liver and glandular stimulant | frankincense, myrrh, patchouli |

# IN OTHER WORDS...
## (A SUMMARY OF CHAPTER 2)

Essential oils should not be approached just like a medicine. They are highly complex molecular compounds that are dynamic and work in dynamic environments. Essential oils are extracted from raw plant material either by a specialized distillation process of the plant matter or for some plants (like citrus fruits) by cold pressing from the rind. They are volatile, water-insoluble oily liquids that are usually colorless and are different than lipid oils in both their molecular structure and volatility.

**Essential oils serve plants and humans in four main ways:**
1. They bring nourishment and participate in metabolic processes
2. They help reduce inflammation and combat infection
3. They help provide and balance hormones (ligands)
4. They help repair damage at the cellular level

**In general, there are three main ways to use essential oils:**
**1. Aromatically through direct inhalation or passive diffusion**
-Direct inhalation usually means applying an oil to your hand, holding over the nose, and inhaling.
-Passive diffusion can happen in a variety of ways, including a special diffuser, clothing, or jewelry.

**2. Topically**
Topical use of essential oils often occurs by rubbing the essential oil on the skin either neat (without dilution) or diluted with a fatty, vegetable oil (like coconut or olive oil).

**3. Internally**
Internal use of essential oils consists of consuming orally an essential oil deemed safe in water, food, or other drink, in a capsule diluted with a vegetable oil, or directly under the tongue. Internal use also could consist of the oil used (especially in a gel capsule) in any orifice of the body except the eyes or ears.

The molecules of essential oils are minuscule and rapidly absorbed in the body. Though they can have similar chemical components to some medications, essential oils are completely different and can't be outsmarted by bacteria and viruses like many synthetic compounds. Essential oils are able to cross the blood-brain barrier and as a result, they can often help with mental and emotional conditions.

Adulterated essential oils won't display the same pharmacological or aesthetic qualities of the natural, pure essential oils. Though the safety of an essential oil is difficult to predict from merely examining its chemical composition, in general, pure, unadulterated essential oils are very safe for use. They are usually more potent than dried herbs and could be considered "nootropics" (substances that can enhance learning, memory, and recall without other effects on the central nervous system).

Essential oils are complex natural mixtures that can vary in their chemical compositions. A typical essential oil can contain, on average, between 20 and 50 various constituents at different concentrations, which in general, can be classified into two major groups: the terpenoids and the phenylpropanoids (or aromatic compounds).

# Glossary of Chemistry Terms

*adulteration:* To make impure by adding extraneous, improper, or inferior ingredients.

*alcohol:* a hydrocarbon group (R) with a hydroxyl radical (OH-) attached. Alcohol names end in -ol.

*aromatherapy:* in a broad sense, the use of aroma to enhance a feeling of well-being.

*aromatic compound:* chemical compounds that contain conjugated planar ring systems with delocalized pi electron clouds instead of discrete alternating single and double bonds. Typical aromatic compounds are benzene and toluene. They should satisfy Hückel's rule.

*blood-brain barrier:* in a broad sense, the barrier in combination with the arachnoid barrier and the choroid epithelium, the three of which collectively isolate the extracellular fluids of the CNS from the general extracellular fluids of the body.

*butyl:* a functional group consisting of an incomplete methane molecule. $C_4H_8$ or $C_4H_7$. Any compound whose name includes "butyl" has incorporated one or more butyl radicals in its molecules.

**chemotype:** a chemically distinct entity in a plant or microorganism, with differences in the composition of the secondary metabolites. Minor genetic and epigenetic changes with little or no effect on morphology or anatomy may produce large changes in the chemical phenotype.

**chirality:** asymmetric in such a way that the structure and its mirror image are not superimposable. Chiral compounds are typically optically active; large organic molecules often have one or more *chiral centers* where four different groups are attached to a carbon atom.

**constituent:** an essential part, component, or element that comprises the whole.

**ester:** an organic compound resulting from the reaction of an alcohol and a carboxylic acid. Ester molecules consist of a carbonyl group with a hydrocarbon group (R) attached to one side of the carbon and an oxygen atom (O) to the other side of the carbon to which is attached another hydrocarbon group (R'). Esters have double names the first ending in -yl, the second ending in -ate.

**ethyl:** a functional group consisting of an incomplete methane molecule. $C_2H_5$ or $C_2H_4$. Any compound whose name ends in "ethyl" has incorporated one or more ethyl radicals in its molecules.

**functional groups:** a group of atoms within a molecule that has a characteristic chemical behavior.

**gas chromatography with mass spectrometry (GC-MS):** Gas chromatography linked with mass spectrometry. In the chromatography step a mixture is separated into its components. The isolated components enter the mass spectrometer where they are identified as a consequence of their molecular mass (weight) and their fragmentation patterns.

**herb:** (sometimes referred to as a botanical) refers to plants used in various forms or preparations, valued for their therapeutic benefits, and often sold as dietary supplements.

**isomer:** From the Greek, meaning "equal (or same), parts". Isomers are compounds with the same chemical formula, but different structural formulas.

*isoprene:* the most common functional group in nature. Its formula is $C_5H_8$. Two isoprene units acting as a functional group form a terpene unit, $C_{10}H_{16}$.

*ketone:* a basic structural element in which oxygen is bound to carbon by a double bond.

*methyl:* a functional group consisting of an incomplete methane molecule. $CH_3$ or $CH_2$. Any compound whose name includes "methyl" has incorporated one or more methyl radical in its molecules.

*molecule:* a group of atoms bonded together, representing the smallest fundamental unit of a chemical compound that can take part in a chemical reaction.

*monoterpene:* a hydrocarbon molecule or functional group with the formula $C_{10}H_{16}$, which is the formula for one terpene unit.

*neat:* term used for describing the application of essential oil without dilution in a carrier oil.

*nootropic:* a substance used to enhance memory or other cognitive functions.

**phenol:** 1. a compound consisting of a hydroxyl radical (OH-) attached to a benzene ring ($C_6H_6$). Its formula is ($C_6H_6O$). 2. a family of compounds containing a phenol molecule as a functional group. Members of this family are also called phenolics.

**phenylpropanoid:** a compound containing a phenol functional group and a propyl radical ($C_3H_7$ or $C_3H_5$). Also, the term for aromatic compounds. Found throughout the plant kingdom, phenylpropanoids serve as essential components of a number of structural polymers. Among other things, phenylpropanoid derivatives, such as floral pigments and scent compounds, provide protection from ultraviolet light, defend against herbivores and pathogens, and mediate plant-pollinator interactions.

**primary metabolites:** all those components that comprise the bulk of the biomass and basically perform a plant's daily activities. They are proteins, carbohydrates, fats and oils, and genetic materials such as DNA.

**propyl:** a functional group consisting of an incomplete methane molecule. $C_3H_7$ or $C_3H_5$. Any compound whose name includes "propyl" has incorporated one or more propyl radicals in its molecules.

**secondary metabolites:** substances that are spun off the biosynthetic pathways that manufacture primary metabolites, and then, coincidentally, help the survival of the plant, for instance by repelling herbivores. Over time, these substances became not only the defense mechanism but also the communication system of the plant. Essential oils are one large group of secondary plant metabolites.

**sesquiterpene:** a compound consisting of or containing a functional group with the formula, $C_{15}H_{24}$—the joining of three isoprene units or one-and-a-half terpene units.

**steam distillation:** a separation process used to purify or isolate temperature sensitive materials, like natural aromatic compounds.

**stereochemistry:** the branch of chemistry concerned with the three-dimensional arrangement of atoms and molecules and the effect of this on chemical reactions.

**terpene:** A large, common functional group found throughout nature formed from a pair of isoprene units and having the formula, $C_{10}H_{16}$. This group consists of volatile unsaturated hydrocarbons, found in the essential oils of plants. These organic compounds are major biosynthetic building blocks within nearly every living creature. They are distinguished by their biosynthetic origin from the terpenoid cholesterol synthetic pathway. Terpenes may be classified by the number of terpene units in the molecule, indicated by a prefix in the name, giving rise to monoterpenes, diterpenes, sesquiterpenes, etc. Countless natural organic compounds from multiples of terpene units.

**terpenoid:** any of a large class of organic compounds including terpenes, diterpenes, and sesquiterpenes. They have unsaturated molecules composed of linked isoprene units, generally having the formula $C_5H_8$.

**Chapter Three**

# UNDERSTANDING THE STRUCTURE

The famed and brilliant Thomas Alva Edison once said that "the chief function of the body is to carry the brain around."

The intricate design of the brain continues to fascinate researchers and scientists, poets and laureates, and philosophers. No matter how much we map it, the brain changes and parts previously unknown emerge like a gift waiting to be unwrapped. I suspect that though we know more in this information age than ever before about the brain, we will never fully comprehend its majesty.[12]

Even an infant is more powerful than we've previously thought. In fact, "the vast computational power of the human visual cortex cannot be overestimated. The brain of even a six-month-old child vastly outperforms the most sophisticated artificial vision systems yet devised."[13]

**The brain is a powerful tool worth maximizing!**

# CNS vs. PNS

Our bodies are comprised of various systems; the main ones related to our brain is the **central nervous system (CNS)** and the **peripheral nervous system (PNS).**

In general, you can think of the central nervous system as everything inside of the head and the peripheral nervous system as everything outside of the head. The PNS is a collection of spinal and cranial nerves that reach virtually every part of the body in order to convey messages to and from the CNS.

The peripheral nervous system is responsible for voluntary and involuntary movement and is subdivided into the autonomic nervous system and somatic nervous system.

The **autonomic nervous system** is responsible for the regulation of your body's internal environment such as heart rate, breathing, perspiration, digestion, sexual arousal, "fight or flight" responses, etc. It is divided into two parts including the **sympathetic nervous system** (the "fight or flight" system) and the **parasympathetic nervous system** (the "rest and digest" system).

The **somatic nervous system** controls the access of the CNS to muscles, joints, tendons, and ligaments involved in voluntary movement.

The normal boundary lines between the PNS and the CNS is at the attachment points of the spinal and cranial nerve roots, where the myelinating glial cells change from Schwann cells to oligodendrocytes.

The CNS is housed in the skull and vertebral column and comprised of two parts: the brain and the spinal cord. The brain then is made of three parts: the **cerebrum** (*"the big brain"*), the **cerebellum** (*"the little brain"*), and the **brainstem**.

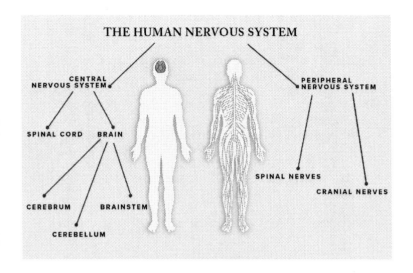

THE HUMAN NERVOUS SYSTEM

CENTRAL NERVOUS SYSTEM

PERIPHERAL NERVOUS SYSTEM

SPINAL CORD    BRAIN

SPINAL NERVES

CRANIAL NERVES

CEREBRUM    BRAINSTEM

CEREBELLUM

# The Cerebrum

Depending on their area of focus or preference, different scientists divide the brain differently. Divisions may be spatial (top to bottom, back to front, outer to inner), anatomical (by lobe, by region, by network), chemical (by neurotransmitter), functional (which parts do which tasks). In general, for the purposes of this book, we will be discussing the brain from the divisions of the anatomy (the structure) and their functions.

The **cerebrum** is the largest part of the brain and is therefore affectionately called, "the big brain". It is divided into two halves, known as **the right hemisphere** and **the left hemisphere**, which are separated by a deep fissure called the **longitudinal fissure**, and the **diencephalon** (literally Greek for "in-between brain" made up mostly of the thalamus and hypothalamus). Connecting the two hemispheres is a large bundle of cells that bridges the two, known as the **corpus callosum**.

If we were examining the cerebrum from the perspective of top to bottom, you would find it is defined by two distinct layers: ***cortical*** and ***subcortical***. The cortex (or the "cortical region") is built by collections of ***neuronal cells*** (collectively known as ***gray matter***) which form the cortex (plural: cortices). A ***cortex*** is a collection of neurons arranged in anywhere from four to six layers that are wired into networks and circuits. The cortex is folded around subcortical regions, which are organized in clumps of neurons (i.e. the amygdala is an example of a subcortical structure). An easy way to remember cortical versus subcortical regions is by imagining a hard-boiled egg. The egg white is the cortical region covering the subcortical region of the yolk.

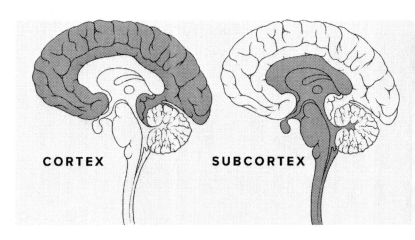

CORTEX          SUBCORTEX

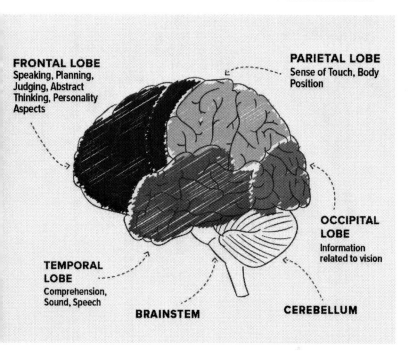

**FRONTAL LOBE**
Speaking, Planning, Judging, Abstract Thinking, Personality Aspects

**PARIETAL LOBE**
Sense of Touch, Body Position

**OCCIPITAL LOBE**
Information related to vision

**TEMPORAL LOBE**
Comprehension, Sound, Speech

**BRAINSTEM**

**CEREBELLUM**

Looking at the cerebrum from an anatomical and functional perspective, the cerebrum itself is divided into five basic lobes, and each falls within the right or left hemisphere. Some parts of the lobe are cortical (on top) and some fall within the subcortical regions (underneath). The lobes are named according to their relative locations and can be imagined as being like the "continents" of the brain.

The *frontal lobe* is the most anterior (in the front) of your brain. It is responsible for motor, premotor, and supplementary motor functions. The prefrontal cortex in this lobe is home to an extensive executive control, which acts like the "boss" of the brain. It is responsible for decision making, judgment, abstract thinking, and working memory, among other things. The frontal lobe is connected to the limbic lobe through bundles of cells that allow it to play a part in re-

gulating emotions, prioritizing bodily and environmental demands, and stabilizing short- and
long-range goal-directed activity, and memory-
related functions. It also contains "***Broca's area***"
(usually in the left hemisphere), which is important in the production of written and spoken
language.

The ***temporal lobe*** sits as the lowest lobe in
terms of location in the brain. It includes areas
that are related to a few main functions: it is
home to the auditory sensory and association
cortex that processes sound and speech; it is involved with the higher-order aspects of processing visual information and associations; it contains the primary and association cortices for
processing smell (olfaction); it is involved in
complex aspects of learning and memory (this is
primarily because it houses aspects of subcortical structures also assigned to the limbic system such as the amygdala, hippocampus, and
the parahippocampal gyrus).

The ***parietal lobe*** is surrounded by the frontal, temporal, and occipital lobes and is responsible for things such as processing touch sensations and complex actions associated with
spatial orientation and perception (directing
attention). It also contains some areas involved
with language comprehension.

The ***occipital lobe*** is the furthest posterior
(back) and includes the primary visual cortex,
which is primarily responsible for processing visual input.

The ***limbic lobe***, is mostly comprised of subcortical structures not visible when looking at
the surface of the brain. It is nestled in the
center of the brain and constructed of individual
parts, which together, are collectively known as
the fifth lobe of the brain. There is no universal
agreement[14] on the total list of structures that
comprise the limbic system.

For this book, the limbic lobe will be defined
as consisting of a continuous border zone of

cortex around the corpus callosum and is primarily comprised of the **cingulate gyrus** (or cortex), **parahippocampal gyrus** (together these are known as the limbic cortex), the **dentate gyrus**, **hippocampus**, and **subiculum** (together this known as the hippocampal formation), the **amygdala**, the **septal area**, and the **hypothalamus**.

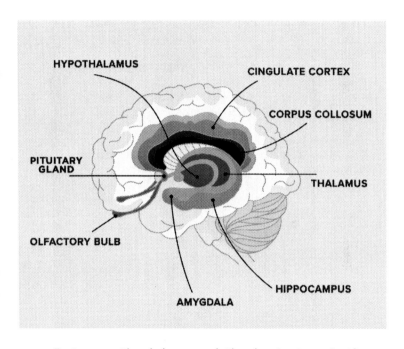

Between the lobes and the brainstem is the subcortical "in-between brain" known as the diencephalon. This area comprises less than 2 percent of the total mass of the brain, but it is highly important as it contains the **pineal gland**, **thalamus**, **hypothalamus**, and **optic nerve**, among other structures.

The **thalamus** is integral for the function of the brain as it serves as the relay station to the brain. No sensory information (with the exception of olfaction) reaches the cerebral cortex without a synaptic stop in some part of the thalamus. The hypothalamus, also located in the diencephalon, controls the autonomic nervous system and is a major visceral control center also involved in limbic functions.

# The Cerebellum

One of the most underrated and misunderstood parts of the brain is the **cerebellum** (literally "*the little brain*"), which sits posterior. The cerebellum comprises only 10 percent of the mass of the brain, but it is densely packed and highly important as it contains as many neurons as the rest of the CNS combined. There is increasing research into the functions of the cerebellum and most scientists will admit that we know very little about it in comparison to other parts of the brain. What is known is that the cerebellum is extensively responsible processing sensory information that includes regulating equilibrium, maintaining muscle tone and postural control, and coordination of voluntary movements. Most functions the cerebellum performs are outside of our conscious awareness (i.e. tuning, timing, posture, movement, and balance). With the exception of olfaction, which proceeds directly to the cerebrum via the cranial nerves, the cerebellum receives from the sensory systems, the cerebral cortex, and other sites virtually every kind of sensory input before they find their way to various sites of the brainstem and thalamus.

# The Brainstem

The **brainstem** is comprised of three parts: the **midbrain**, the **pons**, and the **medulla**. As a whole, the brainstem is responsible for conveying information to and from the cerebrum as well as performing some special functions of its own. The brainstem begins at the top of the spinal cord and it plays a major role in the function of the 12 cranial nerves. In general, we divide the functions of the brainstem into three general types: conduit functions (information passing through the brainstem to get from the spinal cord to the cerebrum or vice versa); cranial nerve functions (these serve as the head's equivalent of spinal nerve fibers that transmit information regarding the special senses like olfaction, sight, hearing, equilibrium, gustation, taste); integrative functions (complex motor patterns, multiple aspects related to cardiovascular and respiratory functions, and even some levels of consciousness).

The midbrain of the brainstem contains parts (the Locus ceruleus, Raphe nuclei, Substantia nigra, Periaquaductal gray, and others) that contain nuclei specifically to form neurotransmitters such as norepinephrine, dopamine, serotonin, as well as regulate the pain-control pathway.

Pons is the Latin word for "bridge" and helps to conduct signals from the cerebrum down to the cerebellum and medulla as well as sensory signals up to the thalamus in the diencephalon. The pons contains nuclei that deal primarily with sleep, respiration, swallowing, bladder control, hearing, equilibrium, taste, eye movement, facial expressions, facial sensation, and posture.

The medulla is a small structure comparatively, but plays a crucial role in regulating vital functions like the respiratory, cardiovascular, and visceral activities. It contains reflex centers used for vomiting, coughing, sneezing, and swallowing and are collectively known as the "bulbar reflexes". It also performs additional integrative activities and most of the sensory and motor tracts of the CNS run through the medulla.

# Neurons and Glia

Now that we've talked about the gross anatomy of the brain, let's dial down to the cellular level. The CNS functions on two main types of cells: neurons and glia.

**Neurons** are electrically active nerve cells that form some of the basic units that process information in the brain and nervous system. The entire job of neurons is to convey information. Neurons do this through a combination of electrical and chemical signaling mechanisms: electrical signals convey information quickly from one part of a neuron to another and chemical messengers are typically used to transmit information between neurons.

Neurons are polarized with their electrical signals traveling in only one direction under normal circumstances. The neuron will "fire" based on an **action potential** (the ability to excite or inhibit it by a depolarizing all-or-nothing electrical signal, which takes about one millisecond in duration). The action potential determines if the neuron will send an electrical signal down the **axon** to the **synaptic terminals** (also known as terminal branches). The synaptic terminals sit at the end of the axon and contain the mechanisms for the release of **neurotransmitters** into the synapses (over what is known as the synaptic cleft), which are picked up by the **dendrites** of other neurons. The neurotransmitters freshly received by the new neuron determine that neuron's action potential, thus exciting or inhibiting its rate of firing. This cascade effect explains how one potential trigger can influence thousands of neurons simultaneously.

**Most neurons are multipolar, meaning they consist of one *cell body* (the soma), *dendrites* that receive incoming information, and one *axon* that sends out information through the *synaptic terminals*.**

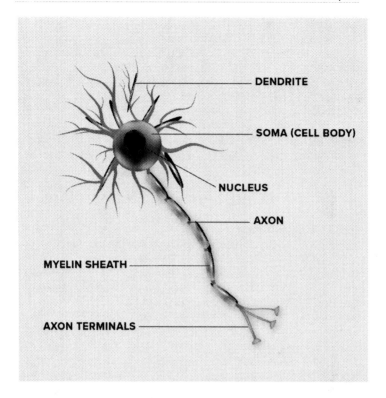

DENDRITE

SOMA (CELL BODY)

NUCLEUS

AXON

MYELIN SHEATH

AXON TERMINALS

Think of neurons like a telephone pole: the dendrites receive incoming information, the cell body is like the telephone pole itself (it provides the support), and the axons are the wires going out to the next dendrites. However, there is a big difference between multipolar neurons and telephone poles. Unlike a one-to-one connection on a telephone pole (one input, one pole, one out-put), due to the synaptic terminals releasing information and the dendrites receiving the neurotransmitters, a single neuron can connect to many, many other neurons just by its axons and dendrites. You will only have one axon per neuron, but you can have possibly thousands of dendritic connections on one neuron. Groups of dendrites are called "dendritic arbors" at times because their connections look so much like the branches and stems of a tree.

There are many different kinds of neurons in both the CNS and PNS. Sensory neurons can be either directly sensitive to various stimuli (such as touch or temperature changes) or receive connecting information directly from noneuronal receptor cells. Motor neurons end directly on muscles, glands, or other neurons in the PNS and like sensory neurons, they live partly in the CNS and partly in the PNS. Most other neurons live entirely in the CNS and serve to interconnect other neurons. Projection neurons serve to project information across long distances and therefore have long axons that connect different areas (an example of this would be a neuron in the cerebral cortex whose axon reaches the spinal cord). The longer the axon of a neuron, the slower the transmission will be because of the length it has to travel in the body. It is estimated that there are no more than 20 million sensory neurons in all of the spinal and cranial nerves and no more than a few million motor neurons. Our human nervous system contains about 100 billion neurons, which means more than 99 percent of our neurons are only used to communicate messages to other neurons (these are called interneurons) within the CNS or are projection neurons with long axons.

**If neurons are the information messengers, then glial cells are the glue that holds the nervous system together.**

A *glial cell* (plural: *glia*) serves to surround and protect neural cells. It's aptly named "glia" as that is the Greek word for glue. Glia was named historically because the cells fill up most of the spaces between neurons and appear to hold them in place like scaffolding. But glial cells also serve many other purposes including: providing support, nutrition, insulation, and helping with signal transmission between neurons. Glial cells make up about half of the mass in your brain and they are very important and underrated.

Most neurons in the PNS and some in the CNS are surrounded like a "pig in a blanket" by a fatty layer known as the **myelin sheath**. The pig-in-a-blanket fatty layer, myelin, is made of a certain kind of glial cell (Schwann cell in the PNS or oligodendrocyte in the CNS) that wraps around the axon of the neuron and allows for messages to transport more quickly between neurons. Think of it like the protective coating around the copper wire of the telephone line. The copper wire is like the axon and the myelin coating surrounding it protects and speeds the transmission.

# Ligands

In addition to the electrical cells (neurons) and the support cells (glia), the nervous system, also influences the body through chemical messengers collectively known as ligands.

**Ligand** is from the Latin term, *ligare*, meaning "that which binds" and is used to describe any natural or manmade substance that binds selectively to its own specific receptor on the surface of a cell. Traditionally, this is viewed as a "lock and key" visual: the ligand substance is the key that unlocks the information when it fits into the matching (or very near matching) proper receptor site in the cell. Once the receptor has received the information from the ligand that "unlocks" its potential, it transmits the information from the surface of the cell to deep in the interior, where the message can dramatically change the state of the cell. Ligands can communicate through cell membranes and talk to the DNA.

**Ligands are divided into three types: *neurotransmitters*, *steroids*, and *peptides*.**

## LIGANDS

fig. 3.6
*ligare:* "THAT WHICH BINDS"

Neurotransmitters are the most familiar ligand class as these molecules are the simplest and smallest and are generally made in the brain to carry information across the synaptic cleft (the space between the synaptic terminals and the dendrites of the neuron). Some of the commonly known neurotransmitters include acetylcholine, norepinephrine, dopamine, histamine, glycine, GABA, and serotonin. They generally begin as simple amino acids (the building blocks of protein) and then other occasional atoms are added here or there until a neurotransmitter is formed. A few neurotransmitters are unmodified amino acids. A chart with more detail on neurotransmitters can be found in the appendices.

The next group of ligands are steroids, which are divided into two classes: corticosteroids and sex steroids. Corticosteroids are typically made in the adrenal cortex and sex steroids are typically made in the gonads (ovaries or testes), by the adrenal glands, or by conversion from other sex steroids in other tissue such as the liver or fat. These two classes of steroids are then subdivided into five subtypes according to the receptors to which they bind: glucocorticoids, mineralocorticoids (corticosteroids), androgens, estrogens, and progestogens (sex hormones including testosterone, progesterone, and estrogen). In general, steroid hormones aid in a variety of ways including: controlling metabolism, regulating inflammation, increasing the ability to withstand illness and injury, monitoring immune function, maintaining salt and water balance, and the development of sexual characteristics.

Peptides (also known as neuropeptides) are larger molecules also built by combining the small protein molecules known as amino acids. The amino acids are formed into long chains and are activated by chemical signals produced in the brain and sent to the body. Peptides comprise probably 95 percent of the ligand family.

Neurotransmitters and neuropeptides are frequently classed together under the header of "neurotransmitter". However, there are far more neuropeptides than classical neurotransmitters. In fact, there have been fewer than 12 small molecule (amines and amino acids) neurotransmitters identified, but well over 100 neuropeptides have been found.

According to Dr. Candace B. Pert, a pioneer in the research of neuropeptides and involved in the discovery of the opiate receptor in the brain, neurotransmitters and neuropeptides can serve similar functions.

"The neurotransmitters seemed to carry very basic messages, either "on" or "off", referring to whether the receiving cell discharges electricity or not," says Pert. "The peptides, on the other hand, while they sometimes act like neurotransmitters, swimming across the synaptic cleft, are much more likely to move through extra-cellular space, swept along in the blood and cerebrospinal fluid, traveling long distances and causing complex and fundamental changes in the cells whose receptors they lock onto."[15]

After decades of new developments in the research, most now believe that ligands and the receptor sites they bind to in the cells should be termed "information molecules" and serve as "the basic units of a language used by cells throughout the organism to communicate across systems such as the endocrine, neurological, gastrointestinal, and even the immune system."

When we talk about the structure and function of the brain and body, it's important to remember that the complex messaging system is produced through a combination of the electrical *and* chemical signals of neurotransmitters *and* hormones. In general, the electrical signals travel and operate quickly in the body, while the chemical process of hormones can take days or weeks to fully express itself.

# How Thoughts Happen

The nervous system is a complex network with intricate moving parts that affect and respond to other systems of the body and environment. But let's discuss for a moment how a few of these parts work to form the basic units of thought. We will discuss in greater detail how these units of thought affect our brains and bodies in later chapters.

Let's go back to the analogy of a garden that we used earlier and imagine that your brain is the soil where your plants (i.e. cognitive functions like memory, emotion, and perceptions) will grow. What you put into the soil will affect the outcome of your crop. Moment by moment, your brain is sending electrical and chemical signals that are like seeds being planted in the soil. By thinking and choosing, the landscape of the brain is redesigned so whatever you think about most will grow. LITERALLY.

When a thought is formed, if the signal is strong enough, it will excite the neuron. The information will flow along the neuron until it reaches the next neuron and then it excites that neuron and it fires. It's one giant game of telephone. With each thought, thousands of neurons may be firing at the same time and each time they are activated, they are firing together in a network.

The firing of neurons is caused by action potentials, which travel down the axon and change the polarity across the membrane of the cell. This is caused because of Na+ and K+ (sodium and potassium) gated ion channels that open and close as the membrane reaches the threshold potential in response to signals from other neurons. In the past, the thought was that the stronger the action potential, the more likely the firing, but research has shown that ligands can influence the permeability of the cell membrane and influence the process.

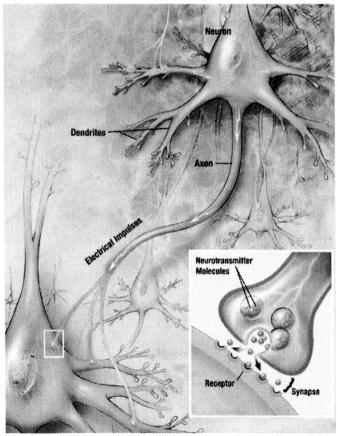

Candace Pert states, "Dr. Eric Kandel and his associates at Columbia University College of Physicians and Surgeons have proved that bio-chemical change wrought at the receptor level is the molecular basis of memory. When a receptor is flooded with a ligand, it changes the cell membrane in such a way that the probability of an electrical impulse traveling across the membrane where the receptor resides is facilitated or inhibited, thereafter affecting the choice of neuronal circuitry that will be used."[16]

In 1949, a researcher by the name of Donald Hebb combined up-to-date data on behavior and the mind and published a highly influential work that coined a phrase we still use today known as Hebb's axiom.[17]

### "Neurons that fire together, wire together."
#### -Hebb's Axiom

Hebb argued that "When an axon of cell A is near enough to excite cell B and repeatedly or persistently takes part in firing it, some growth process or metabolic change takes place in one or both cells such that A's efficiency, as one of the cells firing B, is increased."[18]

Neurons "wire" together when they regularly connect across the synaptic cleft to connect with other neurons, thus creating pathways and networks. One neuron has the capacity to make a synaptic connection with up to approximately 10,000 other cells. That means the total number of possible connecting patterns between all these neurons is virtually infinite.

Since Hebb's axiom, neuroscientists added other phrases along a similar theme including: "Neurons that fire apart, wire apart"; "Neurons out of sync, fail to link"; "Use it or lose it." These speak to the fact that if neurons are not activated, or co-activated, the synaptic connections and neuronal networks are weakened and eventually lost.

**Each time a neuron connects with another neuron by sending changes over the synaptic cleft and starting a new action potential causing neurons to be "wired" together, changes in the structure or function of the nervous system is happening. Changes in the synapses may strengthen and increase, or weaken and decrease the number of connections between neurons. Neurons aren't just creating their own individual pathways, but also huge networks of connections. This ability for the brain to change over time is what science calls neuroplasticity.**

Neuroplasticity, or the changing of neural networks, is not an occasional state. Instead, it is the normal ongoing state of the nervous system throughout your life span. The nervous system, particularly the brain, undergoes continuous changes in response to modifications in the inputs and outputs the brain selects and attends to. The process of neurons wiring and de-wiring (neuroplasticity) happens naturally, over time — sometimes days, weeks, or months.

Think of the soil of your brain like a field that's ready to be plowed. Each neuron firing is like the farmer creating a row with the plow in order to plant the seed of information. The first time the plow makes a path in the ground, it will have a much harder time than if the plow goes back over the ground multiple times to till the soil. Similarly, the more action potential exerted on the neuron and the more it fires repeatedly and wires with other neurons, the stronger the pathway in the brain and mind.

**Neuroplasticity is the natural result of each sensory input, motor act, association, reward signal, action plan, or awareness that feeds your mind. Behavior will lead to changes in how your brain wires and fires, just as changes in brain circuitry will lead to behavioral modifications.**

When a thought is dwelt upon, the network of neurons continues to fire. Each time the neurons fire, they are creating little electrical and chemical grooves in the structure of the brain. They literally become like a freshly plowed row in the soil of the brain. When a thought is stopped, that row of soil is abandoned temporarily and replaced with a new plow row. But the previous plow row is still established and so it will be easy for neurons to run along it unless the new plow row is established as the dominant track.

According to Dr. Caroline Leaf,

"Neurons that don't get enough signal (the rehearsing of the negative event or thought) will start firing apart, wiring apart, pulling out, and destroying the emotion attached to the trauma. In addition, certain chemicals like oxytocin (which bonds and remolds chemicals), dopamine (which increases focus and attention), and serotonin (increases feelings of peace and happiness) all start flowing around the traumatic thoughts, weakening them even more. This all helps to disconnect and desynchronize the neurons; if they stop firing together, they will no longer wire together. This leads to wiping out or popping those connections and rebuilding new ones."[19]

Though the process of neuroplasticity is constantly underway, essential oils can influence the speed and strength with which the brain can change both its structure and function. We'll dive deeper into that in subsequent chapters. For now, let's discuss how the nervous system physically processes the components of essential oils.

# How the Brain Processes Essential Oils

Humans have two main chemical detection systems: olfaction (smell) and gustation (taste). Together, these two senses aid in the basic survival needs by knowing what substances are beneficial (food) and what to avoid (toxins). But olfaction is unique from touch, taste, sight, or hearing. Unlike the other senses, olfaction stands alone as the ONLY sensory input that doesn't have to go through the thalamus in the brainstem before being processed by the brain.

Because of its unique form of processing and the nature of essential oils and olfaction, we will be examining just how the brain responds to olfactory input in greater detail than the other sensory input (see chapter 5 for an example of the other senses).

The neurons in the olfactory system have direct access to the brain and are the only part of the brain exposed to the outside world. Dendrites on the **olfactory sensory neurons** (OSNs) are one of three types of cells in the nasal cavity (along with supporting cells and basal cells). Olfactory sensory neurons are different from all other sensory receptor cells in the body because they are not mediated by a protective barrier (like visual receptors protected by the cornea or hearing receptors by the ear drum) and instead have direct contact with the brain.

The olfactory sensory neurons (OSNs) are small neurons that have **cilia** protruding into the mucus covering the **olfactory epithelium**, a mucous membrane that serves to detect odorants in inhaled air. The cilia (the dendrites of the OSNs) have odorant receptors on their tips that receive the information and then send the information along the axon through tiny sieve-like holes at the top of your nasal cavity, in what's called the cribriform plate. The **cribriform plate** is a bony structure at the level of the eyebrows that separates the nose from the brain.

Once the odorant information has passed along the axon through the cribriform plate, the axons bundle together to form the **olfactory nerve** (cranial nerve I) and then project straight to the olfactory bulb, an extension of the brain just above the nose that is about the size of a blueberry. The **olfactory bulb** is bilateral, existing in both the right and left hemispheres of the brain, but processes information ipsilaterally. This means that the right olfactory bulb gets information from the right nostril and the left olfactory bulb gets information from the left nostril. This is unlike most of the other senses, which are processed contralaterally in the brain (i.e. information from the left hand is processed on the right side of the brain, etc.). Once in the olfactory bulb, the sensory nerve endings gather to form tiny spheres called **glomeruli** (singular: glomerulus).

After passing through the olfactory bulb, the information is processed in the **primary olfactory cortex** (or **piriform cortex**), which includes the amygdala, parahippocampal gyrus, and interconnected areas and interacts intimately with the **entorhinal cortex**. The primary olfactory cortex comprises parts of the brain that are also considered the limbic system, which is involved heavily in emotion, memory, and learning. The amygdala-hippocampus complex conjoined in this region are especially key structures in the regulation of emotion and encoding of memory. They are critically involved in the unique emotional and associative properties of olfactory cognition.

From the primary olfactory cortex, information goes to the thalamus (specifically mediodorsal nucleus) and on to the **orbitofrontal cortex** (known as the secondary olfactory cortex) where conscious smell perception occurs. It is specifically[20] the right orbitofrontal cortex that plays a significant role in the conscious perception of odors, which is significant because this portion of the brain is dominant for emotional processing and has less to do with language. This helps to explain why odors are inherently emotional stimuli and why it can take longer (and sometimes not at all) to formulate words to explain the emotions felt when something has been smelled.[21]

Olfactory sensations are called *odors* (or odor molecules), but not every chemical is an **odorant** (perceived by the brain as having a smell). Odor molecules can have a chemical effect on people with agnosia (loss of the sense of smell) even if they cannot perceive the odorant.

Even though the cells in the nose connect directly with the brain, compared to other sensory experiences, the time it takes to process an odor sensation is long. For instance, from sniffing until the brain actually registers a scent can vary from approximately 400 milliseconds (ms) to almost half a second. Compared to visual input, which takes 45 ms, olfaction is undeniably a slow sense. The time it takes for an odor to clear once your brain has registered the scent can also be a relatively long time.

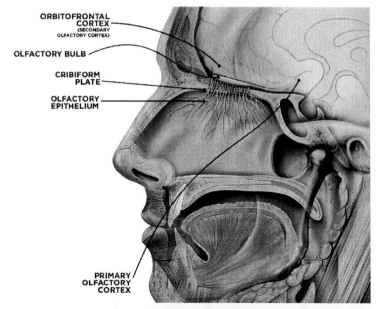

ORBITOFRONTAL CORTEX
(SECONDARY OLFACTORY CORTEX)

OLFACTORY BULB

CRIBIFORM PLATE

OLFACTORY EPITHELIUM

PRIMARY OLFACTORY CORTEX

# Shape-Pattern Theory vs. Vibration Theory

It was Shakespeare in his *Romeo and Juliet* who coined the line, "A rose by any other name would smell as sweet," but how does the brain know what odor is rose and what is peppermint?

The **odorant receptors** (ORs) on the dendrites of the olfactory sensory neurons function on a basic "one-to-one-to-one" receptor rule. This means that when an odor molecule is received it will activate only one type of odorant receptor and all OSNs expressing the same type of receptor will project to the same gathering of OSNs in the specific glomerulus. When the odorant (i.e. rose) meets the corresponding odorant receptor, it creates the action potential and starts the biochemical cascade.[22] An action potential begins when about seven or eight odor molecules bind to a receptor, and about 40 nerve impulses must occur before a smell sensation is reported by the brain.

Recent findings estimate that the human olfactory system can detect over one trillion odors.[23] Far greater than the number of colors we can see (up to about 7.5 million) or tones we can hear (approximately 340,000), the ability to perceive "smellable" molecule mixtures is essentially infinite. This is partly due to the incredible number of olfactory sensory neurons possessed (these have not been able to be counted, but are estimated to be between five and 10 million).[24] Only the sense of vision has more sensory neurons than olfaction. OSNs die and regenerate through stem cells in the olfactory epithelium about once every 28 days.

Even though humans have incredible ability to smell, the number of OSNs pales in compareson to other species who not only have more sensory neurons, but larger brain space dedicated to the processing of scent. For instance, dogs have at least 100 times more OSNs than humans and about 5 percent of their brain dedicated to processing the input compared with 0.1 percent in humans.[25]

There are two theories as to how the brain processes and perceives odor molecules and identifies them as a specific odorant.

**Shape-pattern theory** is the best-accepted theory by most scientists. It was first proposed in the 1950s by John Amoore, and is based on the match between the molecular shape of odorants fitting with the shape of the odorant receptor sites. The theory claims that the olfactory receptor is activated because the molecules of the odorant "fit" into the shape of the receptor that best corresponds to the shape of the odorant. This is like the key fitting into a lock analogy that we used earlier in regards to ligands. When the chemical structure of the odor molecule meets its match in the olfactory receptor, the olfactory receptor creates an action potential and then fires in specific patterns in the olfactory bulb.

It seems that the specific firing in the olfactory bulb may not arise from only a single activation, but rather could be a coded combination of multiple receptors having been "fit" by several or many odorants and may vary in activation to differing degrees. The perception of scent then relies on the activation of specific glomeruli in the olfactory bulb subject to the firing from the various receptor types stimulated by various odorants.

The second theory is less-recognized, but arguably no less valid: **vibration theory**. Championed most recently by Luca Turin,[26] it is similar to shape-pattern theory in that similar odorants are clustered in groups to be processed. But instead of a key inside of a lock, the olfactory sensory neurons are activated chiefly from the vibrational frequency of the odor molecules.

According to vibration theory, odor molecules all vibrate at various frequencies, and molecules that produce the same (or similar) vibrational frequencies will produce a similar smell. If odorants have similar vibrations, the action potential will cause similar neural firing and result in a perception of the same smell.

It should be noted that the vibrational theory cannot easily account for specific agnosias and stereoisomers (molecules that are mirror-image rotations of one another and though they contain the same atoms, they can smell completely different), which can be accounted for by shape-pattern theory.

Both shape-pattern theory and vibration theory can be useful in the context of essential oils and fit the models of chemistry and quantum physics (respectively). Regardless of which theory you ascribe to, the evidence exists that we detect odors based on the pattern of activity (either chemical or vibrational) across various receptor types. The intensity of an odor will change depending on the activation of the receptors, which is why weak and strong concentrations of odorants don't smell quite the same. This explains why diffusing peppermint essential oil may have a different perceived scent than directly inhaling it from the bottle.

Different odor perceptions can happen for two primary reasons: the patterns in which the olfactory receptors fire or the timing and/or sequence in which they fire.

According to Wolfe et al,

> "The timing of olfactory receptor activation also seems to be important; an odorant that activates several receptors will also stimulate them in a specific temporal sequence and speed. Another odorant might stimulate the same receptors in a differ-

ent order and rate, and the difference might lead to the perception of a different scent. Thus, different odor perceptions can be due to different OR [olfactory receptor] firing patterns, or to firing of the same receptors at a different rate and/or in a different sequence.

The flip side of the pattern perception mechanism is that if two odorants, one molecularly simple and the other complex, activate the same receptors in the same way, we end up smelling the same thing. For example, the feature detectors for the single molecule odorant phenylethyl alcohol (which is artificial rose scent) and for a real live rose (whose scent is composed of more than 1,000 different molecules) might both result in the same basic pattern of OR activation and hence the same perception of 'rose'."[27]

Not only does the perception of odors differ from person to person, but the rate, accuracy, and ability to detect odors can vary in an individual for a variety of reasons. As we age, our ability to perceive odors decreases as OSNs decrease in number. Additionally, gender plays a role in the ability to sniff. Women typically outperform men on identifying, detecting, and discriminating odors.[28]

## Passive vs. Direct Inhalation

Do you remember that feeling after you've been away from home for a period of time and you return home to find that your house has a familiar or even "funny" smell that wasn't there when you left? Or maybe you applied an essential oil and found it didn't smell the same a few minutes after you rubbed it on. This is explained by understanding that the sense of smell is a

**change detection system**. A change detection system is when a new chemical comes along that alerts the receptors in your nose and your mind perceives the scent. The olfactory receptors are designed to adapt when an odor is given over time. Receptor adaptation is the term used to describe the biochemical phenomenon that occurs after continual exposure to an odorant whereby the receptors stop adapting and the detection ceases.

How long it takes for receptor adaptation depends on the individual[29] and the odorant.[30] The intensity[31] of an odor affects how much the receptors will adapt—the more concentrated the odorant, the less the cells will adapt. On average, it takes about 15 to 20 minutes of continual exposure to an odorant for the molecules to stop eliciting a response from the mind, but adaptation can occur in less than a minute. The average adaptation of 15 to 20 minutes is interesting in that it correlates to most essential oils being completely absorbed in the body within approximately 20 minutes.

So, what's the best way to absorb the molecules of essential oils to aid your brain? The answer to that question (as with everything brain-related) is nuanced. We spoke earlier about how there are three ways to use essential oils including inhalation (either directly or passively), topical application, or internally.

**Because the only exposed part of the brain to the outside world sits at the top of the nasal cavity in the cribriform plate and due to the direct access to the primary olfactory cor-tex without routing through the brainstem, I am a strong proponent for both passive and direct inhalation as a regular and active way to use essential oils.** The power of sniffing (active, direct inhalation) is that it increases the ability to detect odorants and decreases likelihood of the receptors adapting. Directly inhaling through sniffing has also been shown[32] to produce greater activation in some parts of the brain, including the cerebellum, than passive inhalation. In addition to directly inhaling, adaptation to odorants can be prolonged or avoided by dispensing an odor intermittently, as with a diffuser.

# The Truth About The Blood Brain Barrier

## (Essential Oil Molecules on the Brain)

Whether aromatically, topically, or through ingestion, an amazing thing about essential oils is that they have the ability to cross the **blood-brain barrier**. The term "blood-brain barrier" (BBB) is commonly used to describe the anatomical and physiological complex that regulates the movement of substances from the extracellular fluid of the body to the extracellular fluid of the brain. The BBB is a selective barrier consisting of capillaries and membranes that serves to slow or prevent the passage of substances from entering into the brain. It helps guard the brain from viruses, bacteria, disease-causing-agents, radioactive ions, and toxins (including some drugs). In order for a substance to pass the BBB, it must meet two requirements: be lipid soluble and under 500 amu in weight. Essential oils are lipid soluble (meaning they dissolve in another oil) and they have a small molecular weight (usually no more than 300 amu) and can pass through skin, membranes, and the blood-brain barrier.

According to Dr. David Stewart,

> "Some fatty molecules are light in weight, like caprylic acid (molecular weight: 144 amu) and auric acid (molecular weight: 200 amu), which are comparable to the weights of monoterpenes (136 amu) and sesquiter-

penes (204 amu). Yet these fatty oil molecules do not pass through the blood-brain barrier while monoterpenes and sesquiterpenes do. The difference is in their structural shapes... Essential oil molecules are compact in shape, almost always containing rings while fatty molecules come in long chains with no rings... Thus, essential oil molecules are condensed in size while fatty molecules are strung out and long. All oil molecules (fatty or essential) are lipid soluble but even when fatty molecules are relatively light weight (of the order of essential molecules), they are still not volatile and aromatic and do not penetrate the blood-brain barrier because of their long structure."[33]

The power of essential oils in being able to penetrate skin, cross the blood-brain barrier, and influence cells is incredible and cannot be understated. In addition to essential oils, our brains can be supported by what we feed them. In the next chapter, we're going to examine how to better support the structure of our brains.

# IN OTHER WORDS...
## (A SUMMARY OF CHAPTER 3)

Our nervous system is subdivided into: the central nervous system (everything inside of the head) and the peripheral nervous system (everything outside of the head). The CNS is housed in the skull and vertebral column and comprised of two parts: the brain and the spinal cord. The brain then is made of three parts: the cerebrum ("the big brain"), the cerebellum ("the little brain"), and the brainstem.

The cerebrum is divided into two halves (the right and left hemispheres) and contains five lobes: the frontal, temporal, parietal, occipital, and limbic lobes. The cerebrum, if examined from top to bottom, is defined by two distinct layers: cortical and subcortical. The cortex is built by collections of neuronal cells (collectively known as gray matter) arranged in anywhere from four to six layers that are wired into networks and circuits. The cortex is folded around subcortical regions, which are organized in clumps of neurons (i.e. the amygdala is an example of a subcortical structure).

Contained between the lobes and the brainstem is the subcortical "in-between brain" known as the diencephalon, comprising less than 2 percent of the total mass of the brain and contains the pineal gland, thalamus, hypothalamus, and optic nerve, among other structures.

The cerebellum comprises only 10 percent of the mass of the brain, but it is densely packed and highly important as it's extensively responsible for processing sensory information (including regulating equilibrium, maintaining muscle tone and postural control, and coordination of voluntary movements).

The brainstem is responsible for conveying information to and from the cerebrum as well as performing some special functions of its own.

The CNS functions on two main types of cells: neurons and glia. Neurons are electrically active nerve cells that serve to convey information in the brain and nervous system through a combination of electrical and chemical signaling mechanisms. Most neurons are multipolar, meaning they consist of one cell body, dendrites that receive incoming information, and one axon that sends out information (usually in the form of neurotransmitters) through the synaptic terminals. Glia cells surround and protect neural cells like "glue". Glia cells serve many purposes including: providing support, nutrition, insulation, and helping with signal transmission between neurons. Glia cells make up about half of the mass of the brain and they are very important and underrated. Most neurons in the PNS and some in the CNS are surrounded like a "pig in a blanket" by a fatty layer known as the myelin sheath, made of glia cells.

In addition to the electrical cells (neurons) and the support cells (glia), the nervous system, also influences the body through chemical messengers collectively known as ligands, natural or manmade substances that bind selectively to specific receptors on the surface of a cell (like a "lock and key"). Once the receptor has received the information from the ligand that "unlocks" its potential, it transmits the information from the surface of the cell to deep in the interior, where the message can dramatically change the state of the cell. Ligands can communicate through cell membranes and talk to the DNA and are divided into three types: neurotransmitters, steroids, and peptides.

Moment by moment, the brain is sending electrical and chemical signals like seeds being planted in the soil. When a thought is formed, if a signal is strong enough, it will excite the neuron, travel along the neuron until it reaches the next neuron and then it excites that neuron and it fires. It's one giant game of telephone. With each thought, thousands of neurons may be firing at the same time and each time they are activated, they are firing together in a network. By thinking and choosing, the landscape of the brain is redesigned so whatever you think about most will grow. LITERALLY.

Each time a neuron connects with another neuron by sending changes and starting a new action potential causing neurons to be "wired" together, changes in the structure or function of the nervous system is happening. Changes in the synapses may strengthen and increase, or weaken and decrease the number of connections between neurons. Neurons aren't just creating their own individual pathways, but also huge networks of connections. This ability for the brain to change over time is what science calls neuroplasticity. Neuroplasticity is the natural result of each sensory input, motor act, association, reward signal, action plan, or awareness that feeds the mind. Behavior will lead to changes in how the brain wires and fires, just as changes in brain circuitry will lead to behavioral modifications.

Unlike the other senses, olfaction stands alone as the ONLY sensory input that doesn't have to go through the thalamus in the brainstem before being processed by the brain. The neurons in the olfactory system have direct access to the brain and are the only part of the brain exposed to the outside world.

There are two theories as to how the brain perceives odor molecules as the specific odorant: shape pattern theory and vibrational theory. Shape pattern theory claims that the olfactory receptor is activated because the molecules of the odorant "fit" into the shape of the receptor that best corresponds to the shape of the odorant like a key fitting into a lock. With vibration theory, the olfactory sensory neurons are activated chiefly from the vibrational frequency of the odor molecules.

Both shape-pattern theory and vibration theory can be useful in the context of essential oils and fit the models of chemistry and quantum physics (respectively). Regardless of the theory, evidence exists that we detect odors based on the pattern of activity (either chemical or vibrational) across various receptor types. The intensity of an odor will change depending on the activation of the receptors, which is why weak and strong concentrations of odorants don't smell quite the same. This explains why diffusing peppermint essential oil may have a different perceived scent than directly inhaling it from the bottle.

Because the only exposed part of the brain to the outside world sits at the top of the nasal cavity, both passive and direct inhalation is a powerful way to use essential oils. Whether aromatically, topically, or through ingestion, essential oils have the ability to cross the blood-brain barrier because they are lipid soluble and under 500 amu in weight.

# Glossary of Neuroanatomy Terms

***action potential:*** a depolarizing, all-or-nothing electrical signal, typically about a millisecond in duration, that propagates actively and without decrement along *axons* (and sometimes other parts of neurons) to convey information over longer distances than would be possible using electrotonic (passive) spread.

***amine:*** an organic compound derived from ammonia by replacement of one or more hydrogen atoms by organic groups.

***amino acid:*** the individual building blocks of protein. There are approximately twenty different amino acids. Ten of the amino acids are known as "essential" amino acids, in that the body cannot manufacture them, so it is essential that they are consumed in diets. The remaining ten nonessential amino acids can be manufactured by the body.

***amygdala:*** a collection of cells in the temporal lobe, named for its shape resembling an almond. It is one of the two core structures in the limbic circuits (the other being the hippocampus).

***autonomic nervous system:*** The parts of the PNS (extending slightly into the CNS) that control smooth and cardiac muscle and glands. The autonomic nervous system includes *parasympathetic*, *sympathetic*, and *enteric* subdivisions.

**axon:** the single, cylindrical appendage used by most *neurons* to conduct *action potentials* away from the soma (cell body) and toward axon terminals that make synaptic endings on other neurons.

**blood-brain barrier:** in a broad sense, the barrier in combination with the arachnoid barrier and the choroid epithelium, the three of which collectively isolate the extracellular fluids of the CNS from the general extracellular fluids of the body.

**brain:** the entire CNS, exclusive of the *spinal cord* (i.e., the *cerebral hemispheres, diencephalon, cerebellum,* and *brainstem*).

**brainstem:** in common medical usage, the *midbrain, pons,* and *medulla.*

**Broca's area:** the opercular and triangular parts of the inferior frontal gyrus, usually on the left. Traditionally been considered critical for the production of language, but more recent work indicates that other structures such as the insula and the head of the caudate nucleus may be at least equally important.

**cell body:** the central portion of a nerve cell not including the axon or the dendrites, which includes the nucleus and most of the cell's maintenance structures. Also called soma.

**central nervous system (CNS):** the *brain* and *spinal cord*. The formal CNS/PNS boundary is near the attachment points of the spinal and cranial nerve roots, where the myelinating glial cells change from oligodendrocytes to Schwann cells.

**cerebellum:** a large, convoluted subdivision of the nervous system (*cerebellum* literally means *"little brain"*) that receives inputs from sensory systems, the *cerebral cortex* and other sites and participates in the planning and coordination of movement.

**cerebral hemispheres (right and left):** the telencephalic derivatives on each side of the CNS, together with a few nontelencephalic but adjoining structures. Includes the *cerebral cortex*, striatum, globulus pallidus, *hippocampus, amygdala,* and the white matter pathways interconnecting them.

**cerebrum:** the two *cerebral hemispheres* (right and left) and the *diencephalon*. (*Cerebrum* literally means *"big brain"*).

**cilia:** any of the hairlike protrusions on the *dendrites* of the *olfactory sensory neurons*. The receptor sites for *odorant* molecules are on the cilia, which are the first structures involved in olfactory signal transduction.

**cingulate gyrus**: a broad belt of cortex partially encircling the *corpus callosum*. The cingulate gyrus forms the upper part of the *limbic lobe* (see also *parahippocampal gyrus*) and has extensive limbic connections. Anterior cingulate cortex is closely related to the *amygdala*, posterior cingulate cortex to the *hippocampus*.

**corpus callosum:** (Latin for "hard body"), a massive bridge of fibers, shaped like an overturned canoe that interconnects most cortical areas of the two *cerebral hemispheres* and serves to join them functionally, providing the substrate for a unitary consciousness.

**cortex (or 'cerebral cortex'; plural: cortices):** the 1.5- to 4.5-mm thick layer of gray matter that covers the surface of each cerebral hemisphere. The cerebral cortex includes olfactory areas (paleocortex) and the hippocampus (archicortex), but most of it is six-layered neocortex. The neocortex is made up of a huge number of columnar functional modules, organized into primary sensory and motor areas, unimodal association areas, multimodal association areas, and limbic areas.

**cortical**: relating to the outer layer of the *cerebrum*.

**cranial nerves:** the 12 paired nerves subserving sensory and motor functions for the head and neck. The *olfactory nerve* (CN I) projects directly to the *cerebral hemisphere*, the *optic nerve* (CN II) projects directly to the *diencephalon,* and the *accessory nerve* (CN XI) exits from the upper cervical *spinal cord*; the remaining nine enter or leave the *brainstem*.

**cribriform plate:** a bony structure riddled with tiny holes, at the level of the eyebrows, that separates the nose from the *brain*. The axons from the *olfactory sensory neurons* pass through the tiny holes of the cribriform plate to enter the brain.

**dendrites:** tapering extensions from neuronal cell bodies; the principal but not the only site of synaptic inputs. The dendrites of many neurons have their own extensions, dendritic spines, that may be favored sites for modifying the strength of synapses.

**dentate gyrus:** a part of the hippocampus. In a cross-section, one of two interlocking C-shaped strips of cortex (the hippocampus proper is the other).

**diencephalon:** literally the "in-between brain" made up mostly of the thalamus and hypothalamus.

**entorhinal cortex:** the cortex covering the anterior part of the *parahippocampal gyrus*. Entorhinal cortex receives inputs from the *amygdala*, the *olfactory bulb*, the *limbic lobe* and other cortical association areas, and in turn is the major source of afferents to the *hippocampus*.

**frontal lobe:** the most anterior lobe of each *cerebral hemisphere*. The frontal lobe includes motor, pre-motor, and supplementary motor cortex, an exten-sive prefrontal region, and a large expanse of orbital cortex. The latter two regions have access via long association fibers to all other lobes and also to the limbic system, and are important (in a poorly under-stood way) in working memory, regulating emotional tone, prioritizing bodily/environmental demands, and stabilizing short- and long-range goal-directed acti-vity.

**glial cell (plural: glia):** a diverse collection of non-neuronal cell types that perform a wide variety of metabolic, electrical, and mechanical support func-tions. In the *PNS*, Schwann cells form *myelin*, en-sheath unmyelinated axons, and serve as satellite cells in ganglia. In the *CNS*, oligodendrocytes form *myelin*, astrocytes provide metabolic and mechanical support and help respond to injury, microglia trans-form into phagocytes in response to injury, and ependymal cells line the ventricles.

***glomeruli* (singular: *glomerulus)**: any of the spherical conglomerates containing the incoming axons of the olfactory sensory neurons. Each OSN converges onto two glomeruli (one medial, one lateral).

***gray matter:*** the darker tissue of the *brain* and *spinal cord*, consisting mainly of nerve *cell bodies* and branching *dendrites*.

***gyrus* (plural: *gyri*):** a ridge or fold between two clefts on the *cerebral* surface in the *brain*.

***hippocampus:*** a specialized cortical area rolled into the medial *temporal lobe*. The hippocampus plays a critical role in the consolidation of new declarative memories. Anatomically, it has three subdivisions (until recently, usually referred to collectively as the hippocampal formation rather than the *hippocampus*), from within outward as follows: dentate gyrus, hippocampus proper, and subiculum.

***hypothalamus:*** the most inferior of the four divisions of the *diencephalon*, the hypothalamus plays a major role in orchestrating visceral and drive-related activities.

***ligand:*** an ion or molecule that binds to another (usually larger) molecule.

**limbic lobe:** the most medial lobe of the *cerebral hemisphere*, facing the midline and visible grossly only in sagittal section. The limbic lobes consists of a continuous border zone of cortex around the *corpus callosum*, comprising the *cingulate* and *parahippocampal gyri* and their narrow connecting isthmus; this lobe and its many connections, cortical and subcortical, make up and characterize the limbic system.

**longitudinal fissure:** an extensive vertical cleft, oriented sagittally, separating the two *cerebral hemispheres* around the margin of the undivided *corpus callosum*.

**medulla (medulla oblongata):** the most caudal of the three subdivisions of the *brainstem*. This small structure is important out of proportion to its size: it is crucial to vital functions (respiratory, cardiovascular, visceral activity) and other integrative activities; most sensory and motor tracts of the *CNS* run rostrally and caudally through it.

**midbrain:** the most rostral of the three subdivisions of the *brainstem*. Contains parts necessary for the production of neurotransmitters. Like the *medulla*, a small region of enormous importance.

**myelin:** spiral wrappings of Schwann cell (PNS) or oligodendrocytes (CNS) membranes around *axons*, interrupted periodically by *nodes of Ranvier*, where voltage-gated NA+ channels are concentrated and action potentials are regenerated. Myelin forms a low-capacitance insulating coating around *axons*, creating increasing their conduction velocities by allowing saltatory conduction.

**neuron (neuronal cells):** an electrically active cell that forms one of the basic information processing units of the nervous system. Typical neurons are multipolar and have numerous *dendrites* and a single *axon* emerging from an axon hillock, but some are unipolar and others bipolar. Most are wholly contained within the *CNS*, serving as local interneurons or projection neurons with long axons, some are partly in the *CNS* and partly in the *PNS* and some are entirely in the *PNS*.

**neuropeptide:** a short peptide able to function as a *neurotransmitter* (although many neuropeptides do double duty by serving other functions elsewhere in the body). Neuropeptides are derived from larger precursor proteins synthesized in the cell body and shipped by fast axonal transport to synaptic terminals, where they are released from large dense-core vesicles.

**neuroplasticity:** the ability of neural circuits to undergo changes in function or organization as a result of previous activity.

***neurotransmitters:*** a chemical synthesized by neurons and released into synaptic clefts, where it diffuses to other neurons and causes some specific response. Most neurotransmitters are small amine molecules, amino acids, or neuropeptides that are released from vesicles, although some are gases that simply diffuse across neuronal membranes.

***occipital lobe:*** the most posterior lobe of each *cerebral hemisphere*. The occipital lobe includes the primary visual cortex and adjoining areas of the visual association cortex.

***odor (or odor molecules):*** the translation of a chemical stimulus into a smell sensation. For example, "the cake has a chocolate *odor*."

***odorant:*** a molecule that is defined by its physiochemical characteristics, which is capable of being translated by the nervous system into the perception of a smell. For example, "you were given the *odorant* methyl salicylate to smell, which has the *odor* of wintergreen mint."

***odorant receptors (ORs):*** the region on the *cilia* of *olfactory sensory neurons* where *odorant* molecules bind.

**Olfactory bulb:** the knoblike anterior end of the olfactory tract on the orbital surface of the *frontal lobe*. The olfactory bulb is the site of the central termination of incoming olfactory fibers (Cranial nerve I) from the *olfactory epithelium* in the nasal cavity. It is large and well laminated in animals depending heavily on the sense of smell, but relatively small and poorly differentiated in the human brain.

**olfactory epithelium:** a secretory mucous membrane in the human nose whose primary function is to detect odorants in inhaled air. Located on both sides of the upper portion of the nasal cavity and the olfactory clefts, the olfactory epithelium contains three types of cells: *olfactory sensory neurons*, basal cells, and supporting cells.

**olfactory nerve:** Cranial nerve I, the bundles (olfactory fila) of very thin axon of olfactory receptor neurons that pass vertically through the *cribriform plate* and terminate in the *olfactory bulb.*

**olfactory sensory neurons (OSN):** one of three cell types—the main one—in the *olfactory epithelium*. OSNs are small neurons located beneath a mucus layer in the epithelium. The *cilia* on the OSN *dendrites* contain the *receptor sites* for *odorant* molecules.

**optic nerve:** the second cranial nerve, containing axons of the various types of retinal ganglion cells projecting to the lateral geniculate nucleus and a few other sites.

***orbitofrontal cortex (OFC):*** the part of the frontal lobe of the cortex that lies behind the bone (orbit) containing the eyes. The OFC is responsible for the conscious experience of olfaction, as well as the integration of pleasure and displeasure from food; and it has been referred to as the *secondary olfactory cortex* and the secondary taste cortex. The OFC is also involved in many other functions, and it is critical for assigning affective value to stimuli—in other words, determining hedonic meaning.

***parahippocampal gyrus:*** the gyrus immediately adjacent to the *hippocampus*. Its anterior region contains the *entorhinal cortex*, a meeting ground for cortical projections from multiple areas and the source of most afferents to the *hippocampus.*

***parasympathetic nervous system:*** one of the three divisions of the *autonomic nervous system*, also referred to as the craniosacral system or the "rest and digest" system.

***parietal lobe:*** a cerebral lobe bounded by the *frontal, temporal,* and *occipital* lobes on the lateral surface of each hemisphere, and by the *frontal, limbic,* and *occipital* lobes not the medial surface. The parietal lobe contains primary somatosensory cortex in the post-central gyrus, areas involved in language comprehension (in the inferior parietal lobule, usually on the left), and regions involved in complex aspects of spatial orientation and perception.

**peptide**: a compound consisting of two or more amino acids linked in a chain, the carboxyl group of each acid being joined to the amino group of the next by a bond of the type -OC-NH-.

**peripheral nervous system (PNS)**: the total collection of somatic and visceral afferent and efferent fibers that infiltrate virtually the entire body, conveying messages to and from the CNS. The formal CNS/PNS boundary is near the attachment points of the spinal and cranial nerve roots, where the myelinating glial cells change from oligodendrocytes to Schwann cells.

**pineal gland**: an endocrine gland, a dorsal outgrowth of the *diencephalon,* important in seasonal cycles of some animals; in humans it secretes melatonin with a circadian rhythm and participates in adjusting the phase of the rhythm.

**pons:** the second of three parts of the *brainstem*. It is overlain by the *cerebellum* and includes an enlarged basal region known as the basal pons.

**primary olfactory cortex** (or **piriform cortex**): the neural area where olfactory information is first processed. It comprises the amygdala, parahippocampal gyrus, and interconnected areas; and it interacts closely with the *entorhinal cortex.*

**receptor site:** a molecular site or the docking port on the surface of, or within, a cell, usually involving proteins that are capable of recognizing and binding with specific molecules.

**septal area:** a component of the medial wall of the *cerebral hemisphere*. The septal nuclei are continuous inferiorly with the preoptic area and *hypothalamus*, and are reciprocally connected with the *hippocampus, amygdala, hypothalamus,* and other limbic structures via the fornix, stria terminals, and other tracts. They are also the source of cholinergic input to the *hippocampus.*

**somatic nervous system:** the part of the *peripheral nervous system* associated with the voluntary control of body movements via skeletal muscles. It consists of afferent nerves (or sensory nerves), and efferent nerves (or motor nerves).

**steroid:** includes many biologically important compounds, including cholesterol and other sterols, the sex hormones (such as testosterone and estrogen), bile acids, adrenal hormones, plant alkaloids, and certain forms of vitamins.

**subcortical:** relating to or denoting the region of the brain below the cortex (or the "cortical region")

**subiculum**: a transitional zone between the hippocampus proper and the entorhinal cortex, the subiculum receives afferents from the hippocampus proper and is the principal source of efferents from the hippocampus in general.

**sympathetic nervous system:** one of the three divisions of the *autonomic nervous system*, also referred to as the thoracolumbar system or the "fight or flight" system.

**synapse:** a point of contact at which one neuron influences another; may be electrical, but most are chemical. Typical chemical synapses include a pre-synaptic element with transmitter-filled synaptic vesicles, a synaptic cleft across which released transmitter diffuses, and a postsynaptic element studded with receptor molecules that bind the transmitter Depending on the nature of the receptor, a depolarizing EPSP (excitatory postsynaptic potential) or a hyperpolarizing IPSP (inhibitory postsynaptic potential) may result.

**synaptic terminals:** the location where axons terminate at the synapse for transmission of information by the release of a chemical transmitter.

**temporal lobe:** the most inferior lobe of each *cerebral hemisphere*, inferior to the lateral sulcus and anterior to the *occipital lobe*. The temporal lobe includes auditory sensory and association cortex, part of posterior language cortex, visual and higher-order association cortex, primary and association olfactory cortex, the *amygdala*, and the *hippocampus*. (The *parahippocampal gyrus*, a major part of the *limbic lobe*, is also commonly referred to as part of the medial temporal lobe).

**thalamus:** a collection of nuclei that collectively are the source of most extrinsic afferents to the cerebral cortex. Some thalamic nuclei (relay nuclei) receive distinct input bundles and project to discrete functional areas of the cerebral cortex. Others (association nuclei) are primarily interconnected with association cortex. Still others have diffuse cortical projections, and one has no projections at all.

**white matter:** the paler tissue of the brain and spinal cord, consisting mainly of nerve fibers with their myelin sheaths.

**Chapter Four**

# SUPPORTING THE STRUCTURE

It was Linus Pauling, a two-time Nobel Prize winner (once in 1954 for chemistry and then in 1962 for peace), who said, *"The mind is a manifestation of the structure of the brain itself."* He spent a considerable amount of time in the latter portion of his career examining the link between physiology (note: *not* psychotherapy or psychology) and disturbed mental function. He was the first to call mental disorders "molecular diseases" as a result of abnormalities of the biochemistry of the body.

In this chapter, we will be examining some variables and nutrients that feed the "soil" of our brain. Many functional issues in the mind and body are actually a result of structural deficiencies. In fact, there is data suggesting that the same method used to diagnose ALS (*amyotrophic lateral sclerosis*, a neurological condition that is mainly structural in nature) may also be used to detect Post Traumatic Stress Disorder (PTSD) more quickly than previous diagnosis methods. Countless research studies in the last few decades have repeatedly shown the interaction between the introduction of substances (such as vitamins, minerals, and amino acids through food) to influence the structure and function of the brain in positive ways.

Though this chapter is meant to give a high-level overview of various variables that can aid your brain, it is important to take into consideration the needs of the individual before drastically adding or modifying any of these variables. Just as the soil conditions for one type of plant will vary greatly from the soil conditions necessary for another to thrive, so the biochemistry of our individual bodies can vary vastly. Though there are commonalities amongst all humans of the basic building blocks needed for longevity, it's best to use discretion and consult a doctor (especially one well-versed in functional medicine who knows the variables to look at through quantitative testing) to determine the best course of action for the individual.

# Diet

I likely don't need to convince you on the importance of maintaining a healthy diet for optimal brain health. If you've been around at all in recent years, you likely have already become convinced that the "SAD" (Standard American Diet), complete with the food pyramid taught on *Sesame Street,* is far from ideal. I also probably don't need to convince you that many of the negative effects our society is facing can be linked to poor dietary choices. So, what I *will* do, instead, is give you some basics on how to feed your brain the right way.

The brain is fueled by glucose and oxygen. These are the absolute requirements for energy, development, and survival. And your brain takes those two requirements pretty seriously. In fact, it's pretty selfish when it comes to those two inputs. A typical brain uses 10 percent of the oxygen needed for the body and a whopping 50 to 60 percent of the glucose consumed. If you ever feel like you're starving, it's because your neurons and glia literally *are* starving.

"Short disruptions in blood supply to the brain are either fatal or produce lasting damage. Even in the presence of adequate blood circulation, severe hypoglycemia (low level of blood sugar) produces similar effects," says Govind Dhopeshwarkar, M.D.[34]

Your body will naturally convert *all* foods to glucose (sugar) to feed your brain, but the rate at which the sugar will be broken down into the body depends on the complexity of the source. In the case of simple carbohydrates and highly processed foods, the breakdown into glucose will be quite rapid. In the case of complex carbohydrates (found in whole foods such as vegetables, legumes, and some fruits) the conversion to glucose is much slower and therefore fuels the brain optimally.

The exception to glucose being the sole fuel source for the brain is when the body is in a starvation mode. During starvation, the ketone bodies generated by the liver partly replace glucose as fuel for the brain.[35] This concept is what underlies certain dietary concepts wherein proteins and/or medium or long chain triglycerides (fats) are consumed in order to wean the brain from its dependence on glucose and move the body into ketosis.

There seems to be evidence in both camps for which is the better orientation for fueling your brain and body, and depending on what research you find, you can draw your own conclusions. In general, I ascribe to the belief that a good balance of complex carbohydrates, quality protein sources, and healthy fats are the best way to serve your brain optimal nutrition.

In addition to this balanced approach to the consumption of food, there are three things I'm a strong believer in when it comes to the topic of nutrition. The first is quite simple: don't be a fad dieter. New and improved "diets" will come and go. If it sounds "too good to be true", then the diet probably is. Not to mention, many don't keep the weight off or see the lasting behavioral changes when they haven't taken the steps to make overall lifestyle changes.

The second principle is feeding your body what it specifically needs. Sounds simple? It is. There are two ways specifically I argue this can be achieved: firstly, learn to listen to your body and respond to what it says. If you're craving a certain food (sugars, alcohol, and highly pro- cesssed foods are of course an exception to this), it's likely you're needing certain nutrients from that food. Listen to your body, use discre- tion, and give it what it needs. The contrary is also true: don't consume that which you know is harmful to you. Of course, there are the big "no- nos" we all know about, but also your body has specific needs. Knowing your blood type and eating according to that diet (see *Eat Right 4 Your Type* by Dr. James D'Adamo) can be huge- ly beneficial for consuming the right things (and avoiding the wrong ones) specific to your body's chemistry. Additionally, find out through testing if you have food allergies or aversions and avoid those foods that might cause inflam- mation or adverse reactions.

Thirdly, examine your mindset toward food. In *A Framework for Understanding Poverty*, researcher Ruby Payne examined teachers and students from various socioeconomic classes and their approach to various facets of life in an effort to bridge the communication divide bet- ween classes. One of the most interesting obser- vations was the various approaches toward food varying among the classes.

Payne found that those with "poverty mind- sets" cared most about how much food they possessed; the *quantity* was the important fac- tor. They asked "do you have enough?" as the key indicator. Those who possessed a middle- class mindset wanted to know if the other person liked the food as the *quality* of the food was important. Those who possessed mindsets of wealth cared not for the quantity or the quality, but for the *presentation*; they wanted to know if the food was presented well.[36]

From her research, it's clear that your mindset (poverty, middle-class, or wealth) will greatly influence the relationship you have with food. It's not just what you're feeding your brain that affects your brain. Believe it or not, your brain also affects what you feed it.

# Exercise

Exercise is another key factor for keeping your brain in optimum shape. Once again, depending on which school of thought you ascribe to, the type, frequency and intensity of exercise that is "best" will be highly variable. Similar to the approach of a healthy diet, I'm a believer that the "best" form of exercise is the one that is best suited for your body.

Finding the exercise routine that best suits you can be done in a variety of ways (once again, I think there is some data that supports the idea that exercising for your blood type can be beneficial). The point is to get up and get active. Based on my blood type and my personal preferences, I'm fairly certain I'll never be into high intensity workouts as the most beneficial exercise for me. What my body responds to the most are those workouts that require deliberate movements and concentration (i.e. yoga, dance, etc.). Knowing that allows me to not only stretch my body to the best of its limits and abilities, but give positive reinforcement to my mind so that I actually *enjoy* exercise instead of it being a chore. Again, listening to your body and what it needs is key. Exercise regularly and rest when needed. You have a built-in intuition—use it.

Basic tenets in regards to exercise show that your brain thrives on exercise for a couple of key reasons: increased oxygen/blood flow and decreased stress response. And that increased blood flow doesn't just affect the brain in the moment, it actually has long term benefit, too. Researchers investigated the role of exercise on the neurogenesis (ability for the brain to change over time) in the hippocampus using both human and mouse models.[37] Specifically, two magnetic resonance imaging (MRI) studies were conducted, with the first study imaging cerebral blood volume in the hippocampal formation of exercising mice. The findings revealed that exercise selectively up-regulated cerebral blood volume in the dentate gyrus, which is the only region of the hippocampus that has been observed to support adult neurogenesis. These results indicate that exercise may have a direct effect on the brain's ability to fight aging.

These findings have been substantiated multiple times since the 2007 study, including recent findings by a research team in Finland who found that aerobic exercise, such as running, enhances adult hippocampal neurogenesis (AHN) in rodents.[38] Though they confirmed that little is known about the effects of high-intensity interval training (HIIT) or of purely anaerobic resistance training on AHN, compared with a sedentary lifestyle, a very modest effect of HIIT and no effect of resistance training on AHN in adult male rats. Their results confirmed that sustained aerobic exercise is key in improving the brain's ability to engage in adult hippocampal neurogenesis.

Though the hippocampus responds well to aerobic exercise, various parts of the brain, including the prefrontal cortex and other cortical regions can be greatly affected by even 30 minutes of daily brisk walking. Multiple well-controlled studies in children, adults, and the elderly have shown not just the impact of exercise on memory and learning, but on executive function and decision making. One study on children in the United States found that daily exercise after school increased their executive control and the children became more adept at ignoring distractions, multitasking, and holding and manipulating information in their minds.[39]

Some research is coming forth on how essential oils can aid exercise and athletic performance. One such study showed the consumption of peppermint essential oil before exercise increases performance and endurance. Subjects were given peppermint essential oil in water before exercise and found "improved exercise performance, respiratory function, blood pressure, heart rate, and respiratory gas exchange. It also reduced resting blood pressure and heart rate. The amount of total work performed by the test subjects was increased by a whopping 51 percent, including an increase in the time to exhaustion of about 25 percent."[40]

# Amino Acids

We've already touched briefly on amino acids, the building blocks of proteins, when we discussed neurotransmitters. I want to give you more specifics here on how you can utilize them to benefit your brain and body. Nine "essential" amino acids must be consumed daily in order to support survival. They are called "essential" because they cannot be created by the body and therefore must be consumed through food sources or supplementation. The other 11 amino acids are considered "conditionally essential" meaning that if they're not consumed through dietary means, your body will produce them. However, the energy to produce those conditional amino acids can tax your body, so if you can get them through food sources, that is ideal.

The nine essential amino acids cannot be received in any way other than consumption. Many of our emotions (i.e. neurotransmitters) begin in the form of amino acids—the protein building blocks of our nervous and endocrine systems. Unlike vitamins and minerals, which can take days or weeks to build up in the body, amino acids are absorbed quickly into the brain and body network and if consumed in their free (predigested) form, can be effectively taken orally and do not need digestive enzymes in order to work.

According to Dr. Joan Mathews Larson, "Since our emotions originate as amino acids, we are at a disadvantage when we are denied normal amounts of them. Amino acids alone, or by their transformation into neurotransmitters and neuropeptides, supply us with the chemicals necessary to generate pleasure, alleviate pain, protect against radiation, and combat the aging process. They thereby can treat our depression, anxiety, memory loss, and many other seemingly 'psychological' states."[41]

A serious depletion of amino acids could be labeled "mental illness" and supplementation through drugs is often recommended by the traditional medical community when simply providing natural sources of the missing natural chemicals and the mental or emotional issue typically corrects itself. Not only are natural suplements of amino acids much safer than drugs, they can be suited to the individual's need much more acutely.

According to Dr. Carl Pfeiffer in *Elemental Nutrients*:

> "We have found that, If a drug can be found to do the job of medical healing, a nutrient can be found to do the same job. For example, anti-depressants usually enhance the effect of serotonin and the epinephrines. We now know that if we give the amino acids tryptophan or tyrosine, the body can synthesize these neurotransmitters, thereby achieving the same effect.

Nutrients have fewer, milder side effects, and the challenge of the future is to replace or sometimes combine drugs with the natural healers called nutrients."[42]

Not only do amino acids form the building blocks of neurotransmitters and neuropeptides, but they aid the brain in some key ways including: creating your actual cells and body tissues; promoting the production of blood and the repair and growth of various parts of your body; creating the enzymes necessary for hormone regulation and digestion; creating energy by converting glucose and glycogen; facilitating the intricate communication network between the central nervous system and the endocrine and immune systems.

Essential amino acids are derived from protein. Dietary sources of protein include animal products like meat, poultry, fish, eggs, and dairy as well as vegetarian products such as grains, legumes, nuts, seeds, and vegetables. Some amino acids that can be taken in supplement form (I personally take 500mg of GABA semi-regularly in a capsule I obtain from a health food store). The best way to find out an individual's amino acid availability is through a lab testing either blood plasma or urine.

The nine* essential amino acids are: histidine, isoleucine, leucine, lysine, methionine, phenyla-lanine, threonine, tryptophan, and valine.[43] More information about specific amino acids can be found in the appendices.

*It is worth noting that there is debate amongst the scientific community if there are eight or nine essen-tial amino acids. Technically histidine is "condition-ally essential" to adults, but for infants it must be consumed and therefore I am agreeing the number is nine rather than eight.

# Vitamins

Vitamins are vital to life. Without them, we suffer less than vibrant existences as they aid us by regulating metabolism and assisting the bio-chemical process that release energy from digested food. Vitamins are considered micro-nutrients because they are needed in much smaller quantities when compared to nutrients such as carbohydrates, proteins, fats, and water.

Some vitamins are water-soluble and others dissolve in oil and both kinds are needed for proper functioning in the body. The water-soluble vitamins (such as vitamin C and the B-complex vitamins) must be consumed daily as the body cannot store and thus excretes them within hours. Oil-soluble vitamins (such as vita-mins A, D, E, and K) can be stored for longer periods of time in the body's fatty tissue and the liver.

If enzymes are catalysts for the bodies, then vitamins are considered co-enzymes, working with enzymes to allow the activities within the body to be carried out how they should be. There are both synthetic and natural sources of vitamins to supplement, but as many vitamins as can be consumed through food is optimal. For more information on specific vitamins, see the appendices.

## Minerals + Trace Elements

Most of us are walking around with mineral de-ficiencies and we don't even realize it. Thanks to overly processed food and nutrient-depleted soil where our food is harvested from, our bodies are not absorbing the minerals and trace elements necessary for proper brain function. Of the 44 minerals and trace elements that can be found in the ocean, over 20 of those have disappeared from the land and fertilizers added to the soil are further depleting our minerals. Just as is the case with both amino acid and vitamin deficiencies, lack of proper minerals can result in emotional symptoms.

Be sure to note the source of your minerals for supplementation to be sure the quality of the source is high and can be absorbed properly by your body. Testing to find out an individual's mineral levels can be done through blood, urine, or hair analysis. More information on specific minerals and trace elements can be found in the appendices.

# Essential Fatty Acids

Though the brain feeds off of glucose and oxygen, nearly two-thirds of its mass is comprised of fatty acids. Not only are glia cells primarily comprised of fat (thus constituting the white matter of the brain tissue), but the signal transmission in the central and peripheral nervous system is dependent on fat for proper functioning. When laboratory rats were denied essential fatty acids, their behavior radically changed and within a few weeks, they had become anxious, ceased learning new tasks, and began to panic in stressful situations.[44]

Another great support for your brain is by consuming healthy fats, including omega-3 and omega-6 essential fatty acids. Omega-3 fatty acid deficiency has been repeatedly linked to mental illness and this is due to the fact that omega-3s are the base from which the prostaglandin hormones are created.

There are both vegetarian and non-vegetarian sources of omega-3 and omega-6 fatty acids, but the important thing is to get a lot of them and get them regularly. There are two essential fatty acids, both polyunsaturated fats: linoleic acid (LA) is the precursor to omega-6 fatty acid, and alpha-linoleic acid (ALA) is the precursor to omega-3 fatty acid. Humans cannot synthesize essential fatty acids, so they must be consumed through diet to prevent deficiency. Omega-3 fatty acids play important roles in vision, nervous system function, immune and inflammatory responses, and modulation of gene expression.

What does that mean? Basically, having essential fatty acids helps feed your "blanket around your pig". Lack of essential fatty acids slows the firing between neurons. Healthy levels of essential fatty acids resulted in improved learning and memory function in healthy older adults.

# Antioxidants

Antioxidants serve the body by slowing the natural oxidation process that causes aging. Only recently has this process begun to be understood, but what research increasingly tells us is that the higher our intake of antioxidants, the more vibrant our lives. Because brain cell membranes are the most susceptible to lipid peroxidation (from exposure to sources like paint, cigarette smoke, gasoline, cleaning fluids, and chemicals of all kinds), antioxidants fight the free radical damage and protect the cells and nerves from damage.

Many components of vitamins, minerals, and amino acids can serve in an antioxidant capacity, like beta-carotene, glutathione, and Vitamin C. But one antioxidant fairly new to the Western world, but worth noting, is the wolfberry (also known as the goji berry). Hailing from China, the wolfberry (*Lycium barbarum*) supports the brain and body due to its high antioxidant content. It's been studied for its use providing direct effects at a cellular level and indirectly helping to modulate the immune response in the brain and aiding in aging-associated conditions.

Polysaccharides—the active components in the wolfberry fruit—have been shown to have direct cellular protection against beta-amyloid neurotoxicity—which is a known factor in contributing to brain cell degeneration.

This superfruit has one of the highest percentages of fiber of any whole food. It contains zeaxanthin—a carotenoid, which is important for maintaining healthy vision. It also contains polysaccharides, amino acids, and symbiotic vitamin mineral pairs that when present together, promote optimum internal absorption.

# Enzymes

Enzymes are energized protein molecules and they play a necessary role in virtually all of the biochemical activities in the body including digesting food, stimulating the brain, providing cellular energy, and repairing tissues, organs, and cells. According to Dr. Edward Howell, enzymes are the "sparks of life" and serve as a catalyst for accelerating and precipitate the hundreds of thousands of biochemical reactions in the body.

The body manufactures a supply of enzymes, but it can and should also obtain supplementation of enzymes through food. Sadly, due to processed and highly cooked food, many of our bodies are suffering the ability to make enough enzymes to compensate and further supplementation is needed. According to Joan Mathews Larson, "If your pancreas fails to deliver adequate digestive enzymes to your intestinal tract, your absorption of fats and proteins will be gravely impaired. Even the uptake of B vitamins will partially suffer. The old saying, "You are what you eat" really should be updated to "You are what you *absorb*."[45]

Many people are not receiving adequate enzymes and supplementation by way of a good digestive enzyme can prove to be beneficial and relieve the stress load from the pancreas, especially following ingestion of a meal. The majority of commercially available enzymes are digestive enzymes from various sources. They are not manufactured synthetically and usually come from animal sources. They are typically available over the counter in tablet, capsule, powder, and liquid forms. For maximum benefit, any digestive enzyme supplement you take should contain all of the major enzyme groups: amylase, protease, and lipase. There are many companies with quality enzyme products and research is readily accessible for the best fit for your body.

# Gut/Brain Connection + Probiotics

I'd be doing you a disservice if I spoke about brain health without mentioning gut health. Research is increasingly showing that many physical and emotional conditions are greatly affected and/or relieved by the digestive tract. In fact, 75 percent of your serotonin receptors are in your gut. This is important because serotonin helps in mood regulation and low serotonin levels have been associated with feelings of depression.

Taking a high-potency probiotic to support gut health is a no-brainer. By building and restoring gut and intestinal health through probiotics, you're boosting your brain and your body's ability to combat stress and illness. Probiotics aid the growth of healthy bacteria or intestinal flora that are beneficial for a healthy digestive system.

Understanding that we are more than just the brains that are in our bodies and the things we're consuming (or applying) to affect it is key to improving our bodies and minds. What we put *in* our bodies affects the expression of our minds. In the following chapters, we will see how the function and expression of the mind is played out from our physical body and brain. Setting the foundation with practical tools like

diet, exercise, and healthy supplementation provides us with a strong edifice from which we can
express our lives to the world around us.

# IN OTHER WORDS...
## (A SUMMARY OF CHAPTER 4)

Many functional issues in the mind and body are actually a result of structural deficiencies. Countless research studies in the last few decades have repeatedly shown the interaction between the introduction of substances (such as vitamins, minerals, and amino acids through food) to influence the structure and function of the brain in positive ways.

In short, the brain is fueled by two main things: glucose and oxygen. These are the absolute basic requirements for energy, development, and survival. A typical brain uses about 10 percent of the oxygen needed for the body and a whopping 50 to 60 percent of the glucose consumed, so if you ever feel like you're starving, it's because your neurons and glia literally *are* starving. In general, a good balance of complex carbohydrates, quality protein sources, and healthy fats are the best way to serve your brain optimal nutrition.

Exercise is another key factor for keeping your brain in optimum shape. Once again, depending on which school of thought you ascribe to, the type, frequency and intensity of exercise that is "best" will be highly variable. Similarly to the approach to a healthy diet, the "best" form of exercise is the one that is best suited for your body. Your brain thrives on exercise for a couple of key reasons: increased oxygen and blood flow and decreased stress response. The increased blood flow doesn't just affect the brain in the moment, it actually has long term benefit, too. Exercise may have a direct affect on the brain's ability to fight aging. Though the hippocampus specifically responds well to aerobic exercise, various parts of the brain, including the prefrontal cortex and other cortical regions can be greatly affected by even 30 minutes of daily brisk walking. Multiple well-controlled studies in children, adults, and the elderly have shown not just the impact of exercise on memory and learning, but on executive function and decision making.

Amino acids, the building blocks of proteins, are key for forming and maintaining components in our brains and bodies, including neurotransmitters. There are nine "essential" amino acids that must be consumed daily in order to support survival and because they cannot be created by the body, they must be consumed through food sources or supplementation. The other 11 amino acids are considered "conditionally essential" and the body will produce them if they're not consumed through dietary means. Amino acids are absorbed quickly into the brain and body network and if consumed in their free (predigested) form, can be effectively taken orally and do not need digestive enzymes in order to work.

Without vitamins, we suffer less than vibrant existences, as vitamins assist in regulating metabolism and the biochemical process that release energy from digested food. Vitamins are considered micronutrients because they are needed in much smaller quantities when compared to nutrients such as carbohydrates, proteins, fats, and water. Some vitamins are water-soluble and others dissolve in oil and both kinds are needed for proper functioning in the body. The water-soluble vitamins (such as vitamin C and the B-complex vitamins) must be consumed daily as the body cannot store and thus excretes them within hours. Oil-soluble vitamins (such as vitamins A, D, E, and K) can be stored for longer periods of time in the body's fatty tissue and the liver.

Most of us are walking around with mineral deficiencies and we don't even realize it. Thanks to overly processed food and nutrient-depleted soil where our food is harvested from, our bodies are not absorbing the minerals and trace elements necessary for proper brain function. Of the 44 minerals and trace elements that can be found in the ocean, over 20 of those have disappeared from the land and fertilizers added to the soil are further depleting our minerals. Just as is the case with both amino acid and vitamin deficiencies, lack of proper minerals can result in emotional symptoms.

Nearly two-thirds of the mass of the brain is comprised of fatty acids. Not only are glia cells primarily comprised of fat (known as the white matter of the brain), but the signal transmission in the central and peripheral nervous system is dependent on fat for proper functioning. Consuming healthy fats, including omega-3 and omega-6 essential fatty acids, supports proper brain function. There are both vegetarian and non-vegetarian sources of omega-3 and omega-6 fatty acids, but the important thing is to get a lot of them and get them regularly. There are two essential fatty acids, both polyunsaturated fats: linoleic acid (LA) is the precursor to omega-6 fatty acid, and alpha-linoleic acid (ALA) is the precursor to omega-3 fatty acid. Humans cannot synthesize essential fatty acids, so they must be consumed through diet to prevent deficiency. Omega-3 fatty acids play important roles in vision, nervous system function, immune and inflammatory responses, and modulation of gene expression.

Antioxidants serve the body by slowing the natural oxidation process that causes aging. Because brain cell membranes are the most susceptible to lipid peroxidation (from exposure to sources like paint, cigarette smoke, gasoline, cleaning fluids, and chemicals of all kinds), antioxidants fight the free radical damage and protect the cells and nerves from damage.

Enzymes are energized protein molecules and they play a necessary role in virtually all of the biochemical activities in the body including digesting food, stimulating the brain, providing cellular energy, and repairing tissues, organs, and cells. The body manufactures a supply of enzymes, but it can and should also obtain supplementation of enzymes through food. Sadly, due to processed and highly cooked food, many of our bodies are suffering the ability to make enough enzymes to compensate and further supplementation is needed. The majority of commercially available enzymes are digestive enzymes from various sources and are typically available over the counter in tablet, capsule, powder, and liquid forms. For maximum benefit, any digestive enzyme supplement you take should contain all of the major enzyme groups: amylase, protease, and lipase.

Research is increasingly showing that many physical and emotional conditions are greatly affected and/or relieved by the digestive tract. In fact, 75 percent of your serotonin receptors are in your gut. This is important because serotonin helps in mood regulation and low serotonin levels have been associated with feelings of depression. Taking a high-potency probiotic to support gut health boosts the brain and body's ability to combat stress and illness.

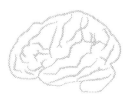

**Chapter Five**

# UNDERSTANDING THE FUNCTION

A friend called me recently to tell me about her shopping excursion. She's a professional decorator so people hire her to come, assess the needs, and then transform the interior of their homes. Sometimes they want the walls repainted and completely new flooring; other times walls are torn out for an "open concept" floor plan; sometimes she is hired to simply shop for the furniture, new fixtures, and fresh decor. Regardless of what is done, the goal is a completely new home.

If we liken the physical brain to the structure of a home and the inner cognitive operations to the function of that structure, it's similar to the physical edifice of a home versus the fixtures and decor inside. The structure serves the function, but they are distinctly different.

Not too long ago I went through a stressful few months of life. I was in the middle of selling a company I owned, running another company, and launching a new brand all while trying to maintain healthy relationships and keep my internal world grounded. Needless to say, I was juggling and life was a little bit hectic. One day, a close friend came over to my apartment and it was an absolute mess. I was embarrassed by the array of my belongings strewn across my one-bedroom place and I am fairly certain I apologized about fourteen times to her for the clutter. She told me later (thankfully, she waited until I was in a healthier place in my life), that she recognized that day that my home had been a reflection of my soul. She knew I was in distress when she saw the environment I had allowed around me. That correlation between the internal and external world isn't always true for everyone, but I knew that day it was true for me. I was stressed; I was tired; I didn't have much capacity; so, it made sense that my home would then reflect that. Sure enough, after the company sold, I had shored up the loose ends in my life that were causing excess stress, and I got internally grounded and decompressed, my home was back in tip-top shape and stayed that way permanently. I can still tell the difference when I'm feeling stressed internally because that is what my body and my environment manifest. When I'm grounded and at peace, my body and environment reflect that reality. And sometimes, just sometimes, I decide what I'm going to feel before it manifests. (But more on that later).

Your home may get cleaned on a regular basis, but never get redecorated. Similarly, your brain engages in a natural cleaning and con-solidation processes (think of this like the on-going maintenance and cleaning in your home). It might come as a surprise that there are people who live their entire lives without ever redecorating the interior of their homes. For my entire childhood, both sets of my grandparents had the exact same decorations and furnishings. This was a far contrast from the home I was raised in that changed decor by the season. For most of us, we're used to redecorating or upd-ating our homes at least every few years. Not many people go decades without updates to their home. But to my amazement, there are many who don't address the "redecoration" of their minds.

If cleaning is your brain's unconscious consolidation of thought, redecorating is choosing to engage in new patterns of thought. It's not uncommon for people to carry around toxic thoughts, old beliefs, negative mindsets, and traumatic memories for years, if not decades. It takes work to consciously alter thought processes or unidentify with stress or trauma. But I'd venture to say that it's better to undergo the work it takes to clean out the closets and redecorate the interior of your "home" (mind) than to live years in an environment where you aren't thriving.

# A New Model of The Mind

Instead of reducing **cognitive functions** to minute parts, I'm going to be working on a new model that is both theoretical and neuroscientifically sound based on the model that we are a spirit, we have a soul (mind, will, and emotions) and we live in a body.

The biological, neurochemical, and metaphysical functions of our bodies (the hardware) operate on the software of our soul (our mind, will and emotions). The functions of the "soul" (mind, will, and emotions) include the cognitive functions: perception (alertness), attention, cognition, memory, emotional regulation, language, motor skills, visual and spatial processing, and executive function.

**There are five main cognitive functions: *perception, attention, cognition, memory*, and *emotional regulation*.**

We will refer to these interchangeably as "cognitive processes" or "cognitive functions", but they are understood to be the functions operating on the structure of the brain and may manifest as "mind", "will", or "emotion" as the expression. Also, for clarification, sometimes the term "cognition" is used as a general term to encompass all cognitive functions. This is meant distinctly from the "cognitive process" of cognition which can be selectively rehearsing information, but usually the broad term is meant as a catchall for the cognitive functions/processes.

**Five principles are true for all brains:**

1.  **The cognitive processes are active, rather than passive.**

2.  **The cognitive processes are efficient and accurate.**

3.  **The cognitive processes handle positive information better than negative.**

4.  **The cognitive processes are interrelated with one another; they do not operate in isolation.**

5.  **Many cognitive processes rely on both bottom-up and top-down processing.**

Regardless of the cognitive function (i.e. perception, attention, cognition, memory, or emotional regulation), the brain engages in different kinds of thought: **conscious** (or **cognitive**) and **unconscious** (or **metacognitive**) through a combination of electrical and chemical signals. (See the discussion about neurons and ligands in Chapter 2).

Conscious thought can be thought of like a straight line—it is ordered thought that has a clear beginning, middle, and end. It is temporal (meaning it has a time effect) that defines its sequence. If the sequential order is broken, the thought no longer makes sense. (Language is a good example of conscious thought).

Unconscious thought, in contrast, is non-linear or seemingly "disordered". Often it is thought to influence our behavior from a level "below the surface" in ways that we're unaware. Unconscious thought happens all the time and can be understood as "running in the background" while we're consciously thinking or even while we're asleep.

Dr. Bruce Lipton states that the conscious mind is the site of our personal identity and forms our creative mind. "It can see into the future, review the past, or disconnect from the present moment as it solves problems in our head... It is the mind that conjures up our 'positive thoughts'. In contrast, the unconscious mind is primarily a repository of stimulus-response tapes derived from instincts and learned experiences. The unconscious mind is fundamentally habitual; it will play the same behavioral responses to life's signals over and over again."[46]

Some scientists argue (and I would agree) that the main difference between conscious cognition and unconscious cognition is simply the amount of neural firing or neuropeptides at work at a given time. The more intense or prolonged the neural network fires, the more a cognition will rise from the unconscious and into the conscious.

**In our working model, we reduce the conscious cognitive functions that combines the mind, will, and emotions into one linear order (though they are happening usually simultaneously and not necessarily in succession).**

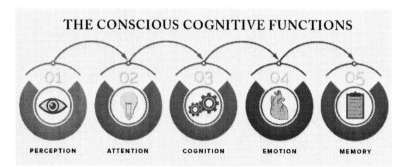

THE CONSCIOUS COGNITIVE FUNCTIONS

01  02  03  04  05

PERCEPTION    ATTENTION    COGNITION    EMOTION    MEMORY

A stimulus prompts an alertness or perception by the senses, if the stimulus is attended to it will then form a cognition (a thought). If this cognition is then dwelt upon (using the principle of Hebb's axiom of "neurons that fire together, wire together") the cognition will be stored in short-term memory and possibly long -term memory depending on the intensity or duration of the stimuli. The likelihood that the cognition will be stored in long-term memory is much higher if it has been attached to an emotion at the time of encoding.

# Neuroplasticity Revisited

**The good news about changing your brain is that you don't have to spend thousands of dollars and time shopping to alter your reality. Your brain is designed to naturally change over time. This is what we call neuroplasticity.** Age affects the level of neuroplasticity as does trauma. But by and large, throughout life, your neurons are going to be constantly shifting and changing depending on what you attend to.

For infants, there are millions of neural connections when they're born. The first eighteen months or so of life, all that the child is doing is pairing down the neural connections. Their brain is constantly changing as they learn and adapt to the world around them. That's why it's so important, especially for the first couple years of a child's life, that they are nurtured, held, spoken to, and have a variety of safe stimuli to help properly shape and guide their neural connections that will have effect for the rest of their life.

Our brains are mostly developed by the time we're young adults—about age 18 for most females and between 20 and 23 for most males. Neuroplasticity continues throughout our lifespan, but slows as we age. When people say that someone is "hard-headed," it can literally mean that they are hard-headed as the neural connections are less pliable and adaptable. As people age, their neural connections increasingly slow. This can create issues with memory, problems with executive function, decision-making, judgment, and even some motor movements.

Neuroplasticity, in short, is the ability of neural pathways to change over time. As we discussed in chapter two, neurons fire in networks. As a neuron is excited by the action potential, it fires and then sends a chain reaction until other neurons excite and also fire along the same bio-electrical pathway. This foundation of understanding is key to understanding how the brain processes sensory and perceptual information along the networks.

## Sensation vs. Perception

Before we talk about stress and trauma, I want to give a framework for how a "neuro-typical" brain processes stimuli and engages in cognitive functions. It will then be much easier to understand what happens to our brains when they undergo stress and trauma and how our functions become more limited. We will then examine how essential oils can aid our cognitive functions and benefit both neurotypical brains, as well as those needing some assistance.

Let's talk about the brain's processes from the perspective of "***sensation*** and ***perception***". ***Psychophysics*** is the study of how perceptions and memory systems link our mental world with the physical world. One of the pioneers of psychophysics, Herman Helmholtz, maintained the belief that it takes examining what the brain and nervous system are doing to fully give you the experience you have. He argued that we need to figure out what is going on internally that gives us the experience from the stimuli. In essence, we don't see the world as it is, we see it filtered through our sensory systems.

We cannot separate perception from memory or from cognition. As soon as you perceive something, it's in your memory. We see a view of the world that's constructed and stored in our memory by the brain. Memory is often not accurate to the specific events, but rather it has been filtered through our sensory systems and perceptual biases. For anyone who doubts this fact, simply engage in an argument with another person and record the entire thing on video. You have one recollection of the event, the other party has a different recollection based on their emotions, cognitions, and perceptions, and then there's the truth recorded on video.

Though there exists some argument from a few scientists, the general notion agreed upon by cognitive scientists is that most of the processing of the world comes from both a "***top-down***" and a "***bottom-up***" approach. Let me elaborate.

Remember that game when you were a child where you were blindfolded, would reach your hand into a bucket full of sand, and pull out one object from a myriad of choices? As you feel around the bucket of sand, you choose an abstract, medium sized object. It feels metallic, but you're not sure. It is rectangle in shape—you can tell because it fits in the palm of your hand. Suddenly you realize what you're holding: a matchbox car. This is an example of what your brain is doing at all times: both bottom-up and top-down processing.

When you reach your hands into the bucket of sand, this begins the "bottom-up" segment of processing. You are feeling the sensation of the grit of the sand; its weight; its cool temperature. All of those feelings are sensations recorded by your fingers, skin, and hand, and sent to your brain from the "bottom, up". When you finally grasp the object, that sensory information is sent from your nerve receptors in your fingertips and palm. From there, it is sent through the brainstem to the motor cortex and association areas of your temporal lobe, where your brain assembles the information to construct a perception of the item in question. When the brain perceives the object, it makes a judgment and decides "matchbox car" is the item you're holding, even though only one sense has informed this judgment. The brain's ability to perceive the object and sending the signal back to the hand from the "top, down". Your brain relies on both the sensory input and the perceptual cues in order to make sense of almost every scenario in life. In a neurotypical brain that isn't suffering from cognitive stress, trauma, or abnormal environmental influences, this is going to be a relatively simplistic and rapid process.

No one has quite figured out the "how", but we know from research that as input is received, the brain paradoxically brings the information from individual features such as color, motion, texture, shape, and orientation together in such a way that the whole is greater than the sum of the parts and it perceives one object. In this way, it could be argued that the literal world is not actually being perceived accurately at all, but rather it is an illusory glimpse that our selective attention and perceptual binding have allowed us to have, absorb, and process.

As we live life, we build experiences, memories, and associations around what we have learned over time and our brains begin to create "shortcuts" to streamline the amount of time it takes to perceive data and process it. Because our brains are wired to make associations rapidly, the brain will look for as many "short-cuts" to the perception as possible. These are what we call *"heuristics"*. It becomes clear that our know-ledge of what is going on around us then feeds into what we perceive is going on. Our expectations—the heuristics our brain creates—feed into what we then perceive through our senses.

In this example, if you were a child who had played hours and hours with a matchbox car before you ever put your hand in the bucket of sand, your brain would perceive "matchbox car" much more quickly than a child who had been exposed to that toy a limited amount, or not at all. Little Johnny, who had grown up on the other side of the world and then moved to your neighborhood, put his hand in the box of sand and grabbed the matchbox car, but had never seen one before, might have a very difficult time accurately perceiving what he held in his hand. The expectation (heuristic) helps to form the reality.

In a top-down recognition, object inter-pretation may not be influenced by the physical form or sensory experience, but rather by the expectations, existing beliefs, and cognitions of the individual. Most of the time the top-down processing is within milliseconds and can often be unconsciously performed. The perceptual system develops heuristics (or shortcuts) to gather information about the continuity, simi-larity, proximity, symmetry, or other rules to quickly define objects in real space. Many of the heuristics are grouped and referred to as the Gestalt grouping principles, which simply de-scribe the natural and learned processing meth-odology. The particular heuristics the individual uses will vary from person to person and object to object based on their biases.

Often when people think about how the brain processes information, they like to localize things to one part of the brain or another in an attempt to simplify their understanding. Though debate still exists amongst scientists about how the brain processes input, it is clear from both what is known of object perception and that which is still unknown, that no one, central process is responsible for recognition. Rather, multiple steps along various tracks in the neural pathways result in sensory perception. It is also notable that the divide between top-down and bottom-up processing is still unclear and it is likely that they occur simultaneously and unconsciously. The amazing thing about the brain is that it is not only adaptable to change over time, but it is complex.

An example of how the brain adapts was detailed by Dr. Richard J. Davidson and Sharon Begley in the book, *The Emotional Life of Your Brain.*

> "Scientists led by Alvaro Pascual-Leone, of Harvard University, had half a group of volunteers learn a simple five-finger keyboard piece, practicing over and over for a week with their right hand. They then used neuroimaging to determine how much of the motor cortex was responsible for moving those fingers, finding that the intense practice had expanded the relevant region. That was not too surprising, since other experiments had found that learning specific movements causes such an expansion. But the scientists had the other half of their group of volunteers only imagine playing the notes; they did not actually touch the ivories. Then the researchers measured whether the motor cortex had noticed. It had. The region that controls the fingers of the right hand had expanded in the virtual pianists just as it had in the volunteers who had actually played the piano. Thinking, and thinking alone, had increased the amount of space the motor cortex devoted to a specific function."[47]

## How a Neurotypical Brain Processes

Most human beings have five senses: sight (vision), smell (olfaction), taste (gustation), hearing (aural), and touch (haptic). (Note: some consider extra sensory perception a sixth sense and though I don't doubt it's reality, we won't be covering it in this forum). With each of the senses, (with the exception of olfaction, covered in chapter 3), most sensory information is processed similarly and passes through the brain stem before localizing in the specific association cortices. There are three distinct phases that start at the neural and chemical level before gathering and being processed and forming the cognitive functions we will discuss shortly.

**When a sensory stimulus comes in through one of the senses, you become alerted to it and if you give it attention, the perception of the stimuli will continue. The attention then gives way to cognition — the conscious mental processing of the stimulus. The more something is attended to and cognitively processed, it will then be stored in short-term memory and potentially in long-term memory. The likelihood of a stimulus being stored in the memory system will be even greater if it is linked to an emotion.**

To give an example of how sensory input (minus olfaction) is processed, let's use a visual cue. The process begins when light enters your eyes. There are then three distinct phases in which light is processed as color through the eyes and in the brain: detection, discrimination, and appearance.

The first phase is known as detection. During detection, light is absorbed by photosensitive receptors which are sensitive to specific wavelengths. Humans have three types of cone receptors: short-wavelength cones (S-cones with about 420 nm peak), medium-wavelength cones (M-cones with about 535 nm peak), and long-wavelength cones (L-cones with about 565 nm peak). These cones are more frequently referred to as the blue, green, and red cones, respectively, as their peak wavelength generally falls within those color ranges. By combining the three cone types, we are able to see wavelengths between approximately 400 nm and 700 nm.

Once the stimulus hits the eyes, the cone receptor cells in the retina detect the disparate light input and travel through the optic nerve to the optic chasm where the signals are crossed before going to the lateral geniculate nucleus in the visual cortex.

Thus begins the second phase of the process: discrimination. This takes place in the lateral geniculate nucleus (in the thalamus) where the ganglion cells within repackage the information into signals that narrow the ability to discern colors. These cellular receptive fields respond either antagonistically or agonistically to the S-, M-, and L-cones.

Once the repackaging of the cone-signals is complete, the third step of color perception commences: appearance. In this stage, the brain assigns perceived colors to the visual light or space input. The assignment of color also is regulated so that it does not change dramatically, but rather maintains constancy despite viewing conditions undergoing alteration (i.e. the color red will always be red even if you are in a room where the light has a blue hue instead of a bright white tone).

The brain then applies a perception to the visual input after it has been identified. All of this takes place beginning in the retinas of the eyes, crosses through the optic nerve, is processed through the thalamus in the limbic lobe, and then through the visual cortices of the occipital lobe before conscious thought and language is applied by the other cortices of the brain like the frontal and temporal lobes. It's a highly complex and dynamic system of neural connections that can adapt and change over time. Regardless of the stimuli, the brain takes largely the same approach to the processing of the input.

Although the brain processes information from the senses in generally the same fashion, research has shown that positive information is better retained than negative information.[48] Similarly, information or experiences are better stored in memory systems (both short-term and long-term memory) when they are attached to an emotion—with positive emotions being more impactful than negative emotions for the retention of the data. The retrieval of those memories is also mood-dependent; we recall positive experiences more readily when in a positive mood, while negative experiences are recalled more easily when in a negative mood.

## The Design of a Healthy Individual

**We've discussed the basics of how a *"neurotypical"* brain processes stimuli, but now let's look at what happens when the brain undergoes stress or trauma.** The amazing thing about humans is that we're built with incredible resiliency and the ability to withstand hardship. From the time that we are born, we are hardwired for struggle and designed to overcome challenges and learn from them as we grow. Under ideal circumstances, challenges are easily overcome and we learn and adapt with each new challenge. If life were a staircase, in a perfect world we'd only ever be ascending and sometimes two steps at a time. Unfortunately, thanks in part to environmental stressors, neglect, abuse, toxic chemicals, and poor choices, we can struggle not just to climb the stairs, but sometimes we might take a tumble down the whole flight.

One of the challenges we face in life is in the form of stress. Not all stress is bad. In fact, stress can be wonderfully helpful to keeping us safe and motivated. But stress unchecked and unfettered can be amazingly destructive.

According to the American Psychological Association, **stress** is defined as "the pattern of specific and nonspecific responses an organism makes to stimulus events that disturb its equilibrium and tax or exceed its ability to cope."[49]

**We're designed to withstand stress and in reality, not all stress is bad. There are two types of stress, one positive and one negative: *eustress* (positive) and *distress* (negative).**

Eustress is a form of positive stress that motivates, allows you to focus energy and achieve. It is short-term and we perceive the stressor as being something within our coping abilities. Often eustress feels exciting and experiencing it improves our performance.

Distress (or stress as we'll use generally in this context) can be acute (brief and with a clear onset and offset), episodic (related to specific incidents and often affects people who are prone to set unrealistic expectations or worry—not as brief as acute, but not lasting like chronic), and chronic stress (brought by long-term exposure to stressors that have not been resolved). Stress comes as a result of a **stressor**, an internal or external event or stimulus that interrupts your equilibrium and prompts a response.

Unresolved stress not only affects our brains, but it can be damaging to our bodies. According to a study from the American Medical Association, 75 percent of all illnesses and dis-eases people suffer from today have stress as a clear factor.[50] In fact, based on the research data, Dr. Caroline Leaf argues that 75 to 98 percent of mental and physical illnesses come from one's thought life and stress plays a huge role.[51]

Stressors are sure to come and trigger us throughout life. The variable in question is not *if* or *when* stressors will happen, but how we will respond. Two individuals can experience the same stressor in very different ways and their responses will be based primarily by how they responded to stressors in the past. Research proves this to be true. Davidson reports that studies on sets of fraternal twins compared to identical twins give indicators that lead us to believe that the level of emotionality expressed and whether an individual will approach situations positively or negatively is related to the resilience and outlook of the individual.[52]

Using the staircase analogy, imagine if identical twin brothers Timmy and Tommy were both standing on a staircase on the second or third step when a strange dog comes into the room growling. Despite having the same genetic predisposition, they responded very differently. Tommy had previously avoided new animals and so this encounter with an unfamiliar dog would likely result in his choosing to stand still, take a step back, or run away (fight, flight, or freeze). Timmy, on the other hand, had petted quite a few dogs and therefore was not intimidated when this strange dog approached. He would likely choose to engage the dog in a non-combative manner rather than avoid or fight. In our analogy, Tommy, avoiding the stressor would remain on the same step as he didn't engage (or maybe even ran) from the stressor. Timmy, on the other hand, would have the ability to move forward because the stressor did not negatively affect him because of previous resilience that informed his outlook.

Our outlook on and resiliency toward stress is constantly changing (just like our brains) based on our choices and responses to our environment. Unfortunately, many of us have outlooks and resiliency factors that started out of our control, but can still very much affect how we approach stress.

Your brain consolidates as much information in as little time as possible (remember Brain Principle No. 2 from earlier? The cognitive processes are remarkably efficient and accurate). Naturally, your brain wants to make work as easy as possible so it begins to automate information—memories, emotions, thoughts—that are stored in the unconscious mind (metacognitive) and only are accessed when they're needed. As we've discussed, your brain (not to mention your human spirit) are learning even from within the womb. Before you're born, your brain is already wiring itself using neurons and neuropeptides for resiliency based upon the experiences affecting you and the environment you're in. Much of this is stored in your unconscious. Data shows that up to 99 percent of the decisions you make are based on what you have built and automatized into your unconscious, metacognitive level.[53]

Many think that sensations, feelings, or decisions simply "happen" to them. We know this to not be the case because the brain is constantly adapting at the unconscious level. The brain works as "a generative model of the world using past experience to construct the present. We speculate that it is not an objective, accurate model, but one that is shaped by the information that the organism has encoded in its history and tailored to its allostatic needs and motivations," according to Chanes and Barrett[54].

The body and mind use neuropeptides as the cue to either retrieve or repress emotions and behaviors. Dr. Eric Kandel and other researchers have shown that biochemical change at the receptor level is what influences our memory. According to Dr. Candace Pert, "The decision about what becomes a thought rising to consciousness and what remains an undigested thought pattern buried at a deeper level in the body is mediated by the receptors." She argues the fact that memory is encoded or stored at the receptor level means "that memory processes are emotion-driven and unconscious (but, like other receptor-mediated processes, can sometimes be made conscious)."[55]

If you've been learning since before you even entered the world, what exactly should you have learned? When law enforcement agents are training in order to identify counterfeit currency, they are not taught by identifying the counterfeit. Rather, they study authentic bills and know those so intimately that they can spot counterfeit immediately. This principle applies when we speak of the development of our metacognition. In order to understand what is "broken" or incorrect in our thought processes and approaches to stress, we have to look at what the truth is in how we were designed to function. This can be observed by identifying our basic needs and whether or not we were given them in both formative years and in pivotal moments (i.e. moments with past stressors) when it mattered most. When it comes to approaching new (and potentially stressful) situations, most individuals who were given their basic needs in the developing years will have a greater level of openness and resiliency than those who did not.

Famed psychologist, Abraham Maslow, developed a "Hierarchy of Needs", a theory of psychological health that is predicated on fulfilling innate human needs in priority, culminating in self-actualization. Though some have taken criticism to both his methods (or lack thereof) and the caveat from Maslow that once a need has been "achieved" it is no longer desired (i.e. stair three has been conquered so therefore it is irrelevant), the hierarchy has stood the test of time and is a useful guide. I will note (despite having used an analogy of a stairwell relating to resiliency and stress), I do disagree with Maslow that the basic needs are hierarchical in nature and therefore are dependent upon each other. Rather, I argue that they are cumulative and not mutually exclusive. I also argue that "self-actualization" is not the pinnacle of a healthy individual, but rather "autonomy"—the ability for a person to achieve their full, individual potential. Therefore, in this model, autonomy—the ability to govern one's self—can be achieved as the basic physical and psychological needs are met.

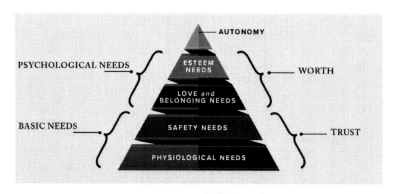

There are a few fundamental needs, that if met, will create a security that enables an individual to exist with resilience and openness. These needs can build upon one another, but also can dynamically innervate to create a "whole" and balanced individual. Humans are wired for connection (attachment, love, or belonging can also be interchangeable terms). The hierarchy of needs defines the ideal conditions in which autonomy, built on trust and worth, can be achieved.

Attachment by an individual precedes the autonomy of an individual and is predicated on two primary forces: trust and worth. Physiological needs and security needs combine to form trust. This trust affirms to the individual that their basic needs will be met in a timely and consistent manner. Psychological needs such as belonging and esteem combine to form worth. A sense of worthiness involves the individual understanding that they are worthy of giving and receiving affirmation and affection. If there is a breach in trust or a lack of understanding of worth, the individual may feel a level of vulnerability that acts as an internal stress. The vulnerability itself is not alarming, but is a gateway either into positive or negative emotions depending on the response of the person.

Dr. Brené Brown has done extensive research on vulnerability, shame, and the connectedness of those who live wholeheartedly. She defines vulnerability as uncertainty, risk, and emotional exposure. Brown states, "Vulnerability is the core of all emotions and feelings. To feel is to be vulnerable. To foreclose on our emotional life out of a fear that the costs will be too high is to walk away from the very thing that gives purpose and meaning to living... We've confused *feeling* with *failing* and *emotions* with *liabilities*. If we want to reclaim the essential emotional part of our lives and reignite our passion and purpose, we have to learn how to own and engage with our vulnerability and how to feel the emotions that come with it."[56]

Stress affects our perceived level of vulnerability, but even more influential is the effect of trauma on an individual's ability to respond properly to stimuli and employ resiliency in the face of vulnerability.

# The Breakdown

### (When Trauma Occurs)

*Trauma* happens when a stressor is either severe, repeated consistently, or happens for a prolonged period of time that we are not equipped to respond. According to Peter Levine, an expert on trauma, trauma happens "when our ability to respond to a perceived threat is in some way overwhelming."[57]

Most researchers disagree on a precise defintion of trauma, but do agree that a typical trauma response might include physiological and psychological symptoms such as numbing, hyperarousal, hypervigilance, nightmares, flashbacks, feelings of helplessness, and avoidance behavior.

A common term used is **Post Traumatic Stress Disorder** (**PTSD**), to explain the effects of intense stress. In general, whether someone has been diagnosed with a condition or not, traumatic stress tends to evoke two emotional extremes: feeling either too much (overwhelmed) or too little (numb) emotion.

Because of the pendulum of feeling overwhelmed or numb, it is not uncommon for some trauma survivors to have difficulty regulating emotions such as anger, anxiety, sadness, and shame. This is even more so when the trauma occurred at a young age—a confirmation of the hierarchy of needs playing a role in the ability to be resilient when trust and worth have been established and the breakdown when they have not. For some with severe trauma, the mental construct of their identity can fragment and they can suffer from **Dissociative Identity Disorder** (**D.I.D.**) and some survivors of trauma can have issues with processing sensory input in a normal fashion (**Sensory Processing Disorder**).

The types of trauma can vary, but may include: violence (community, domestic, school), early childhood trauma, medical trauma, natural disasters, neglect, abuse (physical, sexual, emotional, or verbal), terrorism, and traumatic grief.

For clarity, I will define two types of trauma described by "The Life Model" with a third designation used by the American Psychological Association in the case of extremity.

**Trauma A is everything that you should have received, but did not. This is often referred to as "neglect" because the absence of basic necessities in life is felt as deeply traumatic as if abuse is done to us.** Types of Trauma A include malnutrition, abandonment, insecure emotional or physical bonds, lack of emotional security in the home.

**Trauma B is outside trauma (or overwhelming stimulus) done to you that caused overload and an inability to process. This is often referred to as "abuse" and can be promoted by any variety of stimuli.** Types of

Trauma B include physical, sexual, or emotional abuse, experiences of a natural disaster, an emotionally troubling breach of relationship, death, loss.

**Complex Trauma** is defined as the pervasive impact, including developmental consequences, of being exposed to multiple or prolonged traumatic events. Complex trauma typically involves exposure to sequential or simultaneous occurrences of maltreatment, "including psychological maltreatment, neglect, physical and sexual abuse, and domestic violence.... Exposure to these initial traumatic experiences—and the resulting emotional dysregulation and the loss of safety, direction, and the ability to detect or respond to danger cues—often sets off a chain of events leading to subsequent or repeated trauma exposure in adolescence and adulthood". [58]

According to T.C. Schneirla, "Whether to approach or avoid is the fundamental psychological decision an organism makes in relation to its environment."[59]

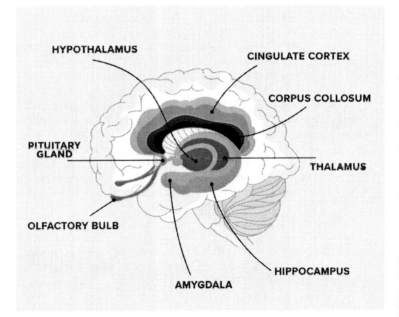

## So, what happens to your brain when it's stressed or suffering from trauma?

It is the job of the nervous system to monitor the environment, assess the situation, interpret the signals, and organize the appropriate responses in the body. There are two systems in your body that assemble to respond to stressors: the ***Hypothalamic-Pituitary-Adrenal Axis (HPA axis)***, which helps to respond to external threats, and the immune system, which helps us respond to threats internally (like viruses or bacteria). For the purposes of this book, we will only be discussing the HPA axis, however much can be said for the immune system and its role.

To illustrate the HPA axis, let's use the analogy of a fire. The fire is the stressor and your goal is to put it out as quickly and efficiently as possible. When your senses (you see, smell, hear, or feel the fire) receive input that is perceived as being potentially dangerous (or novel), it sends the signal through your ***thalamus***, which is situated in the ***diencephalon*** and acts as a relay station for sensory and motor information from the ***brainstem*** to the ***cerebral cortex***. Imagine that your thalamus is the switchboard operator to route the information appropriately. No sensory information, with the exception of olfactory information, reaches the cerebral cortex without stopping first through some part of the thalamus.

The "switchboard" of the thalamus receives the message that there is a potentially dangerous fire and sends the information to the ***limbic lobe***, where the ***amygdala*** receives it first. The amygdala, we know, perceives and assesses objects and situations and initiates an emotional response (positive or negative). When the amygdala is stimulated, most of the time the individual (or animal) stops and becomes very attentive. The amygdala is like the fire alarm that goes off once it has received the message from the thalamus.

As the amygdala is going off like a fire alarm, the alert is sent to the 911 operator for help. The 911 operator is a tag-team of the hypothalamus and the pituitary gland. Together, they call emergency responders to send signals to your body to react appropriately to the stressor (i.e. the fire). The **hypothalamus** controls the **autonomic nervous system** and is a major visceral control center that is also involved in limbic functions. The **pituitary gland** is known as the "master gland" because it is responsible for mobilizing so many emergency responders (50 trillion cells to be exact!). The emergency responders are **adrenaline** and stress hormones like **cortisol** that get pumped into your body to help you overcome the danger.

This information flows in a cascade from the thalamus to the amygdala, to the hypothalamus and then to the pituitary gland. Once the hypothalamus receives the alarm from the amygdala, it secretes a substance called **corticotropin-releasing factor** (**CRF**), which then travels to the pituitary gland. As soon as the pituitary gland realizes that CRF has been released, it activates the release of **adrenocorticotropic hormones** (**ACTH**) into the blood. The ACTH travels to the **adrenal glands** (located on top of the kidneys) and signals to send emergency responders to help.

Emergency responders are adrenaline (produced by the adrenal glands) and stress hormones like cortisol. These are the "fight, flight, or freeze" hormones that mobilize to enable us to respond to the fire. The emergency responders (the stress hormones) are activated, they work by constricting the blood vessels of the digestive tract and visceral organs, which therefore forces the blood flow to the arms and legs where movement can happen to avoid or face the stressor. The visceral organs stop doing their life-sustaining work of digestion, absorption, excretion, and other functions so that the rest of the body can be mobilized using that energy to eliminate the danger.

As adrenaline, cortisol, and the other stress hormones (the emergency responders) show up on the scene and go to work, there is a Fire Chief who comes to oversee the operation and make sure there are enough emergency personnel on the scene to put out the fire. The Fire Chief is your **hippocampus** that communicates back to the 911 Operator (hypothalamus): "even though the alarm is still blaring, we have enough emergency responders and you don't need to send any more." The hippocampus is largely responsible for memory and also aids the body in emotional regulation. Through negative feedback, cortisol begins to control its own secretion, inhibiting the hypothalamus' release of CRH and the pituitary's release of ACTH, thereby bringing the body back to a state of homeostasis rather than arousal.

Once the message is received by the hypothalamus (the 911 operator) that no more help is needed, it sends the signal to the **prefrontal cortex**, where you do your thinking and reasoning, to calm and turn off the alarm. Remember that the prefrontal cortex is not a part of the limbic lobe, but it's the "boss" part of the brain that processes, understands, forms judgments, and modulates our emotions.

When the HPA axis is engaged, not only is blood flow redirected from the visceral organs, but from the cortices of the brain, including the prefrontal cortex in the frontal lobe. This explains why our ability to think logically and rationally is inhibited when we are experiencing a lot of emotion.

Instead of seeing this cascade of events as "emotional regulation", you could say your brain is doing what it always does: identifying, sorting, consolidating, and activating information based on the data it's receiving. This process (negative, positive, or neutral) could also be called the "control network".

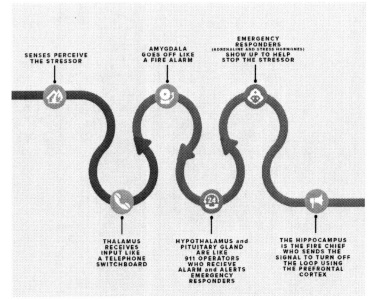

SENSES PERCEIVE
THE STRESSOR

AMYGDALA
GOES OFF LIKE
A FIRE ALARM

EMERGENCY
RESPONDERS
(ADRENALINE AND STRESS HORMONES)
SHOW UP TO HELP
STOP THE STRESSOR

THALAMUS
RECEIVES
INPUT LIKE
A TELEPHONE
SWITCHBOARD

HYPOTHALAMUS and
PITUITARY GLAND
ARE LIKE
911 OPERATORS
WHO RECIEVE
ALARM and ALERTS
EMERGENCY
RESPONDERS

THE HIPPOCAMPUS
IS THE FIRE CHIEF
WHO SENDS THE
SIGNAL TO TURN OFF
THE LOOP USING
THE PREFRONTAL
CORTEX

According to Barrett, "your control network helps select between emotion and non-emotion concepts (is this anxiety or indigestion?), between different emotion concepts (is this excitement or fear?), between different goals for an emotion concept (in fear, should I escape or attack?), and between different instances (when running to escape, should I scream or not?)."[60] Barrett claims that from the brain's perspective, the experience or expression of emotion is nothing more than categorization.

"When you have an experience that feels like your so-called rational side is tempering your emotional side—a mythical arrangement that you've learned is not respected by brain wiring —you are constructing an instance of the concept 'Emotion Regulation,'" says Barrett.[61]

This is good news because it puts the power back in the hands of your conscious mind to make decisions to change emotions, just like any other cognitive process. Emotions in and of themselves are not bad. They are merely matter made up of electrical and chemical components and can be altered.

## What happens when your brain and body are in the cognitive control loop of the HPA axis?

Firstly, when the HPA axis is engaged and mobilizing the body, the work of the immune system is suppressed in order to conserve energy. When the HPA axis has completed its loop and is shut off, the immune system function is restored. If the HPA axis has not been turned off (as can be the case under stress or trauma), immune function is compromised.

Similarly, we mentioned that blood flow is redirected from the visceral organs and the prefrontal cortex, but during this time, memories may not be encoded properly due to reduced hippocampal volume. Learning, memory, and emotional regulation can all be affected by the reduced ability for connections in the hippocampus.

We're going to discuss how essential oils can help this HPA axis and the loop of the cognitive control network, but first, what happens when you can't turn the HPA axis off? For some, this may seem like a normal and natural process and the control loop is working without glitch. But for those under stress, trauma, chronic pain, or in depressed states, the fire alarm that triggers this stress loop might be continually going off and the control loop be severely hindered and not turn off without aid.

To summarize what happens under severe stress and trauma, Dr. J. Douglas Bremner states that patients with post-traumatic stress disorder (PTSD) show "smaller hippocampal and anterior cingulate volumes, increased amygdala function, and decreased medial prefrontal/anterior cingulate function. Additionally, patients with PTSD show increased cortisol and norepinephrine responses to stress."[62] **Specifically, the amygdala, hippocampus, and prefrontal cortex are very strongly affected by stress.**

Research has shown that the left prefrontal cortex contributes to the production of positive emotion and the ability to hold in mind a desired goal and form a plan of action to reach it. Greater activation of the left prefrontal cortex (L-PFC) underlies positive emotions and greater activity in the right prefrontal cortex (R-PFC) is associated with negative emotions. In fact, the left prefrontal cortex has been linked directly with sending inhibitory signals to the amygdala to turn off the fire alarm in the wake of negative experiences. According to Davidson and Begley, research has shown that "individuals with depressive symptoms had significantly less activation in the left frontal region compared with nondepressed participants."[63]

From these and other findings (confirming the L-PFC equates with positive feelings and R-PFC equates with negative feelings), it has been concluded that individuals with *less* activation in certain zones of the frontal lobe have a more difficult time turning off negative emotion when it has been turned on because the communication relays to the amygdala are inhibited. The reverse has also been found to be true. According to Davidson, "activity in the L-PFC *shortens* the period of amygdala activation, al-lowing the brain to bounce back from an upsetting experience."

Studies examining the white matter connections between the PFC and the amygdala prove that strong glial cells improve the number of transmission to turn off the alarm signals and cause greater resiliency.[64] (For ways to increase the white matter tracts, see chapter 4).

**In short, those who are slow to recover from adversity, have fewer signals traveling from the prefrontal cortex to the amygdala. This could happen because of a structural issue (i.e. brain injury) or because of a lack of connecti-**

ons between the two structures. People with trauma have issues with their pre-frontal cortex not shutting off their emotional alarms. They live in constant flight, fight, or freeze. When the prefrontal cortex and the amygdala connection is strengthened, resiliency increases.

After examining infant rats, researchers found that early, unexpected, trauma, and maternal deprivation increases the death of both neurons and glia cells in cerebral and cerebellar cortices.[65] Another study found that increased exposure to cumulative life stress (e.g., exposure to severe marital conflict, severe chronic illness of a close family member or friend) was associated with poorer spatial working memory performance and decreased volumes of white and gray matter in the prefrontal cortex of non-maltreated youth.[66]

The hippocampus, which is highly involved in verbal declarative memory, is very sensitive to the effects of stress. Studies have shown that animals who have damage to neurons in the hippocampus had an inhibition of neurogenesis and learning.[67] High levels of glucocorticoids (caused by increased cortisol being reported to the hippocampus from the adrenals) that can be seen with stress were also associated with deficits in new learning.[68]

Another study showed how feelings of depresssion caused hippocampal volume to decrease by 50 percent causing an impairment of learning, memory, and the regulation of emotion.[69] The study also showed how when the depressive state was turned off, the hippocampal volume increased. Similar studies report that antidepressant treatments have been shown to block the effects of stress and/or promote healthy cellular growth.[70]

We will dive into specific essential oils and how they affect the brain in Chapter 7, but I want to highlight a couple of key studies in this context to give you hope that the fire alarm can, in fact, be turned off.

One of my favorite essential oils of all time is frankincense (also known by its scientific name, *Boswellia*). Boswellia resin contains incensole acetate, a constituent that has been found to modulate the hypothalamic–pituitary–adrenal (HPA) axis and influence hippocampal gene expression. Researchers believe this can lead to beneficial behavioral effects and supports its potential as a novel treatment of depressive-like disorders. In other words, properties in frankincense (incensole acetate) help to balance your limbic lobe when your fire alarm is going off.[71]

According to one Brazilian study, researchers found that inhaling essential oils rich in the monoterpene, linalool, can be useful as a means to attain relaxation, counteract occasional anxiety and aggressive behavior.[72] Some great sources for linalool include: lavender (containing about 35 percent), ylang ylang (containing 25 percent), and rosewood (containing 82 percent). In another study comparing lavender and rosemary, a research team found that "smelling lavender and rosemary decreased the stress hormone, cortisol, which protects the body from oxidative stress." [73]

Essential oils aid the brain and body by supporting the immune system as well as reducing strain on the brain when under stress or trauma. Not only can properties in some essential oils modulate the HPA axis, but they can improve all other the cognitive functions, including perception, attention, cognition, memory, and emotional regulation. Understanding how a healthy brain and body are designed to function allows us to better respond when stress, trauma, environmental factors, or our choices have caused a breakdown in function. In the next chapter, we'll talk about what happens when stress and trauma gets passed down from our parents and how it affects both our conscious and unconscious cognitive functions before we deep dive in the following chapter into how specific oils have been shown to aid our brains and bodies in greater detail. Although the brain and its response mechanisms and control network is complex, the amazing thing is that essential oils can serve to support, modify, and repair this amazing functional masterpiece!

# IN OTHER WORDS...
## (A SUMMARY OF CHAPTER 5)

The biological, neurochemical, and metaphysical functions of our bodies (the hardware) operate on the software of our soul (our mind, will and emotions). The functions of the "soul" (mind, will, and emotions) include the cognitive functions (or "cognitive processes"): perception (or alertness), attention, cognition, memory, emotional regulation, language, motor skills, visual and spatial processing, and executive function.

**Five principles are true for all brains:**
1. The cognitive processes are active, rather than passive.
2. The cognitive processes are remarkably efficient and accurate.
3. The cognitive processes handle positive information better than negative information.
4. The cognitive processes are interrelated with one another; they do not operate in isolation.
5. Many cognitive processes rely on both bottom-up and top-down processing.

The main difference between conscious cognition and unconscious cognition is simply the amount of neural firing or neuropeptides at work at a given time. The more intense or prolonged the neural network fires, the more a cognition will rise from the unconscious and into the conscious. In our working model, we reduce the conscious cognitive functions that combines the mind, will, and emotions into one linear order (though they are happening usually simultaneously and not necessarily in succession): perception, attention, cognition, memory, and emotional regulation. They are understood as the functions operating on the structure of the brain and may manifest as "mind," "will," or "emotion" as the expression.

The brain is designed to naturally change over time through neuroplasticity. Age affects the level of neuroplasticity as does trauma. By and large, throughout life, neurons are constantly shifting and changing depending on what the individual attends to.

We don't see the world as it is, but rather we see it filtered through our sensory systems. We cannot separate perception from memory or from cognition. As soon as you perceive something, it's in your memory. We see a view of the world that's constructed and stored in our memory by the brain. Memory is often not accurate to the specific events, but rather it has been filtered through our sensory systems and perceptual biases. Most of the processing of the world comes from both a "top-down" and a "bottom-up" approach (the brain's ability to perceive the object [top-down] from the senses [bottom-up]). The brain relies on both the sensory input and the perceptual cues in order to make sense of almost every scenario in life. In a neurotypical brain that isn't suffering from cognitive stress, trauma, or abnormal environmental influences, this is going to be a relatively simplistic and rapid process.

As we live, we build experiences, memories, and associations around what we have learned over time and our brains begin to create "shortcuts" to streamline the amount of time it takes to perceive data and process it. Because our brains are wired to make associations rapidly, the brain will look for as many "shortcuts" to the perception as possible (known as "heuristics"). Our knowledge of what is going on around us then feeds into what we perceive about the world. Our expectations—the heuristics our brain creates—feed into what we then perceive through our senses.

With each of the senses, with the exception of olfaction, most sensory information is processed similarly and passes through the brain stem before localizing in the specific association cortices. There are three distinct phases that start at the neural and chemical level before gathering and being processed and forming the cognitive functions. When a sensory stimulus comes in through one of the senses, your brain is alerted to it and if you give it attention, the perception of the stimuli will continue. The attention then gives way to cognition—the conscious mental processing of the stimulus. The more something is attended to and cognitively processed, it will then be stored in short-term memory and potentially in long-term memory. The likelihood of a stimulus being stored in the memory system will be even greater if it is linked to an emotion.

Humans are designed to withstand stress, and in reality, not all stress is bad. There are two types of stress, one positive and one negative: eustress (positive) and distress (negative). Eustress is a form of positive stress that motivates, allows you to focus energy and achieve. Distress (or simply "stress") comes as a result of a stressor—an internal or external event or stimulus that interrupts equilibrium and prompts a response. Unresolved stress not only affects our brains, but it can be damaging to our bodies. According to a study from the American Medical Association, 75 percent of all illnesses and diseases people suffer from today have stress as a clear factor. Dr. Caroline Leaf argues that 75 to 98 percent of mental and physical illnesses come from one's thought life and stress plays a huge role.

Stressors are sure to come throughout life. The variable in question is not if or when stressors will happen, but how we will respond. Two individuals can experience the same stressor in very different ways. Their response will be based primarily in how they have responded to stressors in the past. Naturally, the brain wants to make work as easy as possible so it begins to automate information—memories, emotions, thoughts—that are stored in the unconscious mind (metacognitive) and only are accessed when they're needed. Data shows that up to 99 percent of the decisions you make are based on what you have built and automatized into your unconscious, metacognitive level.

There are a few fundamental needs, that if met, will create a security that enables an individual to exist with resilience to stress and openness. These needs can build upon one another, but also can dynamically innervate to create a "whole" and balanced individual. Humans are wired for connection (a.k.a. attachment, love, or belonging). The hierarchy of needs defines the ideal conditions in which autonomy, built on trust and worth, can be achieved. The autonomy of an individual is built on two primary forces: trust and worth. Physiological needs and security needs combine to form trust, which affirms to the individual that their basic needs will be met in a timely and consistent manner. Psychological needs such as belonging and esteem combine to form worth, which involves the individual understanding that they are worthy of giving and receiving affirmation and affection. If there is a breach in trust or a lack of understanding of worth, the individual may feel a level of vulnerability that acts as an internal stress. The vulnerability itself is not alarming, but is a gateway either into positive or negative emotions depending on the response of the person.

Stress—internal or external—affects our perceived level of vulnerability, but even more influential is the effect of trauma on an individual's ability to respond properly to stimuli and employ resiliency in the face of vulnerability. Trauma happens when a stressor is either so severe, is repeated consistently, or happens for a prolonged period of time that the individual is not equipped to respond or it feels too overwhelming. Traumatic stress tends to evoke two emotional extremes: feeling either too much (overwhelmed) or too little (numb) emotion. The types of trauma can vary, but may include: violence (community, domestic, school), early childhood trauma, medical trauma, natural disasters, neglect, abuse (physical, sexual, emotional, or verbal), terrorism, and traumatic grief. In general, we classify trauma into three types: Trauma A (neglect), Trauma B (abuse), and Complex Trauma.

When the brain is stressed or suffering from trauma, two types of responses are formed to combat the stressor: the Hypothalamic-Pituitary-Adrenal axis (HPA axis) and the immune system. It is the job of the nervous system to monitor the environment, assess the situation, interpret the signals, and organize the appropriate responses in the body. The HPA axis responds to external threats and the immune system responds to threats internally (like viruses or bacteria). When the HPA axis is engaged and mobilizing the body, the work of the immune system is suppressed in order to conserve energy. When the HPA axis has completed its loop and is shut off, the immune system function is restored. If the HPA axis has not been turned off (as can be the case under stress or trauma), immune function is compromised. For those under stress, trauma, chronic pain, or in depressed states, the fire alarm that triggers the HPA axis stress loop may be continually going off and the control loop be severely hindered to not turn off without aid.

Those who are slow to recover from adversity, have fewer signals traveling from the prefrontal cortex to the amygdala, where the HPA axis is turned on and off. A lack of control over the emotional control loop (HPA axis) could happen because of a structural issue (i.e. brain injury) or because of a lack of connections between the prefrontal cortex and the amygdala. People with trauma have issues with their prefrontal cortex not shutting off their emotional alarms. They live in constant flight, fight, or freeze. When the connection between the PFC and the amygdala is strengthened, resiliency increases.

Essential oils aid the brain and body by supporting the immune system as well as reducing strain on the brain when under stress or trauma. Properties in some essential oils have been found to modulate the hypothalamic–pituitary–adrenal (HPA) axis and influence hippocampal gene expression, helping to turn off the fire alarm when it is blaring and increasing effectiveness in all other cognitive functions, including perception, attention, cognition, memory, and emotional regulation.

# Glossary of Functional Terms

**adrenal glands**: located atop the kidney (*renal*), the adrenal gland is composed of the adrenal cortex and the adrenal medulla. This gland produces hormones which regulate bodily homeostasis and energy expenditure.

**adrenaline:** A hormone ($C_9H_{13}NO_3$) and neurotransmitter created in the adrenal glands which acts primarily as an arousal agent. Adrenaline causes an increase in heart rate and heart stroke volume, dilates the pupils, increases blood sugar levels, reduces blood flow to the skin and digestive tract, increases blood flow to the muscles, and suppresses immune function. Adrenaline is used to stimulate the heart in cases of cardiac arrest and sometimes in cardiac arrhythmias. Adrenaline is one of the main neurotransmitters in the fight-or-flight response and in activation of the reticular activating system (RAS). Its action is mimicked by amphetamines, caffeine, and Ritalin.

**adrenocorticotropic hormones** (**ACTH**): a hormone produced in the anterior portion of the pituitary gland. ACTH stimulates neurons in the cortex of the adrenal gland, subsequently leading to the secretion of *cortisol* and other glucocorticosteroids. ACTH is regulated by *corticotropic releasing factor (CRF)* released from neurosecretory cells in the periventricular hypothalamus. ACTH is part of an important feedback loop, the *hypo- thalamic pituitary adrenal (HPA) axis*. This HPA axis takes part in the regulation of stress. In the presence of emotional, physiological, or psychological stress, ACTH responds to CRF and releases cortisol from the adrenal cortex to support a continuation of the organism's response to stress.

**amygdala:** a collection of cells in the temporal lobe, named for its shape resembling an almond. It is one of the two core structures in the limbic circuits (the other being the hippocampus).

**attention:** a concentration of mental activity.

**autonomic nervous system:** The parts of the PNS (extending slightly into the CNS) that control smooth and cardiac muscle and glands. The autonomic nervous system includes *parasympathetic*, *sympathetic*, and *enteric* subdivisions.

**bottom-up processing:** the kind of cognitive processing that emphasizes the importance of information from the stimuli registered on sensory receptors. Any process of analysis which begins with data and seeks pattern or meaning: inductive reasoning. The opposite of deductive reasoning, or top-down processing, which imposes preexisting categories on data.

**brainstem:** in common medical usage, the *midbrain, pons,* and *medulla.*

**cerebral cortex (or 'cortex'; plural: cortices):** the 1.5- to 4.5-mm thick layer of gray matter that covers the surface of each cerebral hemisphere. The cerebral cortex includes olfactory areas (paleocortex) and the hippocampus (archi-cortex), but most of it is six-layered neocortex. The neocortex is made up of a huge number of columnar functional modules, organized into primary sensory and motor areas, unimodal association areas, multimodal association areas, and limbic areas.

**cognition:** mental activities involving the acquisition, storage, transformation, and use of knowledge.

**cognition:** mental activities involving the acquisition, storage, transformation, and use of knowledge.

**cognitive functions** (or **cognitive processes**)**:** a general term for all forms of mental processes including conscious ones such as perception, thought, and memory, as well as nonconscious processes such as grammatical construction, parsing of sensory data into percepts, and the neural control of physiological processes.

**Complex Trauma:** the pervasive impact, including developmental consequences, of being exposed to multiple or prolonged traumatic events.

**conscious** (or *cognitive*): an awareness of the external world, as well as thoughts and emotions about one's internal world.

**corticotropin-releasing factor** (**CRF**) (also **Corticotropin-releasing hormone** [**CRH**])**:** a releasing hormone found mainly in the para-ventricular nucleus of the *hypothalamus* that regulates the release of *corticotropin* (ACTH) from the *pituitary gland*. The paraventricular nucleus transports CRH to the anterior pituitary, stimulating *adrenocorticotropic hormone* (ACTH) release via CRH type 1 receptors, thereby activating the *hypothalamic-pituitary-adrenal axis* (HPA) and, thus, *glucocorticoid* release.

**cortisol:** A glucocorticosteroid hormone released from the adrenal cortex. Cortisol enhances sugar metabolism, thus contributing to increased energy levels. Cortisol also suppresses the immune system via a decrease in lymphocytes, which slows the formation of antibodies. Cortisol also directly affects neurons within the central nervous system, in particular cells in the *hypothalamus* associated with fight-or-flight responses and cells in the *hippo-campus* associated with the consolidation of memory. Cortisol is known as the "healer-killer": low or acute levels of cortisol are useful in healing and in necessary response to stress; high or chronic levels lead to neural and tissue damage and decreased immune function. The secretion of cortisol increases in response to both positive and negative stressors, emotional and physical anxiety, and trauma. Cortisol levels may be measured noninvasively by careful analysis of saliva.

**diencephalon:** literally the "in-between brain" made up mostly of the thalamus and hypo-thalamus.

**Dissociative Identity Disorder** (**D.I.D.**): a disorder characterized by the presence of two or more distinct personalities or identities in the same person, who recurrently exchange control of the person and who may have only some knowledge about each other and the history of the person involved.

**distress** (or **stress**): can be acute (brief and with a clear onset and offset), episodic (related to specific incidents and often affects people who are prone to set unrealistic expectations or worry—not as brief as acute, but not lasting like chronic), and chronic stress (brought by long-term exposure to stressors that have not been resolved). Distress comes as a result of a *stressor.*

***emotional regulation*** (or ***emotion***): in psychological terms, a reaction to a specific stimulus.

***eustress***: a form of positive stress that motivates, allows you to focus energy and achieve.

***heuristic:*** a general strategy that usually produces a correct solution, for example, in language, problem solving, and decision making.

***hippocampus:*** a specialized cortical area rolled into the medial *temporal lobe*. The hippocampus plays a critical role in the consolidation of new declarative memories. Anatomically, it has three subdivisions (until recently, usually referred to collectively as the hippocampal formation rather than the *hippocampus*), from within outward as follows: dentate gyrus, hippocampus proper, and subiculum.

***Hypothalamic-Pituitary-Adrenal Axis*** (***HPA axis***): a complex set of direct influences and feedback interactions among three endocrine glands: the *hypothalamus*, the *pituitary gland*, and the *adrenal glands*. These organs and their interactions constitute the HPA axis, a major neuroendocrine system that controls reactions to *stress* and regulates many body processes, including digestion, the immune system, mood and emotions, sexuality, and energy storage and expenditure.

***hypothalamus:*** the most inferior of the four divisions of the *diencephalon*, the hypothalamus plays a major role in orchestrating visceral and drive-related activities.

*limbic lobe:* the most medial lobe of the *cerebral hemisphere*, facing the midline and visible grossly only in sagittal section. The limbic lobes consists of a continuous border zone of cortex around the *corpus callosum*, comprising the *cingulate* and *parahippocampal gyri* and their narrow connecting isthmus; this lobe and its many connections, cortical and subcortical, make up and characterize the limbic system.

*memory:* the process of maintaining information over time.

*neurotypical:* not displaying or characterized by autistic or other neurologically atypical patterns of thought or behavior.

*perception:* the use of previous knowledge to gather and interpret the stimuli registered by the senses.

*pituitary gland:* an endocrine gland about the size of a pea and weighing 0.5 grams (0.018 oz) in humans. It is a protrusion off the bottom of the hypothalamus at the base of the brain. Hormones secreted from the pituitary gland help control: growth, blood pressure, certain functions of the sex organs, thyroid glands and metabolism as well as some aspects of pregnancy, childbirth, nursing, water/salt concentration at the kidneys, temperature regulation and pain relief.

*Post-Traumatic Stress Disorder* (*PTSD*): an anxiety disorder diagnosable according to the DSM-IV-TR. PTSD occurs in people who have experienced life-threatening events to which they respond with feelings of fear, helplessness, or horror. Not everyone who experiences a traumatic event will develop PTSD, but chances increase with more severe or repeated traumas. PTSD is marked by three distinct sets of symptoms: reexperiencing the trauma, avoiding reminders of the trauma, and experiencing increased physiological arousal. For a diagnosis of PTSD, someone must have experienced a qualifying trauma and have at least one reexperiencing, three avoidance, and two arousal symptoms, and the symptoms must last for at least a month, causing significant personal distress or functional impairment. Symptoms of PTSD typically begin shortly after a trauma; however, they may have a delayed onset, not developing until years later.

**prefrontal cortex:** the part of the frontal lobe anterior (front) to the premotor and supplementary motor areas. One of the two great areas of multimodal association cortex in human brains, important for working memory, planning, and choosing appropriate responses to social and life situations.

**psychophysics:** the study of how perceptions and memory systems link the mental world with the physical world.

**sensation:** the process of detecting and gathering information through external or internal stimulation.

**Sensory Processing Disorder**: a condition in which the brain has trouble receiving and responding to information that enters through the senses. Formerly referred to as sensory integration dysfunction, it is not currently recognized a distinct medical diagnosis. Some people with sensory processing disorder are oversensitive to things in their environment.

**stress:** 1. the pattern of specific and nonspecific responses an organism makes to stimulus events that disturb its equilibrium and tax or exceed its ability to cope. 2. a prolonged state of psychological and physiological arousal leading to negative effects on mood, cognitive capacity, immune function, and physical health.

**stressor:** an internal or external event or stimulus that interrupts your equilibrium and prompts a response.

**thalamus:** a collection of nuclei that collectively are the source of most extrinsic afferents to the cerebral cortex. Some thalamic nuclei (relay nuclei) receive distinct input bundles and project to discrete functional areas of the cerebral cortex. Others (association nuclei) are primarily interconnected with association cortex. Still others have diffuse cortical projections, and one has no projections at all.

**top-down processing:** the kind of cognitive processing that emphasizes the influence of concepts, expectations, and memory. An approach to the analysis of new information based on previously stored information so that new information is compared to stored patterns derived from old information for confirmation or disconfirmation of a match, or the applications of general rules, assumptions, or presuppositions to new information. Also called conceptually driven processing.

**trauma**: 1. any event which inflicts physical damage on the body or severe shock on the mind or both. 2. the damage inflicted by a traumatic event, as in the head trauma caused by a car accident or the stress caused by being falsely prosecuted.

**Trauma A** (or **neglect**): a phrase used to describe the basic needs an individual *should* have received, but did not. It may include, but is not limited to: malnutrition, abandonment, insecure emotional or physical bonds, lack of emotional security in the home.

***Trauma B*** (or ***abuse***): a phrase used to describe outside trauma (or overwhelming stimulus) done to an individual that caused overload and an inability to process. Can be promoted by any variety of stimuli that may include, but are not limited to: physical, sexual, or emotional abuse, experiences of a natural disaster, an emotionally troubling breach of relationship, death, loss.

***unconscious*** (or ***metacognitive***): Of or relating to any process or content of the mind of which the individual is not aware at a particular moment in time; in general usage, any part of the mind outside the awareness of the individual.

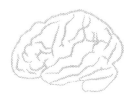

**Chapter Six**

# YOUR MOM'S BRAIN

## The Science of Epigenetics

There I was, sitting in her office one random morning for our set appointment. I was nervous for what she would tell me. A box was checked. And another. And another. Not only was my self-diagnosis of digestive issues and the allergies I suspected confirmed with each check, but a surprise awaited me.

"You have smallpox virus coming up in your cells. Were you aware of that?" the doctor said coolly.

"Uh. No, I had no idea," I responded.

"Did you have the vaccine?" she inquired.

My mind did a quick inventory through my medical history. I was sure there had been no smallpox vaccine. Nor had I manifested symptoms of the virus.

After a few seconds, I spoke up.

"I didn't have the vaccine, but *my mom* did," I stated firmly.

I remembered the scar on my mom's arm—it's distinct, like a round gridiron of honeycomb. She received it as a girl, probably in the third or fourth grade, when everyone was concerned and rapidly eradicating as many destructive viruses as possible. That wasn't the only thing I gained from her. She also gave me my brown hair and brown-green eyes, a fascination for studying the mind, and a slight propensity for fear and worry that ran in her family. Heredity is a fascinating and complicated thing.

What we have intuitively known for centuries, but science is now proving, is we are more than just our own bodies. We are actually compilations of generations encoded and embedded in our DNA. This phenomenon goes beyond just heredity to extend to what science calls "epigenetics." As we will soon see, it plays a major role in how our brains and bodies operate.

Just like the smallpox virus and a familial bent toward fear or worry, my mother (and father) also gave me a host of other things. You can see propensities toward certain emotions, challenges (like substance abuse), or "bents" in families. The bents are collected in a group and then passed down to their children and children's children. We all inherit DNA from our parents, but now science is beginning to show us that we can explain even other factors passed down such as memories, emotions, and even trauma. Epigenetics gives us an explanation for sometimes why we feel the way we do and how things can be imprinted on our subconscious.

The science of epigenetics explains the regulation of gene expression that is not based on DNA sequence but, rather, is controlled by heritable and potentially reversible changes to the DNA (methylation of cytosines) and/or the chromatin structure (acetylation, methylation, phosphorylation, and other modifications of histones).[74]

**Not only can genetic modification of the DNA affect our lives, the epigenetic markers can also play a role in how our genes are expressed.**

We now see from increasing evidence that in order for cells to operate "correctly," both the DNA sequence and the epigenetic factors must be normal. People who have epigenetic misregulation may suffer from a disease or condition, even if their DNA sequences are function-ally impeccable with no disease mutations or pre-disposing DNA sequence variants.[75] And it's not just diseases that can show up because of epi-genetics, but traumatic memories and stress are being shown to pass from one generation to another.

Research has been done on the children of Holocaust survivors who reported having terr-ible nightmares in which they are chased, per-secuted, tortured or annihilated, as if they were reliving the Second World War over and over again. They have been known to suffer from de-bilitating anxiety and depression which reduces their ability to cope with stress and adversely impacts their occupational and social function. The contention is that these individuals, who are now adults, somehow have absorbed the repr-essed and insufficiently worked-through Holoc-aust trauma of their parents, as if they have actually *inherited the unconscious minds* of their parents.[76]

Not only is the transmission of the uncon-scious mind of the parents transferring to the children, but actually may continue beyond the second generation and also include the grand-children, great grandchildren and perhaps oth-ers as well. This process is known as the trans-generational transmission of trauma (TTT) and has been repeatedly described in the academic literature for more than half a century.[77]

The traditional definition of epigenetics is the study of heritable changes in gene expression that are not due to changes in the underlying DNA sequence. But now, we're seeing the results of environmental stress or major emo-tional trauma "marking" the DNA that can be passed down. The stress or trauma leaves cert-ain marks on the chemical coating, or meth-ylation, of the chromosomes.[78] The coating becomes like a sort of "memory" of the cell and since all cells in our body carry this kind of memory, it becomes a constant physical reminder of past events, our own and those of our parents, grandparents and beyond. It's as though the body is keeping the score.[79]

# Just Because It's in Your Genes Doesn't Mean a Thing...

Another way to think about epigenetics is by using the analogy of a computer. Imagine that the genome is the hardware that remains fixed and the epigenome is like the software that has all the memory files. The epigenome can function like a "switch" that turns on or off depending on the stimulus it receives.

Kellermann states that,

> "From such a point of view, offspring of trauma survivors would be somehow 'programmed' to express a specific cognitive and emotional response in certain difficult situations. In effect, these children of PTSD parents would be suffering from a kind of 'software bug,' an error in a computer program or system that produces incorrect or unexpected results, or causes it to behave irrationally. This bug would for example switch on a panic attack and instruct the genes to prepare for 'fight and flight' when triggered, as if the individual were thrown into a Nazi persecution manuscript of catastrophic proportions, even in a relatively non-threatening situation. Metaphorically, such an epigenetic coating would affect the child of survivors in a way which is similar to a computer infected with a malicious virus, a malware that inflicts harm at certain unpredictable points in time."[80]

One of the primary evidences for epigenetics has been repeatedly shown by studying identical (monozygous) twins. They share the same DNA, but depending on the epigenetic markers passed down, the expressions of the twins' lives can be vastly different.

Dr. Richard J. Davidson and Susan Begley explain it this way,

> "The presence of a methyl group sitting on a piece of DNA is called an epigenetic change. It does not alter the sequence of the gene, denoted by the well-known strings of A's, T's, C's, and G's, but it does alter whether that gene will be expressed. And it may explain puzzles like the low concordance for schizophrenia between twins. At birth, identical twins are very similar epigenetically; if a particular gene is silenced in one twin, it is usually silenced in the other. But as we go throughout life, it turns out, we accumulate epigenetic changes. Either through random chance or because of the experiences we have—something akin to being nurtured by a parent, per-haps, but almost certainly many others that reach down into our very DNA—our genes take on more and more epigenetic marks, silencing some genes that had previously spoken and lifting the gag order that others had been under." [81]

Epigenetics explains much more than we have previously known about why we are the way we are. A 2005 study done on identical twins showed that twins who led similar lives and spent more of their lifetimes together were more similar epigenetically than identical twins who had different lifestyles and lived more of their lives apart, which presumably meant they shared fewer experiences. [82]

This is evidence for the old "nature versus nurture" argument. What part of who you are is a result of your genetics and what part is a result of the environment you grew up in and around? A traditional ratio for "nature versus nurture" is 60 percent of who you are is a result of your genetics and 40 percent has to do with your upbringing. However, what we can see from the study of epigenetics is that just because you have the genetic propensity doesn't mean those genes will be turned on (what is also known as the genes being "expressed").

Neuropsychiatrist Eric R. Kandel has repeatedly shown through research that our thoughts, even our imaginations can get "under the skin" of our DNA and can turn certain genes on and certain genes off, changing the structure of the neurons in the brain.[83] The ability to switch on or off our genes can have profound effect on our brains and bodies. According to one study, "thinking and feeling anger, fear, and frustration caused DNA to change shape according to thoughts and feelings. The DNA responded by tightening up and becoming shorter, switching off many DNA codes, which reduced quality expression." Dr. Caroline Leaf continued the conjecture, "So we feel shut down by negative emotions, and our body feels this too. But here's the great part: the negative shutdown or poor quality of the DNA codes was *reversed* by feelings of love, joy, appreciation, and gratitude!"[84]

# In Utero and Newborn Epigenetics

We discussed in the last chapter how love is the foundation of life and that the "soil" to comprise a healthy individual is simply the combination of the elements trust and worth—trust that your basic needs will be met in a timely and consistent manner and an understanding that you are worthy of giving and receiving affirmation and affection.

What many don't realize is that trust and worth aren't just needed when you're a small child who can talk or walk or play, but rather the process of learning trust and worth begins even before your conscious mind is fully developed. The epigenetic expression of your genes begins and is adapting before you even are aware of the world around you. Not only can the epigenetic markers be present on our genes because of our forefathers, but even our time in the womb and as newborn babies profoundly affects how our brains respond to stress, trauma, and establish resiliency in the world.

Karol K. Truman summarizes research done on babies in utero that gives great insight into how our mother's (and even our father's) experiences shape the development of our brains and bodies.

> "Until recently scientists believed that the infant was a virtual blank and, following Freud's dictum, that only at two or three years of age could personality begin to form. Gradually, however, over the last fifty years investigators have begun to break through the ignorance, preconceptions, and lack of data surrounding the prenatal and infant states to reveal a very different picture of these early stages of life. This emerging view gives a broader perspective on human consciousness and the intimate connections among human beings, as well as new insights into the meaning and responsibilities of parenthood.
>
> Recent research on infants shows that even at birth the child has mastered many sophisticated physical and psychological skills. It is increasingly clear that the infant develops these skills in the prenatal period. In *The Secret Life of the Unborn Child*, Dr. Thomas Verny tells us that the unborn child is not 'the passive, mindless creature' of the traditional pediatrics texts.

'We now know that the unborn child is an aware, reacting human being who from the sixth month on (and perhaps even earlier) leads an active emotional life. Along with this startling finding we have made these discoveries:

'The fetus can see, hear, experience, taste and, on a primitive level, even learn in utero... Most importantly, he can feel—not with the adult's sophistication, but feel nonetheless...'

The article discusses the unborn's development and his sensitivity to light at the sixteenth week of pregnancy. By the fourth month the unborn baby has developed his basic reflexes which allow facial expressions. By the fifth or six month the unborn is as sensitive to touch as a newborn.

From the 24th week on he hears all the time—listening to the noises in his mother's body, and to voices, music, etc. Between 28 to 34 weeks his brain's neural circuits are as advanced as a newborn's and the cerebral cortex is mature enough to support consciousness; a few weeks later brain waves... become distinct. Thus, throughout the third trimester he is equipped with most of the physiological capability of a newborn.

Even more intriguing is evidence of the impact of the mother's and father's attitudes and feelings on their unborn child. Based on the findings of many other researchers as well as his own experience as a psychoanalyst, Dr. Verny presents evidence that the attitude of the mother toward the pregnancy and the child, as well as toward her partner, have a profound effect on the psychological development of the child and on the birth experience. The mother, by her patterns of feeling and behavior, is the chief source of the stimuli which shape the fetus.

Communication between mother and her unborn child takes place in several ways: physically (through hormones, for example), in behavior (the child's kicking, the mother's job and [environmental situation], and sympathetically or intuittively [through love, ambivalence, dreams]). One of the main means for communication of maternal attitudes and feelings is the neuro-hormones the mother releases, which increase when she is under stress. These substances cross the placenta as easily as nutrients, alcohol, and other drugs do. In moderation, these hormones cause physiological relations in the child which stimulate his neural and psychological systems beneficially, but in excess they can affect the developing body adversely. Because of the child's resilience, it is only extreme and generally, long lasting stress that leaves marked negative effects, not isolated thoughts or incidents. Moreover, the mother's love, acceptance, and positive thoughts for the unborn child act as a very strong protection, so he will continue to thrive even if her own situation is troubled. But if his needs for affection and attention are not met, 'his spirit and often his body, also, begin wilting.'

What the child experiences in the womb creates predispositions, expectations, and vulnerabilities rather than specific qualities: we are dealing with susceptibility, not pre-determination. Increases in maternal neuro-hormones—such as adrenaline, noradrenaline, and oxytocin—do, however, heighten the child's biological susceptibility to emotional distress by altering the portion of the child's autonomic nervous system which controls physiological processes affecting personality structure. An excess of such maternal hormones has been related to low birth weight, reading difficulties, behavior problems, and gastric disorders. Cigarette smoking, by reducing the amount of oxygen in the mother's blood, has been linked to anxiety in infants traceable to the prenatal period. Most traumatic of all is when the mother, due to an illness, a severe loss, or hostility to the pregnancy, withdraws her love and support from her unborn child. He then falls into a depression, is apt to emerge as an apathetic newborn, and may be plagued with depression throughout his life....

The unborn child appears to distinguish very clearly between different types of maternal stress... As Dr. Verny puts it: 'If loving nurturing mothers bear more self-confident, secure children, it is because the self-aware "I" of each infant is carved out of warmth and love. Similarly, if unhappy, depressed or ambivalent mothers bear a higher rate of neurotic children, it is because their offsprings' egos were molded in moments of dread and anguish. Not surprisingly, without redirection, such children often grow into suspicious, anxious and emotionally fragile adults.'

He further informs us that, the second most important prenatal influence is the father's attitude toward the pregnancy and his commitment to the relationship with the mother. One investigator has estimated from his studies that women trapped in a stormy marriage run 'a 237% greater risk of bearing a psychologically or physically damaged child than a woman in a secure, nurturing relationship'—putting her child at greater risk than would many physical illnesses, smoking, or very heavy manual labor.

The article continues: The birth experience itself is influential; very detailed birth memories can be retrieved, and the more traumatic the birth experience, the higher the correlation with physiological and psychological problems, including serious disorders such as schizophrenia and psychosis. Again, the mother's attitude has been demonstrated to be the most important factor in determining the character of the birth. The vital factors in predicting the ease and speed of labor are the mother's attitudes toward motherhood, her relations to her own mother, and the presence of habitual worries, fears, and anxieties going beyond normal apprehension."[85]

Not only is our experience in the womb and at the moment of our birth of critical importance for the shaping of our emotional and physical resiliency, but the moments immediately after and shortly following birth are of great importance as to whether or not epigenetic markers will begin to potentially be "unlocked" or expressed at a later time. We see from the previous chapter that our responses to stress are mediated by regulation of the hypothalamic–pituitary–adrenal (HPA) axis. After our "fire alarm" goes off and neural stimulation occurs, the release of corticotropin-releasing factor (CRF) activates the HPA axis and the feedback loop eventually blocks synthesis and "turns off" the emergency responders, reducing HPA responses to stress. Recent research by Weaver et al, is now showing us that the more maternal care received following birth, the better our resiliency in response to stress. The researchers studied adult rats that have experienced high levels of maternal care (measured by the extent of licking and grooming behavior) during the first week of life. They found that mice who experienced a higher level of maternal care had reduced levels of hypothalamic CRF and lower HPA responses to stress in adulthood compared with those that have received relatively low levels of maternal care early in development.[86]

Alison Rowan summarizes that these results "indicate that the enzymatic mechanisms that underlie DNA methylation and demethylation might be activated not only during development but also in adult post-mitotic hippocampal neurons. Stable epigenetic changes therefore seem to be susceptible to plasticity in adulthood."[87]

**In short, though a person may have experienced stress or trauma before or after birth and it *has* caused epigenetic changes to their DNA, they are not without hope of change.**

DNA (Deoxyribonucleic acid) is the building block of our bodies. They are the molecules that carry the genetic instructions used in the growth, development, function, and reproduction of all known living organisms. Like it or not, we receive DNA from both our mother and our father. But DNA isn't the only factor at play. If DNA is the building block, RNA is the blueprint for the building.

RNA (Ribonucleic acid) is a nucleic acid present in all living cells and its principal role is to act as a messenger, carrying instructions from DNA for controlling the synthesis of proteins. Specifically, mRNA (messenger RNA) bears the coded blueprints for the cell and the tRNA (transfer RNA) makes sure the instructtions can be carried out.

One researcher put it this way,

> "RNA's mission is to travel away from the DNA in order to produce the proteins, more than 2 million in number, that actually build and repair the body. RNA is like active knowledge, in comparison to DNA's silent intelligence. This is how the cells know how and in what way to function, not only during these times of development, but in times of sickness, trauma, emotional stress, accidents, healing and regenerating. In other words, the

DNA is the blueprint and the RNA carries out the building instructions.

There is a mind-body connection to the DNA. We can liken it unto a radio broadcast. The mind is sending out impulses of intelligence, DNA receives them.

You may not think that you can 'talk' to your DNA, but in fact you do continually. Thinking happens at the level of DNA, because without the brain cell sending out a neuropeptide or other messengers, there can be no thought... Everything in life pours out of DNA—flesh, bones, blood, heart, and nervous system; a baby's first word and a toddler's first step; the maturing of reason in the brain's cortex; the play of emotions, thoughts, and desires that flicker like summer lightning through every cell. All of this is DNA."[88]

**Each cognitive function—every thought, feeling, or memory—we engage in, whether consciously or unconsciously, sends an electrical or chemical signal to our body that can change the expression of our genes and alter each cell in our body.**

# The Law of Sowing and Reaping

There's something my Grandpa Cain, a farmer his entire life, knew well: what you plant in the ground will grow in like kind. The universal law of "sowing and reaping" exists whether you believe in it or not, just like gravity is not predicated on our agreement. Sowing and reaping says that whatever seed you put into the ground *will* produce a fruit according to its kind. If you plant a lavender seed, you'll receive a lavender plant. If you plant an orange seed, you'll receive an orange tree. A lavender seed won't produce an orange tree and an orange seed won't produce a frankincense tree. Each seed produces after its own kind and each seed has its own time for harvest.

It takes about two weeks to germinate a lavender (*Lavandula angustifolia*) seed and the time for its maturity can vary. Some types of lavender will bloom the first year when seeded in springtime, but it might be more mature the second year. Cultivars of English lavender like "Lady," are fast-growing and will bloom at the end of one season. Orange trees, on the other hand, can take up to three years to begin producing fruit and another 12 years for the tree to grow completely from the seed.

Time is a huge factor in the process of sowing and reaping. In our minds and bodies, most of the memories, decisions, thoughts, and words sown are not "harvested" back in life until days, weeks, months, or years later. In fact, epigenetics shows us that the choices our parents and grandparents made "back in the day" can be passed down to us and "reaped" in our lives years after the incidents occurred.

It might not seem fair that we carry around the seeds sown by our forefathers, but the wonderful thing is that we don't *have* to live with their negative effects. The universal law of sowing and reaping was designed to bring favorable outcomes if good seed is sown correctly. We can reap the good or the bad from the choices of not just our lives, but those who went before us. But just because the epigenetic change has been "sown" or marked on our DNA, doesn't mean that we have to live with it forever.

We've seen how nature versus nurture plays a role and what happens with stress and trauma, but what many people don't realize is that their genes turning on and off has much to do with the conscious decisions they are making every day. Because the principle of sowing and reaping is at work in the universe, the judgments and decisions we make about others actually affects our lives—positively or negatively.

Instead of debating our nature versus nurture or how much of who we are is made of who we were from the past, we have the opportunity to participate in "renurture." In psychology, the process of helping someone learn a new task or activity is known as "scaffolding" wherein they are coached and assisted in every way possible and as the skill is mastered, support is increasingly and incrementally withdrawn to match the skill level and need as it grows.

You may have received all of the right nutrients—physically, emotionally, spiritually—from the time before you were born, through your infancy and childhood and to the present. However, the reality for most people is that they carry unresolved, repressed or expressed epigenetic markers from both of their parents, their parents' parents, their parents' parents' parents and others. It can be easy to continue carrying the weight of all that happened to you up to this point, but it's important to not just let go of the trauma, but to forgive and let go of those who failed to give you what you needed or desired. This act of release of others allows us to walk forward into freedom in a new way.

In his book *Transforming the Inner Man*, John Sandford states:

> "Our life with our parents, or whoever raised us, is the root and trunk of our life. Whatever manifests in the present derives from those roots... It is not that the parents are to blame. Whatever parents were, saints or hellions, normal people or psychos, what is important is the child's reactions... We are not interested in finding out whose fault (whose blame) anything is. We are interested in seeing what events and reactions happened and what

resultant character structures were built... Once we see that every human being is sinful by inheritance, blame dies... The greatest difficulty concerning forgiveness is that most often we do not know we still cherish resentment or that we have lied to ourselves and forgotten.... If a bad fruit exists, a hidden unforgiveness must lie at the root."[89]

Sandford's claim is that if the problem is still there, forgiveness has not yet been complete, but it can be accomplished in the inner world and the root is dealt with and gratefulness takes root for what was, what is, and what is to come. As goes the root, so goes the fruit. And there's always a chance to tear up and replant. *That* is nature and nurture and re-nurture.

# IN OTHER WORDS...
## (A SUMMARY OF CHAPTER 6)

We all inherit DNA from our parents, but now science shows us that other factors can be passed down such as memories, emotions, stress, and even trauma. The science of epigenetics gives us an explanation for sometimes why we feel the way we do and how things can be imprinted on our subconscious mind. Epigenetics explains the regulation of gene expression that is not based on DNA sequence but, rather, is controlled by heritable and potentially reversible changes to the DNA by way of methylation or modification to the chromatin structure.

Not only can genetic modification of the DNA affect our lives, the epigenetic markers can also play a role in how our genes are expressed. In order for cells to operate "correctly," both the DNA sequence and the epigenetic factors must be normal. People who have epigenetic misregulation may suffer from a disease or condition, even if their DNA sequences are functionally impeccable with no disease mutations or pre-disposing DNA sequence variants. Traumatic memories and stress are being shown to pass from one generation to another. The transmission of the unconscious mind may continue beyond the second generation and also include the grandchildren, great-grandchildren and perhaps others as well and is known as the transgenerational transmission of trauma.

The traditional definition of epigenetics is the study of heritable changes in gene expression that are not due to changes in the underlying DNA sequence. The coating on the DNA sequence becomes a sort of "memory" of the cell and since all cells in our body carry this kind of memory, it becomes a constant physical reminder of past events, our own and those of our parents, grandparents and beyond. It's as though the body is keeping the score.

What part of who we are is a result of our genetics and what part is a result of the environment we've grown up in and around? A traditional ratio for "nature versus nurture" is 60 percent of who you are is a result of your genetics and 40 percent has to do with your upbringing. However, what we can see from the study of epigenetics is that just because you have the genetic propensity doesn't mean those genes will be turned on (what is also known as the genes being "expressed"). Our thoughts, even our imaginations can get "under the skin" of our DNA and can turn certain genes on and certain genes off, changing the structure of the neural pathways in the brain. The ability to switch on or off our genetic expression can have profound effect on our brains and bodies.

Trust and worth, the elements necessary for a healthy autonomous individual, aren't just needed when you're a small child who can talk or walk or play. Rather, the process of learning trust and worth begins before your conscious mind is fully developed. The epigenetic expression of your genes begins adapting before you even are aware of the world around you. Not only can the epigenetic markers be present on our genes because of our forefathers, but our time in the womb and as newborn babies profoundly affects how our brains respond to stress, trauma, and establish resiliency in the world. Recent research now shows that the more maternal care received following birth, the better the individual's resiliency in response to stress is later in life.

In short, though a person may have experienced stress or trauma before or after birth and it *has* caused epigenetic changes to their DNA, they are not without hope of change. Each cognitive function—every thought, feeling, or memory—we engage in, whether consciously or unconsciously, sends an electrical or chemical signal to our body that can change the expression of our genes and alter each cell in our body.

The universal law of "sowing and reaping" exists whether you believe in it or not, just like gravity is not predicated on our agreement. Sowing and reaping says that whatever seed you put into the ground *will* produce a fruit according to its kind. Time is a huge factor in the process of sowing and reaping. In our minds and bodies, most of the memories, decisions, thoughts, and words sown are not "harvested" back in life until days, weeks, months, or years later. In fact, the choices our parents and grandparents made "back in the day" can be passed down to us and "reaped" in our lives years after the incidents occurred. It might not seem fair that we carry around the seeds sown by our forefathers, but the wonderful thing is that we don't *have* to live with their negative effects. The universal law of sowing and reaping was designed to bring favorable outcomes if good seed is sown correctly. We can reap the good or the bad from the choices of not just our lives, but those who went before us. But just because the epigenetic change has been "sown" or marked on our DNA, doesn't mean that we have to live with it forever.

You may have received all of the right nutrients—physically, emotionally, spiritually—from the time before you were born, through your infancy and childhood and to the present. However, the reality for most people is that they carry unresolved, repressed or expressed epigenetic markers from both of their parents, their parents' parents, their parents' parents' parents and others. It can be easy to continue carrying the weight of all that happened to you up to this point, but it's important to not just let go of the trauma, but to forgive and let go of those who failed to give you what you needed or desired. This act of release of others allows us to walk forward into freedom in a new way. It is nature and nurture and *renurture*.

**Chapter Seven**

# SUPPORTING THE FUNCTION

It can be quite inconvenient and it can also be a gift, but I have an unusually acute sense of smell. It might be because I've trained my brain to respond to sensory experiences or because I regularly use essential oils, but I can smell even the smallest amounts of an odorant and often am quick to identify the source. But even more curious and something that most everyone has experienced, is the phenomenon of retrieving a memory when you encounter a scent.

A certain perfume reminds me of ballet recitals as a girl because it's how the dressing rooms smelled. A familiar lake house reminds me of playing and exploring my grandparents' basement. Hugging someone right after they've been outside reminds me of when my mom would come back from a walk and I learned to associate joy with exercise and sunlight.

Those memories and associations are all positive, but smell can also bring back trauma or unresolved emotion buried deep. For a long time after a breakup, every time I'd smell his cologne, memories and negative emotion would flood and almost overwhelm me. Scent can trigger extreme emotion, but it also can be a useful marker for the level of emotional health.

When you encounter the scent and it no longer triggers you, can be a good marker of when you are no longer impacted negatively by the memory, traumatic or stressful incident, or toxic relationship. A sign of true freedom is how you respond when you encounter the trigger stimulus.

Memories that are triggered by scent are known as "Proustian memories" after the tale told by Marcel Proust in his book, *In Search of Lost Time,* where the aroma of linden tea and a madeleine cookie suddenly triggered the recollection of a long-forgotten event. Differing from semantic memory (information storage) and other types of episodic memory (storage of specific events), Proustian memories aren't triggered by the same cues (like visual and verbal). Research has shown that odors elicit more affective, old, rare, and evocative personal memories.[90]

Odors also evoke more emotional memories than musical or tactile cues. Odors are powerful for awaking memories and one reason is because of their direct access to the neural substrates of olfaction, emotion, associative learning, and memory.

Studies done by Herz, compared recollections stimulated by the familiar smell of popcorn with memories evoked by the sight of popcorn, the sound of popcorn popping, the feel of popcorn kernels, or simply the word *popcorn.* According to Wolfe, "consistently, memories that were triggered by odors were experienced as more emotionally intense, and participants felt more transported back to the original time and place of the event, than when memories were triggered by cues in any other modality."[91]

Since essential oils are aromatic compounds, they naturally can have a profound effect on the ability to retrieve memories and prompt emotions. But how else can they help the brain? In the following pages, we're going to examine the data for what many intuitively know and confirm how the chemical compounds of essential oils are affecting the brain and body in our five main cognitive functions: perception, attention, cognition, memory, and emotional regulation.

# This Is Your Brain On Essential Oils

We understand from Chapter 2 that essential oils are chemical compounds (naturally occurring in pure oils) that can positively affect the structure and function of the brain and body because the molecules are minuscule and complementary to our systems. Essential oils provide many of the same functions in humans as they do in plants like bringing nourishment and participating in metabolic processes, promoting homeostasis and restoring equilibrium, reducing inflammation and infection, providing hormonal balancing and regulating effects, and repairing cellular damage in the DNA.

When we discuss the research, we are examining the chemical properties (such as the sesquiterpenes, monoterpenes, phenols, esters, etc.) that are the building blocks of the essential oil. The basics about these building blocks can be learned in Chapter 2.

Just like essential oils are created to help balance the plant, they also can have profound effect on our cells and even fill in the gaps where we need a little extra balancing.

**Chemically, essential oils can act on our cells in a few distinct ways:**

**1. They engage in selective binding with specific molecular targets such as neuro- or hormone receptors.**

According to Kurt Schnaubelt, "plants [mostly among plant alkaloids] have managed to model secondary metabolites to closely resemble neurotransmitters such as acetylcholine, serotonin, noradrenaline, dopamine, GABA, and histamine, and hormones like endorphins. This type of secondary metabolite can attach to the same receptors as the endogenous messenger molecules."[92]

Human hormones and neurotransmitters are nearly identical in molecular structure to those produced in plants. This fact is not only astounding, but it provides amazing hope for the ability to change our brain chemistry simply by using the secondary metabolites of essential oils.

## 2. They non-selectively cause a disturbance of the three-dimensional structure of proteins (known as protein conformation).

The process of protein conformation appears to be a way to select molecules for defense for the plant. Basically, they change the protein structure to impair or alter the proper functioning in the target. For example, an enzyme like histamine is made from a precursor molecule that leads to inflammation. Essential oils can adapt to change the expression of the enzyme histamine and stop the cascade.

Schnaubelt states, "as the overall chemical structure of the protein changes through the addition (binding) of the additional molecule, so does its conformation. Essential oil molecules that can react in this way and significantly distort protein conformation by nonselective binding are, for instance, terpene aldehydes as found in Melissa or Lemongrass.

Protein conformation can also be modified when terpenes of an essential oil interact with the lipophilic areas of a protein. The small lipophilic terpenes can insert themselves into lipophilic areas of a protein and thereby change its conformation. Such interactions are called weak interactions because no actual chemical bond is formed."[93]

### 3. They bond covalently to DNA and RNA, modifying gene expression.

Just as we discussed in the previous chapter, we are not just a product of our DNA, but are a result of how those genes are expressed. Thanks to essential oils, the ability to modify how our genes are expressed is possible due to the same covalent and non-covalent modifications of proteins.

### 4. They change membrane permeability and the function of membrane proteins.

Essential oils can also change the permeability of membranes. Most water-soluble molecules cannot penetrate cell membranes, only non-polar or very small molecules (like oxygen, carbon dioxide, or water) can get through un-inhibited. Inside the cell membrane is where all of the activity of the cell takes place like the necessary exchanges of amino acids, sugar, and signaling—all controlled by proteins integrated in the membrane.

Once again, Schnaubelt summarizes this process:

> "One of the most outstanding qualities of nerve and sensory cells is their ability to generate and conduct electric signals. This is the result of the membranes' ability to separate charges and the ability of specific membrane proteins (ion pumps) to affect controlled changes in conductivity. Many of the effects of essential oil molecules are a consequence of their ability to modify this electric signaling. They do so by modifying membrane functions in two ways:
>
> 1. They can insert themselves into the lipid membrane, creating hydrophobic inter-

actions with the lipophilic chains of the phospholipids or cholesterol. In this fashion the terpenes in essential oils change membrane fluidity or permeability and ultimately structure and functionality.

2. Essential oil molecules can change membrane function by attaching to the lipophilic areas of membrane proteins, that is, receptor proteins. As terpenoids form hydrophobic interactions with those segments of the receptor, they modify its conformation (its three-dimensional structure) and hence functionality. A well-known example for this is the interference of terpenoids with the ion channels in nerve cell membranes, modifying neuromuscular activity to relieve spasms at smooth intestinal muscle cells. Interference of high concentrations of terpenoids with membranes also mediates their narcotic and anesthetic effects." [94]

Imagine that essential oils are like the person holding the wire cutters and they are systematically cutting through the metal fence in order for larger molecules to pass through. Instead of a child being the only one small enough to able to get through (i.e. small molecules like oxygen or water), essential oils open the way for larger substances to be able to get through the "fence" of the cell.

## The PSM Paradigm

Not only can essential oils affect the cell membranes, but that is where the work of changing the DNA and RNA of the cell actually begins. One simple theory on how essential oils work at the cellular level in our brains and bodies is known as **PSM Paradigm** (also known as the PMS Paradigm). PSM stands for three different chemical component types contained in some essential oils (or mixed in a custom blend) that speed cellular healing. The "P" stands for **phenol** or **phenylpropanoid**, the "S" is for **sesqui-terpene**, and the "M" for **monoterpene**. This chemical combination in a single oil or layering of multiple oils high in these three compounds helps to explain how a single anointment or application of essential oils is able to bring about an instant and permanent healing.

When an oil or a blend of oils is applied that contains the balanced amount of these three constituents the oil goes to work in this way. First, the phenols clean the receptor sites. Then the sesquiterpenes delete bad information from cellular memory. Lastly, monoterpenes restore or awaken the correct information in the cell's memory (DNA).

If you think of your cognitive functions (or expressions of cells) as the software on a computer hard drive that has been corrupted by a virus, the phenols will first identify the corrupt information and clean what it can. Then the sesquiterpenes come in and delete the old, bad information from the memory so it's not clog-ging your computer. Then the monoterpenes come in and reboot and restore the application so it can work properly now that it's debugged.

According to Dr. David Stewart, "The PMS [sic] Paradigm is a useful working hypothesis that provides practical guidance for mixing and applying oils in an effective, therapeutic way. Let's express it another way: 1. When cellular intercommunication is restored in the body by clean, well-functioning receptor sites; 2. When garbled or miswritten information in the cellular job description has been erased; and 3. When God's image of perfection, that was always there in the field of the cell from our creation, has been revived and reinstalled, then whatever our disease or condition had been, the cond-itions for its presence exist no more. **Our dise-ase or condition was the consequence of mis-communications between cells that caused**

**them to malfunction. When these basic errors have been corrected, as is possible with PMS [sic], the problem disappears. It can take time, like days, weeks, or months, but it can also be instantaneous."**[95]

According to Stewart, the best way to create a PSM oil is to blend several oils to provide a proportion of all three classes of compounds. He also states that the cleaning of receptor sites can be done just as effectively and efficiently by ketones and/or alcohols (though alcohols are less aggressive so it takes more of them to accomplish the job). Therefore, we could also be discussing a KSM and/or ASM blend of oils. A therapeutically effective PSM proportion seems to lie in the range of:

> 10-50%  Phenols/Ketones/Alcohols
> 3-20%  Sesquiterpenes
> 10-60%  Monoterpenes.

**Single oils that contain a balanced PSM proportion include Tea Tree (*melaleuca altern-ifolia*) with 33% phenols, 17% sesquiterpenes, and 52% monoterpenes. Marjoram and Hyssop are also both fairly balanced in their composition of PSM constituents. Lavender does not contain any phenols, but it does have 44% alcohols, 6% sesquiterpenes, and 16% monoterpenes, making it an effective and accessible oil for use.**

**There are single oils that contain balanced compositions of PSM/ASM/KSM, but there is no one "magic" oil. This is why understanding that the layering or blending of essential oils is a powerful tool for maximizing the value, potency, and efficacy of single essential oils.**

The PSM paradigm—along with the other components that make up essential oils like alcohols, ketones, ethers, and esters—help to defragment the brain and allow the chance to create lasting change at a cellular level. However, this paradigm is only one possible mechanism for how and why essential oils work so powerfully. We can also argue that electrical, magnetic, and vibrational etiologies are also explanations for the effectiveness of essential oils.

# PHENOLICS

Phenolics are unruly little boys, full of energy, but needing guidance. They are fighters, the purgative ones. They are the ones who clean the receptor sites, clearing out any unwelcome guests that don't belong in those areas. They are warriors and policeman, looking for invaders such as viruses, bacteria, parasites, petrochemicals, heavy metals, pharmaceutical drugs, and other aliens. When they find them, they destroy them and/or usher them out of the body. Phenols and phenylpropanoids are initiators of healing processes, clearing the way for the many other types of healing compounds in an oil, to carry out their divinely designated assignments. In the absence of phenols, the ketones of an essential oil will take over and perform their purgative tasks.

# SESQUITERPENES

Sesquiterpenes are wise, responsible ones who will see a job through to the end, the ones who help pace everyone so that they all finish the race. They are the sensible big brothers watching over every one else and gently guiding them in ways of benefit and healing. Sesquiterpenes are the ones who do what no one else wants to do, like emptying the trash, clearing flawed files, and cleaning out cellular information that is no longer useful. They will also corral an unruly companion, kindly and firmly, taking it under its big brother wing, helping it to behave in a positive and beneficial way. Sesquiterpenes are chaperones of the more aggressive molecules, making sure their work in the body is productive and constructive and not destructive. They are the illuminated ones who, like the monoterpenes, don't mind to work in service and humility, seeing that everyone gets the best job done and not caring who gets the credit.

# MONOTERPENES

Monoterpenes are like mothers. They are coordinators, quenchers, unifiers, and organizers—providing balance and coherence to the actions of the hundreds of participants in an essential oil. Monoterpenes are the ones that see that the healing objectives are not forgotten while supplying encouragement and support to everyone along the way. Monoterpenes don't mind if another constituent gets credit for a job well done. They are content to be of support and to make good things happen behind the scenes, creating an environment of resonance and harmony. Monoterpenes are humble servants, working quietly and hard to make everyone else look good.

# Essential Oils to Aid Your Brain

Now that we understand the science behind how essential oils can modify our cells, let's examine some of the data on common essential oils, some of the main constituents in essential oils (i.e. alpha pinene, linalool, etc.) and what research is showing in how they can affect the five main cognitive functions: alertness (or perception), attention, cognition, memory, and emotional regulation.

There are many more varieties of essential oils and constituents that could be covered as they effect the entire body, but for the scope of this book, we will be looking at just some of the oils most commonly available *and* shown by the research to be useful for the nervous system. Some essential oils or their properties have been better researched than others and there is considerable research yet to be performed.

Though there are several ways to conduct scientific studies on essential oils, one of the best ways to assess brain activation of essential oils is by recordings of spontaneous electro-encephalogram (EEG) activity during the administration. When examining the data, researchers often pay particular attention to changes within the alpha and beta bands, sometimes also the theta band of the EEG in response to olfactory stimulation since these bands are thought to be most indicative of central arousal processes.

Alpha waves are slow brain waves within a frequency range of 8–13 Hz and amplitudes between 5 and 100 mV, which typically occur over posterior areas of the brain in an awake but relaxed state, especially with closed eyes. The alpha rhythm disappears immediately when subjects open their eyes and when cognitive activity is required, for example, when external stimuli are processed or tasks are solved.

Beta waves are faster brain waves with smaller amplitudes (2–20 mV) and frequencies between 14 and 30 Hz. The beta rhythm, which is most evident frontally, is characteristic of alertness, attention, and arousal.

Theta waves are very slow brain waves that occur in the frontal and temporal lobes primarily and consist of amplitudes between 5 and 100 mV in the frequency range between 4 and 7 Hz. Often the theta rhythm is most commonly associated with drowsiness and light sleep, but actually some researchers have found that theta activity can be correlated with memory processes[96] and creativity.[97] There also has been data to show correlations between theta activity and ratings of anxiety and tension.[98] Some have even proposed that sniffing odors activates theta rhythm generated by the hippocampus and allows for encoding and integration of olfactory information with other cognitive and motor processes.[99]

In general, the brain wave patterns on the EEG varies depending on the level of arousal in the CNS. So, depending on the state of consciousness (i.e. sleep, wakefulness, or meditation), brain waves can easily be distinguished based on their characteristic EEG patterns. For instance, an increase in central activation is typically characterized by a decrease in alpha brain waves and an increase in beta activity.[100] Researchers have found data that indicates that pleasant odors increases the alpha wave activity in the brain, while unpleasant odors decreases it.[101]

# Basil
## (*Ocimum basilicum*)

Basil, from the Lamiaceae family, has been known to alleviate anxiety, agitation, stress, challenging behaviors, and aids in recovery from mental exhaustion and burnout.[102] The essential oil is steam distilled from the leaves, stems, and flowers of the plant and contains methylchavicol (estragol) (70-90%), linalool (1-20%), and 1,8-Cineole (Eucalyptol) (1-7%) as its key constituents. The name "basil" is from the Greek name for king, *"basileum"* and traditional uses for basil included the treatment of migraines and chest infections as it contains antispasmodic, anti-inflammatory, and muscle relaxant properties, in addition to antiviral and antibacterial functions. It may also help to restore olfaction where a loss of smell has occurred.[103]

*Note: avoid use if epileptic.

# Bergamot
## (*Citrus aurantium bergamia*)

Bergamot is from the same family as lemon and other citrus fruits known as Rutaceae. It's been known for years as a mainstay in traditional Italian medicine and serves as a calming agent that supports hormones, alleviates depression and can affect anxiety, agitation, stress, and challenging behaviors.[104]

In one study on bergamot, 41 healthy females were tested using a random crossover study design in order to test the oil's effect on psychological stress and anxiety. The endocrinological, physiological, and psychological effects of inhaling bergamot was done by observing effects to three experimental setups: (rest (R), rest + water vapor (RW), rest + water vapor + bergamot essential oil (RWB)) for 15 min each. Immediately after each setup, saliva samples were collected and the volunteers rested for 10 minutes. Subsequently, they completed various stress and anxiety inventory levels as well as measured saliva to determine cortisol levels. The researchers found that inhaling bergamot essential oil together with water vapor exerted positive psychological and physiological effects in a relatively short time.[105]

*Note: Avoid applying to skin that will be exposed to sunlight or UV light within 36 hours.

# Cedarwood
## (*Cedrus atlantica*)

Cedarwood, from the Pinaceae family, is most closely related to the ancient Cedars of Lebanon. It contains alpha-himachalene (10-20%), beta-himachalene (25-55%), gammahimachalene (8-15%), and deta-cadinene (2-6%) and has been known to stimulate the limbic lobe, including the pineal gland.

The variety, *Cedrus deodara* has been used traditionally in Ayurveda medicine for the treatment of central nervous system disorders. Specific constituents were isolated from heart wood and was shown to have antiepileptic and anxiolytic activity. In one study, aimed to explore its anti-depressant effect, it was found to increase serotonin and noradrenaline levels of brain.[106]

Another study found that seven days of treatment with an alcoholic extract of *Cedrus deodara* (30 mg/kg, 100mg/kg.p.o. of ALCD) showed significant enhancement of GABA levels in the cerebellum and the whole brain other than the cerebellum, compared to the control group. These findings suggest that Cedarwood might possess significant anxiolytic and anti-convulsant activity through modulation of GABA levels in brain. GABA appears to play an important role in the pathogenesis of several neuropsychiatric disorders. Many of the traditional agents used to treat psychiatric disorders are known to act, at least in part, by enhancing GABA activity, while some of the newer agents may exert their therapeutic effects exclusively via GABAergic actions.[107]

# Clary Sage
## (*Salvia sclarea*)

Clary sage is from the same family (Lamiaceae) as lavender, but it is different from *Salvia offi-*

*cinalis* or common sage. It has been known to enhance the immune system, address skin issues, calm digestion and muscle spasms, balance hormones, and alleviate pain and inflammation.[108] It is steam distilled from flowering plants and has a calming scent good for relieving stress. It contains mainly linalool (7-24%), linalyl acetate (56-78%), alpha-terpineol, germacrene D, and geranyl.

In recent studies, clary sage oil was found to be very effective in controlling cortisol levels in women.[109] Another study in the UK investigated the use of aromatherapy within a healthcare setting for 8,058 women in childbirth. A total of 10 essential oils were used, plus carrier oil, and were administered via skin absorption and inhalation. Two essential oils, namely chamomile and clary sage, were effective in alleviating pain. It is not clear whether the oils were administered individually or in combination. They were described only by common name.[110]

# Clove
## (*Syzgium aromaticum*)

Clove contains a high amount of eugenol, known for its analgesic effects. From the botanical family, Myrtaceae, it is steam distilled from the flower bud and stem and has been known for centuries for its antimicrobial, antifungal, antiviral, analgesic, and anti-inflammatory properties (among others). It can act as a mental stimulant and also can encourage sleep and feelings of rest. It has also been studied for its effect on the thyroid and its effect on memory, cognition and altering mood.[111]

*Note: Caution should be used if combined with War-farin, aspirin, etc. as anticoagulant properties can be enhanced.

# Eucalyptus
**(Eucalyptus citriodora, E. bico-stata, E. dives, E. globulus, E. polybractea, E. radiata, E. staigeriana)**

There are multiple varieties of eucalyptus essential oil available and though there are powerful crossover properties as an antiviral, anti-inflammatory, and antifungal, and mucolytic, research has shown that *Eucalyptus citriodora* leaf extract may have a beneficial effect in affecting Parkinson's disease and other degenerative neurological conditions.[112]

All the varieties of eucalyptus are in the Mytraceae family and are steam distilled from the leaves. Depending on the variety, they may contain high levels of 1,8-cineole, alpha-pinene, citronellal, and alpha- and beta-phellandrene. Its oils have been used to regulate and activate the various systems like nervous system for neuralgia, headache and physical weakness and has been known as an antidepressant as it promotes clarity of mind.

# Frankincense
**(Boswellia sacra, B. carterii, B. frereana, B. serrata)**

Boswellia, most commonly known as frankincense, is frequently used for uplifting emotions, aiding cognitive function, facilitating muscle relaxation, and promoting cellular health.

The Boswellia shrubs and small trees belong to the Burseraceae botanical family, the same as the trees that produce myrrh.* They are typically native to the dry tropics of Africa (especially the northeast) and Asia.

The essential oil is steam distilled from the fragrant resins taken from various species of Boswellia and is known as frankincense (or oleogum olibanum). For thousands of years, frankincense (from the Medieval French word for "real incense") has been used for incense, anointing oil, embalming liquids, and medicinal purposes around the world.

There are multiple varieties of frankincense including: *Boswellia sacra, Boswellia carterii, Boswellia frereana,* and *Boswellia serrata.* Depending on the variety of frankincense, some its main constituents include: alpha-pinene (30-65% in *boswellia carterii,* and 53-90% in *boswellia sacra*), alpha-thujene (23-45% in *boswellia frereana*), and incensole acetate.

Boswellia resin contains incensole acetate, a constituent that has been found to modulate the hypothalamic–pituitary–adrenal (HPA) axis and influence hippocampal gene expression. Researchers believe this can lead to beneficial behavioral effects and supports its potential as a novel treatment of depressive-like disorders.[113] This research indicates that properties in frankincense (incensole acetate) help to balance your limbic lobe when your fire alarm is going off.

One study found that boswellia resin may affect sensation and emotional states by affecting the TRPV3 channel that is involved in emotional and behavioral processes in the CNS in addition to its known effects on the perception of warmth (thermosensation). They argue that it is possible that incensole acetate augments the euphoric feeling produced during religious functions, due to both the positive, presumably mild, emotional effects and the warm sensation.[114]

Another study found that Boswellia resin acts as a major anti-inflammatory agent to help the brain following major head trauma. They found that incensole acetate (IA) inhibits a protein complex (NF-$\kappa$B) that controls the transcription of DNA, cytokine production and cell survival and protects against ischemic (stroke) neuronal damage. They also found that incensole acetate is shown to have a therapeutic window of treatment up to 6 hours after ischemic injury. This study suggests that the anti-inflammatory and neuroprotective activities of incensole ace-tate may serve as a novel therapeutic treatment for restoring blood flow after a stroke or injury. [115]

One study found that oral doses of AKBA (acetyl-11-keto-beta-boswellic acid) (100mg/kg) and nimesulide (2.42mg/kg) for 15 days significantly reversed the age-induced deterioration of memory, cognitive performance and meta-function in mice. [116]

Multiple studies have been done on the effects of boswellic acids on brain tumors.[117] Malignant brain tumors produce highly active forms of leukotrienes and this causes localized fluid build-up in the brain around the tumor, which damages healthy nerve cells. In one study, 12 patients with malignant glioma, a type of brain tumor, were given 3600mg/day of Boswellia extract (standardized to 60% boswellic acids) for 7 days prior to surgery. Ten patients showed a decrease in fluid around the tumor, with an average reduction of 30 percent in eight of the 12 patients. Signs of brain damage decreased during the treatment; one patient became worse. Vomiting as a side effect was observed in one patient.[118] This resulted in the European Commission declaring Boswellia as an orphan drug (a drug with no sponsors to fund the registration process) for the treatment of oedema resulting from brain tumors.[119]

*Note: Myrrh (*Commiphora myrrha*) essential oil is in the same family as frankincense and though it is less-researched on how it functions on the brain, it is high in sesquiterpenes and could be beneficial in similar ways to frankincense essential oil. Elemi (*Canarium luzonicum*) is also in the Burseraceae family and has been used historically in similar ways to frankincense; it's even been known as the "Poor Man's Frankin-cense" due to its similarities in function. It has been known to alleviate muscle and nerve pain and be conducive toward mediation as well as clearing and grounding the mind.

# Geranium
## (*Pelargonium graveolens*)

Geranium, originating first in Egypt and India and from the family Geraniaceae, contains a strong amount of the constituent citronellol (typically between 25-36%), a moderate amount of geraniol (10-18%) as well as citronellyl formate and linalool and is useful for the release of negative memories and nervous tension. It helps to balance emotions and the aroma is uplifting to the nervous system. It is steam distilled from the flowers and leaves and has been known to help balance hormones and improve circulation. Researchers have found that inhaling geranium essential oil led to subjects reporting significantly lower levels of anxiety.[120]

Uses for geranium essential oil have reportedly included the treatment of inflammatory and pain associated ailments (i.e., headache, neuralgia), nervous system-related ailments (i.e., restlessness, nervousness, anxiety anger, frustration, emotional upsets) and most of these claims have been confirmed via *in vitro* and *in vivo* evaluation.[121]

# Lavender
## (*Lavandula angustifolia*)

Lavender, sometimes known as the "Swiss army knife" of essential oils because of the variety of uses, has been shown to affect all five of the main cognitive functions: alertness, attention, cognition, memory, and emotional regulation. It has been shown to have main properties acting as an analgesic, antidepressant, anticonvulsant, anxiolytic, calming, hypnotic, relaxing, sedative.[122]

The floral plant is from the Lamiaceae or Labiatae (mint) family and the essential oil is produced by steam distillation of the flowering top. Its constituent varies in concentration and therapeutic effects with the different species, but often contains strong concentrations of Linalyl Acetate (24-45%) and Linalool (25-38%), as well as camphor, terpinen-4-ol, beta-ocimene and 1,8-cineole. Linalool shows sedative effects and linalyl acetate shows marked narcotic actions. Overall, lavender essential oil is common and safe for humans of all ages as well as animals.

Studies have shown that lavender increased drowsiness[123] and has sedative effects, which produced an improvement in productivity[124]. One study found that the theta and alpha brain wave activity increased after inhaling lavender oil,[125] while another showed that alpha 1 waves decreased in the parietal and posterior temporal regions resulting in the subjects feeling more comfortable.[126] Another study confirmed these findings, showing that the absolute theta waves increased at the right prefrontal region resulting in significant differences in the relative fast and slow alpha waves. Both the physical and mental states of the subjects became more stable and relaxed.[127] Lavender was shown to help sleep by increasing the percentage of deep or slow-wave sleep in men and women and decreasing rapid-eye movement sleep.[128]

Researchers have found that lavender essential oil not only helps people feel more relaxed, but they also had more mental focus when performing math computations after inhalation.[129] Researchers found that lavender odorants were associated with reduced mental stress and increased arousal rate.[130]

Lavender can be wonderful to help with generalized emotional distress as well as acute symptoms of stress and can help in overcoming anxiety and depression. In one study, researchers gave lavender essential oil in a capsule to patients suffering from mild-to-moderate depression. They reported that it led to a better and earlier improvement in the depression symptoms among patients.[131]

Several studies found that lavender helped to relax not just the brain, but the body. Specifically, the inhalation of favorite odors suppressed the muscle sympathetic vasoconstrictor activity and attenuates the blood pressure increase by affecting the central nervous system higher than the midbrain.[132] Relaxing odors decreased heart rate and skin conductance, with stimulating odors producing reverse effects under equivalent conditions.[133] Aromatherapy massage using lavender has been found to exert positive effects on reducing anxiety and increasing feelings of self-esteem.[134]

Lavender has been shown to have neuroprotective effects with linalool inhibiting acetylcholine release and altering ion channel function at the neuromuscular junction.[135] These findings indicate several targets relevant to treatment of Alzheimer's disease as anti-cholinergic, neuroprotective, and antioxidant activities could be found in lavender. It is suggested that lavender oil might protect against injuries from cerebral blood loss and stroke due to its antioxidant effects.[136]

It has been reported to be useful in the treatment of acute as well as chronic or intractable pain.[137] Inhalation of lavender essential oil was suggested to be an effective and safe treatment modality in acute management of migraine headaches.[138]

Lavender has been suggested as an excellent natural remedy to treat insomnia and improve the sleep quality. Single-blind randomized studies investigated the effectiveness of lavender odor on quality of sleep showed that lavender improved the mean scores of sleep quality in 15 healthy students[139], in 64 ischemic heart disease patients[140], and in 34 midlife women with insomnia[141]. Ten individuals with insomnia, verified by a score of 5 or more on the Pittsburgh Sleep Quality Index (PSQI), were treated with lavender odor. Six to eight drops of lavender oil added each night to the cartridge improved the PSQI score by –2.5 points. More notable improvements were seen in females and younger participants. Milder insomnia also improved more than severe ones.[142]

*Note: Beware of purchasing adulterated lavender essential oil. Many sources of lavender essential oil on the market have been adulterated with hybrid lavender (lavandin), synthetic linalool and linalyl acetate, or synthetic fragrance chemicals like ethyl vanillin.

# Lemon
## (*Citrus limon*)

Lemon essential oil has a warm, uplifting fragrance and can improve mood. From the Rutaceae family, lemon is cold pressed from the rind and is high in limonene (59-73%) with smaller amounts of gamma-terpinene (6-12%), beta-pinene (7-16%), alpha-pinene (1.5-3%) and sabinene (1.5-3%).

It has been studied mostly for its effectiveness for boosting the immune system, but recent research has also arisen in how it can improve productivity[143], positively decrease anxiety, and boost self-esteem.[144]

Research on lab rats given a lemon aroma compared to a control group indicates that lemon essential oil can affect learning. The results showed a connection between the olfactory tract and the hippocampus of the rats exposed to the lemon aroma who spent less time finding the target than the ones in the control group. The researchers attributed the positive results to an increased attention level resulting from the stimulated CNS of the rats exposed to lemon oil and increased attention level leads to enhanced memory.[145]

One study in particular found that lemon oil can have an anxiolytic, antidepressant-like effect that reduces distress by modulating the systems in the brain that produce GABA, serotonin, and dopamine. They specifically found that lemon oil "significantly accelerated the metabolic turnover of DA [dopamine activity] in the hippocampus and of 5-HT [serotonin] in the prefrontal cortex and striatum. These results suggest that lemon oil possesses anxiolytic, antidepressant-like effects via the suppression of DA [dopamine] activity related to enhanced 5-HTnergic neurons."[146]

Another study found evidence to strongly support the hypothesis that oxidative stress in the hippocampus can occur during neurodegenerative diseases, but that lemon could have a strong protective effect as an antioxidant.[147] They report that lemon "significantly reduced the lipid peroxidation level and nitrite content but increased the glutathione reduced GSH levels and the superoxide dismutase (SOD), catalase, and glutathione peroxidase (GPx) activities in mice hippocampus."

*Note: Avoid applying to skin that will be exposed to sunlight or UV light within 24 hours.

**Note: Orange (*Citrus sinensis*), Lime (*Citrus latifolia* or *C. aurantifolia Swingle*) and other citrus essential oils may have similar effects on the CNS as lemon due in part to their high limonene content, but are less researched.

# Melissa
## (*Melissa officinalis*)

Melissa, also known as Lemon Balm, comes from the Lamiaceae family and is steam distilled from the aerial parts before flowering. In ancient traditions, Melissa was commonly used for nervous conditions and ailments related to the heart and emotions. Its properties are calming and uplifting, containing geranial (25-35%), neral (18-28%), and beta-caryophyllene (12-19%).

Melissa has been known to help with promoting feelings of calm and aiding with sleep and throughout history was used to treat migraines, neuroses and hysteria.[148] It has been reported to be a CNS depressant, analgesic, sedative, cholinergic, and antioxidative.[149]

It has also been researched highly (in addition to lavender) for its use in patients with dementia. In a meticulously conducted double-blind study involving 72 dementia patients with clinically significant agitation treated with melissa oil, researchers found reduced levels of aggression after four weeks of treatment. The agitation amongst the dementia patients had included anxiety and irritability, motor restlessness, and abnormal vocalization—symptoms that often lead to disturbed behaviors such as pacing, wandering, aggression, shouting, and night-time disturbance, all characterized by appropriate inventories. The authors concluded that the melissa treatment was successful, but pointed out that there was also a significant, but lower, improvement in the control group and suggested that a stronger odor should have been used. [150]

## Oregano
### (*Origanum vulgare*)

Oregano, from the Lamiaceae family, is oil steam distilled from the leaves and powerful for its anti-aging, anti-inflammatory, antioxidant, anti-bacterial, antinoiceptive, radioprotective, and immune stimulating properties. It is high in carvacrol (60-70%) and constituents include gamma-terpinene (3.5-8.5%), para-cymene (5.5-9%), beta-carophyllene (2-5%), myrcene (1-3%), and thymol (0-5%). Because it contains a high level of phenols, oregano may irritate the nasal membranes or skin if inhaled directly or applied neat.

One study found that oregano may possess antinociceptive (the blocking of detection of a painful or injurious stimulus by sensory neurons) activity in a dose-dependent manner that might be mediated, at least in part, by both GABA receptors. [151]

Oregano has also been shown to be beneficial in aiding the gut and acting as an antiparasitic, which may have positive connotations on the gut-brain connection. [152]

*Note: Caution — oregano is high in phenols and therefore may cause irritation to the nasal membranes or skin if inhaled directly from the diffuser or applied neat.

**Note: There are more than 60 plant species used under the common name "oregano" and showing similar flavor profiles characterized mainly by cymyl compounds (i.e. carvacrol and thymol).

# Peppermint
## (*Mentha piperita*)

Peppermint is one of the most commonly available essential oils and is known for its uplifting, clear, and bright aroma. From the Lamiaceae family, peppermint has been known to contain anti-inflammatory, antibacterial, anti-viral, anti-fungal, and antiparasitic properties as well as acting as a digestive stimulant and pain reliever. It contains menthol as a main constituent (25-50%), menthone (12-44%) as well as smaller amounts of menthofuran (0.5-5%), 1,8-cineole (1-8%), isomenthone (1-7%), neomenthol (1.5-7%), pulegone (0.5-3%), and menthyl acetate (1-18%).

Researchers have found that inhaling peppermint can increase attention, focus, and performance during mental tasks.[153] Studies have shown peppermint to have awakening effects resulting in decreased alpha and beta activities and increased alertness.[154]

Other studies have shown peppermint to effect emotions by reducing fatigue and improving mood. An application of peppermint in water was rated by participants as more pleasant, intense, stimulating, and elating than water alone.[155] Peppermint was shown in another study to enhance memory and increase alertness.[156] It is commonly used as a well-documented and effective remedy for pain associated with headaches and tension. [157]

*Note: Avoid contact with eyes, mucus membranes, sensitive skin, or fresh wounds or burns. Use caution (some argue it's not recommended) on infants younger than 18 months of age.

# Roman Chamomile
## (*Anthemis nobilis*)

Roman Chamomile, from the asteraceae family, is steam distilled from the flowering top and has been used for centuries by mothers to calm their crying children. Research now shows that roman chamomile made subjects in one study "more comfortable" and the alpha 1 waves decreased at the parietal and posterior temporal regions.[158]

Key constituents in roman chamomile include: isobutyl angelate + isamyl methacrylate (30-45%), isoamyl angelate (12-22%), methyl allyl angelate (6-10%), isobutyl n-butyrate (2-9%), and 2-methyl butyl angelate (3-7%). The essential oil is known for its relaxant, antispasmodic, anti-inflammatory, antiparasitic, antibacterial, and anesthetic properties.

One study found that an aromatherapy massage including chamomile exerted positive effects on anxiety and self-esteem.[159] It is thought that because of its calming properties, roman chamomile may be beneficial in alleviating depression, insomnia, nervous tension, and stress as well balancing emotions.[160]

# Rose
## (*Rosa damascena*)

Rose is commonly recognized for its floral and uplifting fragrance. From the Rosaceae family, it is steam distilled from flowers in a two-part process. It contains a high amount of citronellol

(24-50%) as well as geraniol (10-22%), nerol (5-12%), beta-phenylethyl alcohol (0.5-5%) and is known to have anti-inflammatory, antioxidant, anxiolytic, heptoprotective properties as well as serving as a relaxant, immunomodulating and serving to protect DNA.

Rose is a highly valuable essential oil because of the complex distillation that now almost always involves a solvent. An ethanolic extract of the flowering tops of *R. damascena* has been shown in research to possess a potent depressant activity on CNS in mice.[161] Some of these effects evaluated showed rose to be hypnotic, anticonvulsant, anti-depressant, anti-anxiety, analgesic effects, and perform nerve growth.[162]

Several studies confirm that *Rosa damascena* inhibits the reactivity of the hypothalamus and pituitary systems and can suppress the reactivity of central nervous system.[163]

One research study found a chloroform extract of rose to have significantly reduced cell atrophy and death, which gives indication that rose might have possible health benefit for the patients suffering from dementia.[164]

*Note: *Rosa damascene* (high in citronellol) is different from the Moroccan variety, *Rosa centifolia* (high in phenyl ethanol) and have differences not only in color and aroma, but in therapeutic benefit.

# Rosemary
## (*Rosmarinus officinalis CT Cineole*)

Rosemary, from the Lamiaceae family, is steam distilled from the leaves and flowering tops and the oil has been known for its variety of properties including: antibacterial, antifungal, anti-bacterial, antidepressant, and enhances mental clarity and concentration.

Studies have shown that rosemary increased alertness,[165] produced a significant enhancement of performance for overall quality of memory,[166] and can have positive effects on anxiety and self-esteem.[167] In one study, participants inhaled rosemary oil and following the inhalation, subjects were found to have become more active and stated that they felt "fresher". The analysis of EEGs showed a reduction in the power of alpha1 (8–10.99 Hz) and alpha2 (11–12.99 Hz) waves. Moreover, an increment in the beta wave (13–30 Hz) power was observed in the anterior region of the brain. These results confirm the stimulatory effects of rosemary oil and provide supporting evidence that brain wave activity, autonomic nervous system activity, as well as mood states are all affected by the inhalation of the rosemary oil.[168]

Other studies have shown rosemary to help balance emotions by reducing anxiety[169] and feelings of depression.[170]

*Note: Do not use on children under 4 years of age. Do not use rosemary for high blood pressure if already taking ACE inhibitor prescription drugs.

# Sage
## (*Salvia officinalis*)

Sage is distinct from clary sage (*Salvia sclarea*) though they are both in the Lamiaceae family. It was known as a sacred herb by the Romans and its name is derived from the word for "salvation". It contains antibacterial, antiviral, anti-inflammatory, antioxidant, antifungal, and anxiolytic properties in addition to assisting in regulating hormones. It contains fair amounts of alpha-thujone (18-43%), beta-thujone (3-8.5%), 1,8-cineole (5.5-13%), camphor (4.5-24.5%), camphene (1.5-7%), alpha-pinene (1-6.5%) and alpha-humulene (trace-12%).

Studies have shown sage to have a cholinergic, stimulatory, GABAergic, and antioxidant effects on the central nervous system. Ethanolic extracts of certain *Salvia sp.* displaced [3H]-(*N*)-

nicotine and [3H]-(N)-scopolamine in receptor binding studies using human cerebral cortical cell membranes. Other studies have shown that sage might be a useful remedy for patients with dementia.[171]

*Note: In (very) high does, thujone can be neurotoxic. Avoid if epileptic or on persons with high blood pressure.

**Note: Spanish Sage (*Salvia lavandulifolia*) has also been researched for its neuroprotective properties against brain cell death and age-related memory loss.

# Sandalwood
## (*Santalum album*)

Sandalwood, found mostly in India, is from the Santalaceae family and is steam distilled from wood. High in sesquiterpenes such as alpha-santalol (41-55%) and beta-santalol (16-24%), it is extremely useful for removing negative information from cells and stimulating the limbic system.

One study found sandalwood beneficial for enhancing memory. They reported that "the aqueous extract of *Santalum album* increased the level of Acetyl cholinesterase helpful in the brain for storing the memory, decreased levels of GSH, due to excess release of Glutathione may cause the excitotoxity and decreased the formation of reactive oxygen species due to its antioxidant activity."[172]

Other studies have found that sandalwood promotes feelings of relaxation resulting in sub-jects feeling more comfortable[173] with alpha 1 decreased at parietal and posterior temporal regions as well as improvements in productivity due to its sedative effect.[174] Researchers have also found that not only can sandalwood be calming to the nervous system, but the results can linger even up to 24 hours after the stressor was presented.[175]

# Valerian
## (*Valeriana officinalis*)

Valerian, from the Valerianaceae family, has been clinically investigated over the last few decades for its tranquilizing properties. The plant is steam distilled from the root and contains high levels of bornyl acetate (35-43%), camphene (22-31%) in addition to smaller amounts of alpha-pinene (5-8%), beta-pinene (3-6%), limo-nene (1-3%), valerenal (2-8%), and myrtenyl acetate (2-5).

Research has shown that the sesquiterpenes in valerian act in a sedative, tranquilizing, and antispasmodic way to the central nervous system as has been used in treatments of insomnia and anxiety. Studies are now showing that the active valerenic acid within interacts with the GABAergic system, a mechanism of action similar to the benzodiazepine drugs.[176] It serves the body by calming, grounding, promoting feelings of relaxation, and emotional balancing.[177]

# Vetiver
## (*Vetiveria zizanioides*)

Vetiver is from the family Poaceae and is known for its antiseptic, antispasmodic and historically anti-inflammatory properties as well as a relaxant and circulatory stimulant. It is steam distilled from the root and contains iso-valencenol (1-16%), khusimol (7-21%), alpha-vetivone (2-7%), beta-vetivone (4-14%) and beta-vetivenene (1-8%).

It is known to contain calming, nerve tonic, sedative, and uplifting properties. One study found that the anxiolytic properties of vetiver might be associated with altering neuronal activation in the central amygdaloid nucleus therefore promoting relaxation.[178]

Researchers have also found that vetiver can enhance memory and learning activity. Specifically, they found that *"vetiveria zizanioides pretreatment significantly prevented the rise in AchE levels suggesting that it attenuates the excessive formation of reactive oxygen species (ROS).* Treatment groups were efficient to overcome the learning and memory deficits created by scopolamine induced amnesia except chloroform, presenting efficient learning and memory response than the negative control. The treatment groups ethanol and aqueous elaborated better responses of acquisition and retention as compared to the positive control. This is in agreement with the observations that *Vetiveria zizanioides* possesses significant memory and learning activity."[179]

# Ylang Ylang
## (*Cananga odorata*)

Ylang Ylang is steam distilled from the flowers and usually originates from either Madagascar or Ecuador. A member of the Annonaceae family, ylang ylang has been known to be involved in mood regulation and regulates heartbeat in addition to its antispasmodic, vasodilating, anti-inflammatory, antiparasitic capabilities.

It contains linalool (2-16%) known for its calming properties, in addition to Germacrene D (14-27%), (E,E)-alpha-farnesene (5-23%), benzyl acetate (1-15%), geranyl acetate (1-15%), beta-caryophyllene (2-19%), benzyl benzoate (4-8%), paracresyl methyl ether (0.5-9%), methyl benzoate (1-5%), and benzyl salicyclate (1-5%).

Ylang ylang has been shown to increase positive energy and focus of thoughts, restore confidence, peace, and has throughout history been used to decorate the beds of newly-weds.[180]

Research has shown ylang ylang to have awakening effects causing a decrease in alpha and beta activities.[181] Another study participants reported feeling "more calm and more relaxed."[182] Another study showed ylang-ylang to decrease alertness as it promoted feelings of tranquility.[183]

*Note: Use sparingly if you have low pressure.

# The Crossover Properties of Essential Oils

Several other single essential oils including Spruce (*Picea mariana*), Tea Tree (*melaleuca alternifolia*), and Copaiba (*copaifera reticulata, C. Langsdorfii, or C. multijuga*) are readily available and can be beneficial for the central and peripheral nervous systems. However, they are not mentioned in detail here as more clinical research needs to be performed before their efficacy on the brain can be measured.

The wonderful thing about essential oils is that many of them have crossover properties chemically and can do functions because of their ability as secondary metabolites to adapt to environments. Since essential oils are extremely diverse, resilient, resourceful, and intelligent, it stands to reason that many, many more varieties of essential oils could be beneficial for the brain. Even more powerful than their chemical adaptability is the power of quantum physics. In the following pages, let's explore more why and how essential oils can affect our brains and bodies in profound ways.

# IN OTHER WORDS...

## (A SUMMARY OF CHAPTER 7)

Odors are powerful for awaking memories partly because of their direct access to the neural substrates of olfaction, emotion, associative learning, and memory. Memories that are triggered by scent are known as "Proustian memories" and differ from semantic memory (information storage) and other types of episodic memory (storage of specific events). Proustian memories aren't triggered by the same cues (like visual and verbal). Odors elicit more affective, old, rare, and evocative personal memories. Since essential oils are aromatic compounds, they naturally can have a profound effect on the ability to retrieve memories and prompt emotions. But how else can they help the brain? The chemical compounds of essential oils can affect the brain and body in our five main cognitive functions: perception, attention, cognition, memory, and emotional regulation. Just like essential oils are created to help balance the plant, they also can have profound affect on our cells and even fill in the gaps where we need a little extra balancing.

Chemically, essential oils can act on our cells in a few distinct ways:
1. They engage in selective binding with specific molecular targets such as neuro- or hormone receptors.
Human hormones and neurotransmitters are nearly identical in molecular structure to those produced in plants. This fact is not only astounding, but it provides amazing hope for the ability to change our brain chemistry simply by using the secondary metabolites of essential oils.

2. They non-selectively cause a disturbance of the three-dimensional structure of proteins (known as protein conformation).

3. They bond covalently to DNA and RNA, modifying gene expression.
Thanks to essential oils, the ability to modify how our genes are expressed is possible due to the same covalent and non-covalent modifications of proteins.

4. They change membrane permeability and the function of membrane proteins.
Essential oils can change the permeability of membranes. Most water-soluble molecules cannot penetrate cell membranes, only non-polar or very small molecules (like oxygen, carbon dioxide, or water) can get through uninhibited. Inside the cell membrane is where all of the activity of the cell takes place like the necessary exchanges of amino acids, sugar, and signaling—all controlled by proteins integrated in the membrane.

Not only can essential oils affect the cell membranes, but that is where the work of changing the DNA and RNA of the cell actually begins. One simple theory on how essential oils work at the cellular level in our brains and bodies is known as PSM Paradigm. PSM stands for three different chemical component types contained in some essential oils (or can be mixed in a custom blend) that speed cellular healing: phenols (or phenylpropanoids), sesquiterpenes, and monoterpenes. This chemical combination in a single oil or layering of multiple oils high in these three compounds helps to explain how a single anointment or application of essential oils is able to bring about an instant and permanent healing. First, the phenols clean the receptor sites.

Then the sesquiterpenes delete bad information from cellular memory. Lastly, monoterpenes restore or awaken the correct information in the cell's memory (DNA).

The PSM paradigm—along with the other components that make up essential oils like alcohols, ketones, ethers, and esters—help to defragment the brain and allow for the chance to create lasting change at a cellular level. However, this paradigm is only one possible mechanism for how and why essential oils work so powerfully. We can also argue that electrical, magnetic, and vibrational etiologies are also explanations for the effectiveness of essential oils.

The wonderful thing about essential oils is that many of them have crossover properties chemically and can do functions because of their ability as secondary metabolites to adapt to environments. Since essential oils are extremely diverse, resilient, resourceful, and intelligent, it stands to reason that many, many more varieties of essential oils than even those covered in this chapter could be beneficial for the brain.

# Glossary

***alcohol:*** a hydrocarbon group (R) with a hydroxyl radical (OH-) attached. Alcohol names end in -ol.

***analgesic:*** remedy or agent that deadens or relieves pain

***antibacterial:*** agent that resists or destroys bacterial organisms

***anticholinergic:*** agent that blocks the neurotransmitter acetylcholine in the central and the peripheral nervous system

***antifungal:*** agent that resists or destroys fungal organisms

***anti-inflammatory:*** reduces inflammation

***antimicrobial:*** agent that resists or destroys pathogenic microorganisms

***antioxidant:*** natural or synthetic substance that helps inhibit destructive oxygen- and free radical-induced deterioration (oxidation) of substances and tissues in the body.

***antiparasitic:*** agent that resists or destroys parasitic organisms

***antispasmodic:*** prevents and eases spasms or convulsions

***antiviral:*** inhibits the growth of virus

***anxiolytic:*** agent that inhibits feelings of anxiety

**keytone:** a basic structural element in which oxygen is bound to carbon by a double bond.

**monoterpene:** a hydrocarbon molecule or functional group with the formula $C_{10}H_{16}$, which is the formula for one terpene unit.

**phenol** (or **phenylpropanoid**): 1. a compound consisting of a hydroxyl radical (OH-) attached to a benzene ring ($C_6H_6$). Its formula is ($C_6H_6O$). 2. a family of compounds containing a phenol molecule as a functional group. Members of this family are also called phenolics.

**PSM paradigm:** a paradigm for applying essential oils for therapeutic purposes where oils are used such that the combination of them provides certain amounts of the phenols (P), monoterpenes (M), and sesquiterpenes (S). Few single oils contain these three classes of compounds in the right proportions. Blends of oils or layering of oils one after the other are usually necessary to achieve a PSM anointing. A PSM blend is a therapeutic combination or sequence of essential oils with a 10-50% phenols, 10-60% monoterpenes, and 3-20% sesquiterpenes, where ketones or alcohols may be substituted for phenols.

**sesquiterpene:** a compound consisting of or containing a functional group with the formula, $C_{15}H_{24}$—the joining of three isoprene units or one-and-a-half terpene units.

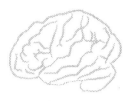

**Chapter Eight**

# WHY "MIND OVER MATTER" MATTERS

Although I skipped studying physics in school (I doubled up on anatomy and physiology instead, which ended up being a smart choice), the field of quantum physics (used interchangeably with "quantum mechanics") has long fascinated me. As I delved deeper into the world of neuroscience and crossed the axioms of both faith and the supernatural as well as that of essential oils, I cannot escape the concrete reality found in these fields and the infinite possibilities afforded by the laws and principles of physics.

This is my attempt at a synthesis and summary of how the mechanics and laws of physics and their quantum possibilities applies to our spirits, souls, and bodies rather than a thorough examination of the topic. There are many hard scientists (as well as philosophers) who have long studied this field and have written books on the topic. The groundwork I lay here is based on my research and synthesis of both the science of the physical and metaphysical as it applies to essential oils, the brain and body, and the nature of healing.

In order to understand the quantum nature of matter, let us first revisit briefly a few principles of classical physics that have informed and suspended when we reach the discussion of quantum.

# Particles or Waves: Classical Physics

In classical physics, defined largely by the principles laid out by Sir Isaac Newton, the study is governed by two fundamental concepts:

1. The concept of a particle: a discrete entity with definite position and momentum that moves in accordance with Newton's laws of motion.

2. The concept of a wave: an extended physical entity with a presence at every point in space that is provided by electric and magnetic fields which change in accordance with Maxwell's laws of electromagnetism. [184]

In the view of classical physics (also called Newtonian physics), matter is either a particle *or* a wave. It cannot be both. It's a neat and tidy picture wherein the laws of particle motion account for the material world around us and the laws of electromagnetic fields account for the light waves which illuminate this world.

This was the firmly held viewpoint until around 1900 when a researcher by the name of Max Planck began experimenting (followed by subsequent experiments by other scientists in later decades) that shifted the view. It is now a firmly held belief that quantum physics explains what classical physics cannot in regards to minuscule matter. **According to quantum mechanics, matter can be both a particle *and* a wave. What used to be thought of as either/or can now be considered both/and.**

In general, it can be difficult connecting with the concept of physics because it involves a great amount of math (certainly not my forte!) and a great amount of imagination (especially when dealing with quantum). Many prefer the concrete. Quantum theory is largely misunderstood by even the most prestigious in the scientific community, but that isn't stopping the world from believing in or using quantum physics.

Einstein's theory of relativity (as proven by the equation $e=mc^2$) changed everything for science and gave an explanation for the concept and matter of time unlike anything the world had seen before or since. Whereas the theory of relativity deals with the nature of large (infinitely large) substances, the theories of quantum mechanics deal with the miniscule. The atoms examined in physics are so small they almost are incomprehensible to the human mind. Let's dive into the microscopic world of atomic mass.

The historical view of the atom according to classical physics was best defined by Niels Bohr who came up with an explanation in 1913 that ultimately won him a Nobel Prize.

Fig. 8.1

# BOHR'S ATOMIC MODEL

A brief introduction to the nature of the classic atomic model.

SOURCE: THE DANCING WI LI MASTERS: AN OVERVIEW OF THE NEW PHYSICS BY GARY ZUKAV

It was a Danish physicist named Niels Bohr who came up with an explanation (in 1913) that made so much sense that it won him a Nobel Prize. Like most ideas in physics, it is essentially simple. Bohr did not start with what was theoretically "known" about the structure of atoms. He started with what he really *knew* about atoms, that is, he started with raw spectroscopic data. Bohr speculated that electrons revolve around the nucleus of an atom not at just any distance, but in orbits, or shells, which are specific distances from the nucleus. Each of these shells (theoretically there are an infinite number of them), contains up to a certain number of electrons, but no more.

If the atom has more electrons than the first shell can accommodate, the electrons begin to fill up the second shell. If the atom has more electrons than the first and second shells combined can hold, the third shell begins to fill, and so on, like this:

| Shell number | 1 | 2 | 3 | 4 | 5 . . . |
|---|---|---|---|---|---|
| Numbers of electrons | 2 | 8 | 18 | 32 | 50 . . . |

His calculations were based on the hydrogen atom, which only has one electron. According to Bohr's theory, the electron in the hydrogen atom stays as close to the nucleus as it can get. In other words, it usually is in the first shell. This is the lowest energy state of a hydrogen atom. (Physicists call the lowest energy state of any atom its "ground state".) If we excite an atom of hydrogen we cause its electron to jump to one of the outer shells. How far it jumps depends upon how much energy we give it. If we really heat the atom up (thermal energy), we cause its electron to make a very large jump all the way to one of the outer shells. Smaller amounts of energy make the electron jump less far. However, as soon as it can (when we stop heating it), the electron returns to a shell closer in. Eventually it returns all the way back to shell number one. Whenever the electron jumps from an outer shell to an inner shell, it emits energy in the form of light. The energy that the electron emits is exactly the amount of energy that it absorbed when it jumped outward in the first place. Bohr discovered that all of the possible combinations of jumps that the hydrogen electron can make on its journeys back to the ground state (the first shell) equals the number of lines in the hydrogen spectrum!"

# Both/And - Why Quantum Physics

It was at the beginning of the 20th century that quantum physics came on the scene. The study of quantum mechanics was not a replacement for Newtonian physics, which remains valid within its limits, but rather is like flipping over the other side of the coin to discover a new face. Classical physics applies still to the large-scale world whereas the study of quantum units lies in the subatomic realm—the invisible universe underlying, embedded in, and constructing the fabric of everything around us.

A "quantum" is a quantity of something, a specific amount. "Mechanics" is the study of motion and "physics" the branch of science concerned with the nature and properties of matter and energy. Therefore "quantum physics" or "quantum mechanics" is the study of the nature, properties, or motion of quantities of matter and energy. Quantum theory states that the universe comes in bits and pieces (quanta) and the physics or mechanics examines the study of this phenomenon.

When discussing the changing world of physics, Einstein summarized,

> "...creating a new theory is not like destroying an old barn and erecting a skyscraper in its place. It is rather like climbing a mountain, gaining new and wider views, discovering unexpected connections between our starting point and its rich environment. But the point from which we started out still exists and can be seen, although it appears smaller and forms a tiny part of our broad view gained by the mastery of the obstacles on our adventurous way up."[185]

Before we apply the principles of quantum physics to our minds and bodies, we must understand the nature forming the underlying grid of the study: matter existing and functioning as both particles and waves.

## A summary of the basic tenants of quantum physics is this:

1. A most basic (subatomic) piece of matter **can** behave as either a particle or a wave without violating its status as little hunks of something. This fact has been repeatedly quantified by physicists (and was first proven by Max Planck).

2. The piece of matter **will** behave as either a particle *or* a wave depending on the role of the individual and their relation to the matter.

3. Unlike classical physics that has defined predictions of the outcome, in quantum, the predicted outcome of the matter is not only infinite and variable, but can actually be influenced by the individual and their relation to the matter.

| Fig. 8.2 | A brief introduction to the nature of the uncertainty principle. |
|---|---|
| **THE UNCERTAINTY PRINCIPLE** | SOURCE: JAMES FREDERICK IVEY |

The uncertainty principle, formulated in 1927 by Werner Heisenberg, demonstrated that we can never simultaneously know the velocity and the location of an elemental particle of force or matter because measuring the one of these instantly changes the other. Besides showing more forcefully yet the nebulosity of material objects by demonstrating that their components can be localized only in terms of statistics, chance, Heisenberg's discovery carries us further yet along in our development of the theme that it is mind and not matter that is primary in the universe. On the quantum level of size, when a mind makes a measurement of any sort, that act of measurement causes change in that which is measured; therefore, either mind is primary in the universe or the uncertainty principle is invalid. Our minds do not seem to be this potent when we measure things such as the length of an automobile, but when we measure the mass of a subatomic particle, an entirely different story pertains.

**Fig. 8.3**

# CLASSICAL AND QUANTUM COMPARED

An introductory comparison between classical Newtonian physics and quantum physics.

SOURCE: ADAPTED FROM GARY ZUKAV

| CLASSICAL PHYSICS | QUANTUM PHYSICS |
|---|---|
| Can picture it. | Cannot picture it. |
| Based on ordinary sense perceptions. | Based on behavior of subatomic particles and systems not directly observable. |
| Describes *things*; individual objects in space and their changes in time. | Describes statistical behavior of *systems*. |
| Predicts events. | Predicts probabilities. |
| Assumes an objective reality "out there". | Does not assume an objective reality apart from our experience. |
| We can observe something without changing it. | We cannot observe something without changing it. |
| Claims to be based on "absolute truth"; the way that nature really is "behind the scenes." | Claims only to correlate experience correctly. |

The short way to summarize decades of research in quantum mechanics is to say that we are dealing with units of energy that exist in patterns of probability waves. It isn't to predict what will actually happen, but only to predict the probabilities of various possible results.

Most of quantum physics is actually just mathematical computations to explain a myriad of possible outcomes. Instead of traditional statistical analysis like in other forms of science wherein probabilities are defined and fixed, quantum mechanics explains how an infinite number of possibilities could be probable.

A good example of applying quantum theory and probabilities to our brain is by examining synaptic connections between neurons. Each neural cell has the capacity to synapse with up to approximately 10,000 other cells. That means the total number of possible connecting patterns between all these neurons is virtually infinite by sheer numerical standards. By applying quantum theory, this cascade has unfathomable potential.

# Summary of Quantum Theory

One of the guiding principles of quantum physics states that matter in particle form is thought to exist if/until there are potential choices to be made and then the matter takes on a wave form depending on the expectation or intended outcome.

**So how does quantum physics apply to the structure and function of our brains? In short, quantum physics helps us to explain:**

1. How the brain functions in endlessly resilient and creative ways beyond what we can know from just examining the data and/or anatomical structure.

2. How and why directed mental effort produces systematic and predictable changes in brain function.

3. How and why essential oils can do unexpected things to/on our brains beyond
   their chemical components.

**Quantum physics provides the "why" be-
hind how mind is greater than just the matter
of our brains and the essential oils we use on
them.** To convey how quantum physics affects
the mind and brain, let me define for you a new
model.

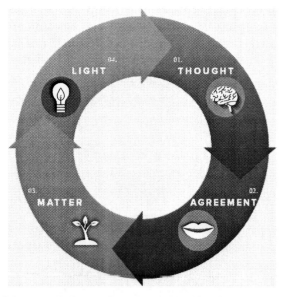

This model works on a cyclical process beginning with the thought, adding agreement,
resulting in physical matter, then the manifestation of the light (life).

Conscious thought (what we see from the
data as being electrical and chemical energy)
requires agreement in order to produce matter. Agreement can come in the form of a con-

scious attention to the thought—some call this **"mindfulness", but even more powerful than just mindfulness is verbal agreement. Words are energy and energy affects (and even creates) matter. Once agreement (whether in conscious acknowledgement or verbally) has been made, the matter can exist.**

Under Newtonian physics, the old question of if a tree (the particle or wave) falls in the forest, it will fall because the law of gravity requires it to regardless if a person is there to observe it. In the realm of quantum physics, the tree (the subatomic particle or wave) might not even be visible *unless* the observer is there to watch it fall. Matter can only exist in some cases when an individual is present to see it exist. There is a dependence then on the individual for the matter to exist in the first place and then their influence (through conscious choice) can allow the matter to change forms and beget new possibilities (light/life).

A new term has emerged recently, "self-directed neuroplasticity", as a general descripttion of the principle indicating that focused training and effort can systematically alter brain function in a predictable and potentially thera-peutic manner.[186] **We've discussed in detail how the brain naturally engages in neuroplasticity, but self-directed neuroplasticity gives language to the process of consciously choosing to engage in agreement in order to modify the matter of your spirit, soul, and body.**

**As we have seen and what has been con-firmed from the data, in the molecular world, many possibilities exist and your conscious choice to agree with them or not will dictate the outcome. Some scientists say it's like a "packet of possibilities"—a yeast that acts like a catalyst on the matter changing it from one form to another. Another way of defining this is "faith".** Using that term is risky as it can con-jure a variety of images depending on your experience and biases. However, when I use "faith", I would like to apply the definition, "the hopeful expectation of good."

Joseph Murphy put it aptly, "It is a well-known fact that all the various schools of healing bring about documented cures of the most wonderful character. The most obvious conclusion that strikes your mind is that there must be some underlying organ and process that is common to them all. Indeed, there is. The organ of healing is the subconscious mind, and the process of healing is faith."[187]

The subconscious mind can be influenced by a variety of things (our spirits, memories, emotions, epigenetic expression, etc.), but it serves as the birthplace of the thoughts we then can choose to apply agreement (faith) to in order to shape and form our reality.

A version of this model can be backed by quantum physics, but it also appears in sacred texts. Looking to the biblical account of the Messiah Yeshua in John 1, the writer notes the following.

> "In the beginning was the Word, and the Word was with God, and the Word was God. He was in the beginning with God. All things were made through Him, and without Him nothing was made that was made. In Him was life, and the life was the light of men. And the light shines in the darkness, and the darkness did not comprehend it."[188]

The existence "began" as a thought and the Word agreed, which then manifested in human form and dwelt on the earth, thus producing eternal light for the world.

## Scale of Efficacy

**If there were levels of potency or speed of change or healing they would function in this**

**order and scale according to quantum theories:**

1. **Neuroplasticity alone**

2. **Neuroplasticity (with essential oils)**

3. **Self-directed neuroplasticity (without essential oils)**

4. **Self-directed neuroplasticity (with essential oils)**

The slowest process and one that requires no effort from the individual is the brain's natural change over time through the neural wiring and dewiring process of neuroplasticity. We have seen this from the research previously discussed. Some "natural" neuroplasticity will increase just by the use of essential oils due to their physical and chemical properties.

The next best thing would be for the brain to engage self-directed neuroplasticity by choosing to add agreement to thought therefore modifying or creating matter through both spiritual (quantum) and physical (neural) means. Studies have shown that using "mindful awareness" (agreement) specifically modulates the activity of the prefrontal cortex.[189] Because of the well-established role of this cortical area in the planning and willful selection of self-initiated responses.

Whereas, much of what we have discussed in the book thus far has been looking at the structural and functional systems of the brain and body, giving agreement (or not) is a conscious choice that involves a person's free will.

Schwartz states,

> "When people practice self-directed activities for the purpose of systematically

altering patterns of cerebral activation they are attending to their mental and emotional experiences, not merely their limbic or hypothalamic brain mechanisms. Although no scientifically oriented person denies that brain mechanisms play a critical role in generating those experiences, precisely what the person is training him- or herself to do is to willfully [sic] change how those brain mechanisms operate—and to do that requires attending to mental experience per se. It is, in fact, the basic thesis of self-directed neuroplasticity research that the way in which a person directs their attention (e.g. mindfully or unmindfully) will affect both the experiential state of the person and the state of his/her brain."[190]

An example is given by Schwartz and colleagues from an experiment done by Ochsner *et al* with quantum theory applied. In the 2002 study, subjects in the experiment were taught in a training phase how to distinguish, and respond differently to, two instructions given while viewing emotionally disturbing visual images. They were told to "attend" (meaning passively "be aware of, but not try to alter, any feelings elicited by") or "reappraise" (meaning actively "reinterpret the content so that it no longer elicits a negative response"). Data from the brains of these subjects was then recorded while they performed these mental actions. The visual stimuli, when passively attended to, activate limbic brain areas, and when actively reappraised, activate regions in the prefrontal cortex.[191]

According to Schwartz and colleagues, "From the classic materialist point of view this is essentially a conditioning experiment where, however, the 'conditioning' is achieved through linguistic access to cognitive faculties. But how do the cognitive realities involving 'knowing', 'understanding' and 'feeling' arise out of motions of the miniature planet-like objects of classic physics, which have no trace of any experiential quality? How do the vibrations in the air that carry the instructions get converted into feelings of understanding? And how do these feelings of understanding get converted to conscious effort, the presence or absence of which determine whether the limbic or frontal regions of the brain will be activated?"

The researchers continue to note that there are "important similarities and also important differences between the classic and quantum explanations of the experiments of Ochsner et al. (2002). In both approaches the atomic constituents of the brain can be conceived to be collected into nerves and other biological structures and into fluxes of ions and electrons, which can all be described reasonably well in essentially classic terms. In the classic approach the dynamics must in principle be describable in terms of the local deterministic classic laws that, according to those principles, are supposed to govern the motions of the atomic-sized entities... Within the context of the experiment by Ochsner et al. (2002), quantum theory provides, via the process 1 mechanism, an explicit means whereby the successful effort to 'rethink feelings' actually causes—by catching and actively holding in place—the prefrontal activations critical to the experimentally observed deactivation of the amygdala and orbitofrontal cortex. The resulting intention-induced modulation of limbic mechanisms that putatively generate the frightening aversive feelings associated with passively attending to the target stimuli is the key factor necessary for the achievement of the emotional self-regulation seen in the active cognitive reappraisal condition."

**Essentially, just by choosing conscious agreement with a thought (or consciously choosing to discard one thought and agree with**

**another) can produce a quieting in the areas of the limbic system producing emotions of fear and restore regulation of emotion.**

**Even more optimally is the brain engaging in self-directed neuroplasticity with the addition of essential oils. This adds the physical and quantum possibilities from the matter of essential oils to speed the physical and quantum progression of the neural wiring and dewiring. In this sense, it is taking matter from multiple sources to modify and create matter through both spiritual and physical means.**

# Essential Oils and Frequency

We've talked previously about how the chemistry of essential oils affect the cells in our body. But quantum mechanics has another explanation: frequency. The behavior of vibrational frequencies (like we've seen is the case when matter acts as energy waves) can alter the physical and chemical properties of an atom just as much as electrical or chemical signals (like neuropeptides).

According to Oschman, each individual atom is unique because of the distribution of its negative and positive charges, coupled with the rate at which it spins. The combination of the electrical charges and the motion, that generates the frequency pattern or rate of vibration. [192]

**Science has shown that every living thing carries a frequency, the measurable rate of electrical energy between two points.** Another way of looking at frequency is the rate at which molecules expressed as waves, vibrate. **Every living thing has a frequency.** Sound is a vibration. Light is a vibration. Sound molecules can travel as a wave in the air, water, or in a solid. That vibration is in every living thing and is referred to as frequency or energy.

Chemicals in our environment, bad food and water, stress, fear, negative thinking, and lack of sleep can all lower the frequencies of our bodies. A healthy body typically has a frequency between 62 and 78 MHz (megahertz). When our body dips below the normal frequency range, even to 58 MHz, sickness and diseases can begin.

Royal Raymond Rife, one of the early researchers of frequency, said that every disease has its own frequency and a substance with a higher frequency will alter the disease with the lower frequency. **The great news is that essential oils range in frequency from 52 MHz all the way up to Rose, which has a frequency of 320 MHz. When we use and diffuse essential oils we are raising our frequency and strengthening our bodies and brains.**

Lipton states, "To increase an atom's vibration rather than stop its movement, researchers select light waves with vibrations that are harmonically resonant and in phase with those of the atom. The vibrations can be of electromagnetic or acoustic origin... the science of physics implies that the same harmonic resonance mechanism, by which sound waves destroy a goblet or a kidney stone, can enable similar energy harmonics to influence the functions of our body's chemistry."[193]

According to David Stewart, "essential oils should not be thought of as having fixed and specific chemical or physical qualities and characteristics. That is classical thinking. They should be thought of as consisting of sets of probabilities. The specific probability that ultimately manifests is determined by the intentions of and choices made by the person applying and/or receiving the oil. Until the choices are made, the oil does not possess any particular property—only a set of possibilities."[194]

**Instead of saying what an essential oil *will* do or what issues it *will* address, rather the manifestation of the potential of the oil is dependent on the hopeful expectation of good (faith) of the user.**

**Therefore, based on the data and according to our model, the most advantageous and fastest way to change both the structure and function of your brain and your body is to engage first in self-directed neuroplasticity (agreement in your mind) *and* state verbally the expected outcome while using essential oils (aromatically, topically, or internally). This combination of multi-frequency agreement (i.e. sound and light) engages the thought with intention to manifest matter and form the light of new possibilities in your life and world.**

Changing your mind takes effort to achieve true, lasting, therapeutic results. This is because to actually change your mind requires a re-direction of the brain's resources away from your first (instinctual), lower level limbic responses and toward higher level, conscious choices and prefrontal functions. This doesn't happen passively. Rather, changing your mind requires both willful training and directed mental effort. The beauty of understanding quantum mechanics is that each and every intentional agreement affects the state of either your body, your soul (mind, will, and emotions), or your spirit. It really *is* mind over matter.

# IN OTHER WORDS...
## (A SUMMARY OF CHAPTER 8)

According to quantum mechanics, matter can be both a particle and a wave. What used to be thought of as either/or can now be considered both/and. The study of quantum mechanics was not a replacement for Newtonian (or "classical") physics, which remains valid within its limits, but rather is like flipping over the other side of the coin to discover a new face. Classical physics applies still to the large-scale world whereas the study of quantum units lies in the subatomic realm—the invisible universe underlying, embedded in, and constructing the fabric of everything around us.

Quantum physics is the study of the nature, properties, or motion of quantities of matter and energy. Quantum theory states that the universe comes in bits and pieces (quanta) and the physics or mechanics examines the study of this phenomenon.

**The basic tenants of quantum physics states:**
1. A most basic (subatomic) piece of matter **can** behave as either a particle or a wave without violating its status as little hunks of something.
2. The piece of matter **will** behave as either a particle *or* a wave depending on the role of the individual and their relation to the matter.
3. Unlike classical physics that has defined predictions of the outcome, in quantum, the predicted outcome of the matter is not only infinite and variable, but can actually be influenced by the individual and their relation to the matter.

We are dealing with units of energy that exist in patterns of probability waves. It isn't to predict what will actually happen, but only to predict the probabilities of various possible results. Matter in particle form is thought to exist if/until there are potential choices to be made and then the matter takes on a wave form depending on the expectation or intended outcome.

**In short, quantum physics helps us to explain:**
1. How the brain functions in endlessly resilient and creative ways beyond what we can know from just examining the data and/or anatomical structure.
2. How and why directed mental effort produces systematic and predictable changes in brain function.
3. How and why essential oils can do unexpected things to/on our brains beyond their chemical components.

Quantum physics provides the "why" behind how mind is greater than just the matter of our brains and the essential oils we use on them. To convey how quantum physics affects the mind and brain, we defined a new model. This model works on a cyclical process beginning with the thought, adding agreement, resulting in physical matter, then the manifestation of the light (life).

**If there were levels of potency or speed of change or healing they would function in this order and scale according to quantum theories:**
1. Neuroplasticity alone
2. Neuroplasticity (with essential oils)
3. Self-directed neuroplasticity (without essential oils)
4. Self-directed neuroplasticity (with essential oils)

We've talked previously about how the chemistry of essential oils affect the cells in our body. But quantum mechanics has another explanation: frequency. Science has shown that every living thing carries a frequency, the measurable rate of electrical energy between two points. Another way of looking at frequency is the rate at which molecules expressed as waves, vibrate. Every living thing has a frequency. Sound is a vibration. Light is a vibration. Sound molecules can travel as a wave in the air, water, or in a solid. That vibration is in every living thing and is referred to as frequency or energy.

Chemicals in our environment, bad food and water, stress, fear, negative thinking, and lack of sleep can all lower the frequencies of our bodies. A healthy body typically has a frequency between 62 and 78 MHz (megahertz). When our body dips below the normal frequency range, even to 58 MHz, sickness and diseases can begin. Royal Raymond Rife, one of the early researchers of frequency, said that every disease has its own frequency and a substance with a higher frequency will alter the disease with the lower frequency. The great news is that essential oils range in frequency from 52 MHz all the way up to Rose, which has a frequency of 320 MHz. When we use and diffuse essential oils we are raising our frequency and strengthening our bodies and brains.

Instead of saying what an essential oil *will* do or what issues it *will* address, rather the manifestation of the potential of the oil is dependent on the hopeful expectation of good (faith) of the user.

Therefore, based on the data and according to our model, the most advantageous and fastest way to change both the structure and function of your brain and your body is to engage first in self-directed neuroplasticity (agreement in your mind) *and* state verbally the expected outcome while using essential oils (aromatically, topically, or internally). This combination of multi-frequency agreement (i.e. sound and light) engages the thought with intention to manifest matter and form the light of new possibilities in your life and world.

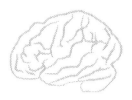

**Chapter Nine**

# DOORS: HEALING THE MIND

*"But sometimes illumination comes to our rescue at the very moment when all seems lost; we have knocked at every door and they open on nothing until, at last, we stumble unconsciously against the only one through which we can enter the kingdom we have sought in vain a hundred years — and it opens."*

-Marcel Proust, *"In Search of Lost Time"*

Recently, I was several hours into talking with a friend when the conversation took a turn in an unexpected direction. I don't remember the specific topic we were discussing, but I know we were processing some fairly innocuous version of life events I'd been experiencing. The conversation seemed normal until we hit one moment when I had an epiphany about a portion of my life and why I was behaving in a certain manner. It was as though I had been walking through the house of my mind and had discovered an entirely new wing hidden behind a door I didn't even know existed.

In the course of that evening, I'd not only discovered the door, but I had opened it to reveal a dusty, dark, and distinct part of my person that I was unfamiliar with. Either I'd not let myself previously be acquainted with this part because of cognitive dissonance or enough other mental "furniture" had been moved around so I couldn't see the door. Either way, there was a door to a part of me I wasn't aware of and it needed to be illuminated. Through the course of that conversation and others, illumination has happened to rooms of my mind and heart day by day.

As you embark on a journey of inner healing in your spirit, soul, and body, you'll discover that there are doors and secret passageways you never knew existed. Sometimes you find the doorway and open it to discover there are glorious secrets and brilliant thoughts on the other side. But more often than not, those doors have been sealed by trauma nestled deep in the subconscious and opening them reveals dank, dark rooms. Let me assure you as you open the door; there's no need to be afraid of what you find. You just need to bring in the light. Go into every room with light and see what needs to be cleaned. Your mind will become new as you illuminate the newly discovered parts that used to be closed to the world.

If our cognitive functions are like seeds planted in our minds, then toxic thoughts, stress, trauma, epigenetic markers negatively expressed could all be like weeds polluting our crop. In this brief chapter, I want to equip you with tools to walk out in practical ways how to reverse negative thinking, trapped emotions, and release your spirit, soul, and body.

In my experience with essential oils and inner healing, we're not talking about mind erasing where you apply an essential oil and suddenly your memory of a traumatic event or stressor is gone and you have a new memory in its place. Not at all. Instead, what I've experienced and what the data shows is that the memory itself will still be there, but the pain, shame, or trauma attached to the memory of the event is gone. You can remember without pain or fear or negativity.

# Practical Healing

Just using essential oils alone will have beneficial effects on our bodies, as does the simple process of engaging in conscious redirection of thought patterns to promote neurogenesis. However, the best and most effective way to facilitate the practice of "inner healing" is to engage the spirit, soul, and body in directed neuroplasticity with the addition of essential oils. This provides a combination of the physical, chemical, and quantum possibilities of essential oils to speed the physical and quantum progression cleaning and redecorating your "house."

The decision to engage in the process of inner healing is yours and yours alone. It is with an act of your will that you consciously choose to engage in the clearing and restoration process. And it is precisely because it is an act of your will that there is power for healing. In proportion to your expectancy it will be done to you.

There are a variety of methodologies that can be effective for processing stress, trauma, and overcoming blocks. Most of them can easily be combined with essential oils to increase their efficacy. Specific quantitative research on the rate at which a healing process is sped up due to essential oils is not yet available, but countless qualitative stories exist. Protocols like the Aroma Freedom Technique (AFT) incorporate essential oils in a type of guided imagery to address blocks and the process has been shown to have positive effects.

Eye Movement Desensitization and Reprocessing (EMDR) can be a useful technique for relieving trauma that has been stored in the subconscious. The methodology has been deemed valuable and effective by many professional counselors who are now utilizing it in addition to or instead of talk-therapy.

One of my favorite therapy methods is Trauma-Focused Cognitive Behavioral Therapy (TF-CBT). This methodology takes the highly effective method of Cognitive Behavioral Therapy (CBT) and specifically adds elements that aid in overcoming trauma. The method has been noted as one of the "best-researched and empirically supported treatment methods for adults and children. Its theoretical framework is based on the assumption that emotions and behaviour are largely a product of cognitions; thus psychological and behaviour problems can be reduced by altering cognitive processes."[195]

**Regardless of what method you use, essential oils can be combined either aromatically, topically, or internally—depending on the desired outcome. One of my favorite methods for using essential oils when doing an emotional release is to apply a few drops of the preferred oil(s) to the trauma point in the middle of the forehead and a few drops to the back of the head on the occipital bone near the foramen magnum—the opening to your brainstem (sometimes marked by a little notch at the base of your head). The subject then directly inhales by cupping hands over the nose and mouth, breathing in both nostrils together and then each nostril one at a time. This combined application is the fastest way to get the essential oil into the frontal lobe, limbic lobe, and brainstem.**

**After applying the oil, the subjects then puts one hand on the forehead and one over the heart. Then you repeat a simple phrase three times choosing to release the trauma behind the trapped emotion you're experiencing (even if it doesn't feel trapped or traumatic) and embracing the opposite experience. In one sense, this is the most basic form of "cognitive behavioral therapy" as you unidentify with the old thought pattern and come into agreement with the new thought, by an act of your will. Though you could simply think the new thou-**

**ght and not do a vocalization at the same time, as we saw previously, the activation of your voice carries a frequency that contains even more quantum potential for changing the ecosystem than simply the thought.**

To engage in the unidentification/agreement process I use a simple script adapted from a few sources and taught to me by Dr. Corinne Allen. There are books that can guide you in identifying what the negative belief or emotion is and subsequently, what the opposite belief or emotion to come into agreement with. I will note however, that I find that the activation of the Spirit is often the most accurate guide for determining what needs to be processed.

Because you are a spirit first, your mind and body are designed to come into submission under the spirit. As you go through the script to come out of agreement with the trapped emotion behind the trauma, you are repeating the script three times to bring your spirit, soul, and body all into proper alignment.

This isn't a magic formula or designed to be a "quick fix" that instantly changes everything. It's actually quite the opposite. By your conscious choice to engage in the process of un-identifying with the toxic thought and agreeing with the new, healthy thought is nothing more than engaging in the neural dewiring and wiring process. Sometimes it will take days, weeks, months, or years to "clean and re-decorate the house" and sometimes it can happen in a moment.

| Fig. 9.1 | A simple method for clearing stress and trauma when it's been trapped in the subconscious or manifesting in conscious thought. |
|---|---|
| **SCRIPT FOR CLEARING STRESS AND TRAUMA** | SOURCE: DR. CORINNE ALLEN (brainadvance.org) |

I choose to release the trauma behind the trapped emotion of:
_____ [state emotion] that no longer serves me in
a positive or productive way.
*(Repeat 3x)*

I choose _____ [affirm opposite emotion or state]
*(Repeat 3x)*

I believe _____ [affirm opposite emotion or state]
*(Repeat 3x)*

I manifest _____ [affirm opposite emotion or state]
*(Repeat 3x)*

| Fig. 9.2 | A simple method for clearing the atmosphere around you when it is filled with negativity. |
|---|---|
| **SCRIPT FOR CLEARING NEGATIVE ATMOSPHERES** | SOURCE: DAWNA DE SILVA (dawnadesilva.com) |

[Begin by calling by name the feeling or atmospheric condition;
i.e. fear].

_____, I see you. I do not partner with you.
I send you back.

*(Repeat as often as necessary.)*

# Another Realm

The amazing thing is that as your spirit and soul become realigned, your body follows suit and it manifests in your DNA. In his book, *Quantum Healing*, Deepak Chopra puts it this way,

> "...The mind and the body are like parallel universes. Anything that happens in the mental universe must leave tracks in the physical one... your body is the physical picture, in 3-D, of what you are thinking. We don't see our bodies as projected thoughts because many physical changes that thinking causes are unnoticeable. They involve minute alterations of cell chemistry, body temperature, electrical charge, blood pressure, and so on, which do not register on our focus of attention. You can be assured, however, that the body is fluid enough to mirror any mental event. Nothing can move without the whole.
>
> The latest discoveries in neurobiology build an even stronger case for the parallel universes of mind and body. When researchers looked further, beyond the nervous system and the immune system, they began to discover the same neuropeptides and receptors for them in other organs, such as the intestines, kidneys, stomach, and heart. There is every expectation of finding them elsewhere, too. This means that your kidneys can 'think', in the sense that they can produce the identical neuropeptides found in the brain. Their receptor sites are not simply sticky patches. They are questions waiting for answers, framed in the language of the chemical universe. It is very likely that if we had the whole dictionary and not just our few scraps, we would find that every cells speaks as fluently as we do."[196]

Candace Pert is the woman who coined the term "bodymind". She is also the one responsible for the discovery of the oxytocin receptor, and has pioneered the research of ligands and how neuropeptides innervate in our bodies. In her book, *Molecules of Emotion*, she tells a story that gives an explanation for why there is more than just what meets our eyes.

"Originally, we scientists thought that the flow of neuropeptides and receptors was being directed from the centers in the brain—the frontal cortex, the hypothalamus, the amygdala. This fit our reductionist model, supporting the view that thoughts and feelings are products of neuronal activity, and that the brain was the prime mover, the seat of consciousness. Then, as a result of my own and other people's work in the laboratory, we found that the flow of chemicals arose from many sites in the different systems simultaneously—the immune, the nervous, the endocrine, and the gastrointestinal—and that these sites formed nodal points on a vast superhighway of internal information exchange taking place on a molecular level. We then had to consider a system with intelligence diffused throughout, rather than a one-way operation adhering strictly to the laws of cause and effect, as was previously thought when we believed that the brain ruled over all.

So, if the flow of our molecules is not directed by the brain, and the brain is just another nodal point in the network, then we must ask—Where does the intelligence, the information that runs our bodymind, come from? We know that information has an infinite capability to expand and increase, and that it is beyond time and place, matter and energy. Therefore, it cannot belong to the material world we apprehend with our senses, but must belong to its own realm, one that we can experience as emotion, the mind, the spirit— an inforealm! This is the term I prefer, because it has a scientific ring to it, but others mean the same thing when they say field of intelligence, innate intelligence, the wisdom of the body. Still others call it God.

Although it's a simple concept, it's hard for the Western mind to understand. But I recall one person who was able to grasp it instantly, a cameraman working on the set of Bill Moyers's PBS special *Healing and the Mind*. As I was groping to explain how the innate intelligence, generated by subtle energies from flowing biochemicals, all converged in the inforealm, what came out was puzzling to Bill, but not to the cameraman. When taping was over and everyone was packing up, the gentle, soft-spoken man approached me and said, almost whispering it in my ear, "You were talking about the Holy Spirit, weren't you?"

Feeling a bit embarrassed, I had to admit that, yes, maybe I was."[197]

It's been said that if you behold light, you will be filled with light. One of the things I want to note is that just like we can't always isolate the sources of our stress, the emotions, trauma, and diseased states we experience don't happen in insolation either. The plants our essential oils are coming from live in an ecosystem, an environment with many factors like varying sunshine, amount of rainfall, soil conditions, environmental chemicals, and humans and animals. All of those conditions affect the plant in various ways and it responds to the biodynamic environment it's around.

Even so, your spirit, soul, and body are biodynamic. Not only is it important to not just treat symptoms, but to examine underlying structures, lifestyle choices, and the environment you are surrounded by. Your physical body, your mind, will, and emotions, and your spirit are all interconnected. It's possible that as you clear trauma, stress, or diseased states, other things will pop up that need to be dealt with. That's alright and very normal. You'll discover new doorways and there is grace for the process of illumination, cleaning, and restoring. It's important to listen to your spirit, soul, and body and respond to your needs and recognize this is a journey over time.

# IN OTHER WORDS...
## (A SUMMARY OF CHAPTER 9)

As you embark on a journey of inner healing in spirit, soul, and body, you'll discover that there are doors you never knew existed. Sometimes you find the doorway and open it to discover there are glorious secrets and brilliant thoughts on the other side. But more often than not, those doors have been sealed by trauma nestled deep in the subconscious and opening them reveals dank, dark rooms. As you open the door, there's no need to be afraid of what you find. You just need to bring in the light. Go into every room with light and see what needs to be cleaned. Your mind will become new as you illuminate the newly discovered parts that used to be closed to the world.

If our cognitive functions are like seeds planted in our minds, then toxic thoughts, stress, trauma, epigenetic markers negatively expressed could all be like weeds polluting our crop. In regards to essential oils and inner healing, we're not talking about mind erasing where you apply an essential oil and suddenly your memory of a traumatic event or stressor is gone and you have a new memory in its place. Instead, what I've experienced and what the data shows is that the memory itself will still be there, but the pain, shame, or trauma attached to the memory of the event is gone. You can remember without pain or fear or negativity.

Just using essential oils alone will have beneficial effects on our bodies, as does the simple process of engaging in conscious redirection of thought patterns to promote neurogenesis. However, the best and most effective way to facilitate the practice of "inner healing" is to engage the spirit, soul, and body in directed neuroplasticity with the addition of essential oils. This provides a combination of the physical, chemical, and quantum possibilities of essential oils to speed the physical and quantum progression cleaning and redecorating your "house."

The decision to engage in the process of inner healing is yours and yours alone. It is with an act of your will that you consciously choose to engage in the clearing and restoration process. And it is precisely because it is an act of your will that there is power for healing. In proportion to your expectancy it will be done to you. There are a variety of methodologies that can be effective for processing stress, trauma, and overcoming blocks. Most of them can easily be combined with essential oils to increase their efficacy.

Regardless of what inner healing method you use, essential oils can be combined either aromatically, topically, or internally—depending on the desired outcome. One of my favorite methods for using essential oils when doing an emotional release is to apply a few drops of the preferred oil(s) to the trauma point in the middle of the forehead and a few drops to the back of the head on the occipital bone near the foramen magnum—the opening to your brainstem (sometimes marked by a little notch at the base of your head). The subject then directly inhales by cupping hands over the nose and mouth, breathing in both nostrils together and then each nostril one at a time. This combined application is the fastest way to get the essential oil into the frontal lobe, limbic lobe, and brainstem.

After applying the oil, the subjects then puts one hand on the forehead and one over the heart. Then you repeat a simple phrase three times choosing to release the trauma behind the trapped emotion you're experiencing (even if it doesn't feel trapped or traumatic) and embracing the opposite experience. In one sense, this is the most basic form of "cognitive behavioral therapy" as you unidentify with the old thought pattern and come into agreement with the new thought, by an act of your will. By your conscious choice to engage in the process of unidentifying with the toxic thought and agreeing with the new, healthy thought is nothing more than engaging in the neural dewiring and wiring process. Sometimes it will take days, weeks, months, or years to "clean and redecorate the house" and sometimes it can happen in a moment.

As your spirit and soul become realigned, your body follows suit and it manifests in your DNA. If you behold light, you will be filled with light. Just like we can't always isolate the sources of our stress, the emotions, trauma, and diseased states we experience don't happen in insolation either. The plants our essential oils are coming from live in an ecosystem, an environment with many factors like varying sunshine, amount of rainfall, soil conditions, environmental chemicals, and humans and animals. All of those conditions affect the plant in various ways and it responds to the biodynamic environment it's around.

Even so, your spirit, soul, and body are biodynamic. Not only is it important to not just treat symptoms, but to examine underlying structures, lifestyle choices, and the environment you are surrounded by. Your physical body, your mind, will, and emotions, and your spirit are all interconnected. It's possible that as you clear trauma, stress, or diseased states, other things will pop up that need to be dealt with. That's alright and very normal. You'll discover new doorways and there is grace for the process of illumination, cleaning, and restoring. It's important to listen to your spirit, soul, and body and respond to your needs and recognize this is a journey over time.

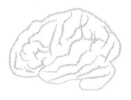

**Chapter Ten**

# SEEDS

*"From a small seed a mighty trunk may grow."*
                                        -Aeschylus

It was a cool morning in March 2011. I was in New York with a friend when our host, a new acquaintance, walked up the dark paneled stairs with a stack of books in his hands. Without prompting or inquiry, he handed me the stack and said gruffly, "These are my favorite books. I just thought I would share."

I thanked him and accepted the pile. I thought to myself the delivery was odd, but then again I *do* have a certain affection for books (especially non-fiction), so I did not protest. One in particular caught my eye. In fact, I can't even tell you the other books he brought because I only ever examined the one. The cover was a deep red with an antiqued image of some sort of a tree. The cover read, *Ruthless Trust* by Brennan Manning (a philosopher, spiritual guide, and author).

I walked into the next room, opened a page at random and began reading aloud with my friend overhearing. When I had finished reading approximately one chapter, I put the book down and my friend and I entered the city. A week later we left New York and returned to our respective homes. I knew that book was special, but I thought I had gleaned all I needed.

Fast forward a few months later, the summer was stifling and my life was in shambles. Every dream and plan I thought was supposed to be happening looked to be the opposite. I was jobless, husbandless, brokenhearted, depressed, and without a plan (which at the time, was the hardest part to deal with).

All I could do most days was my best to avoid having a panic attack and try not to be depressed by using every natural and practical method I could muster as I plugged along professionally as a freelance writer and photographer.

I had purchased my own copy of that book at some point after I returned home earlier in the year, but it had been sitting idly on my bookshelf along with five or six others all begging for me to crack them open and explore. None of them were appealing. I was at the height of depression-induced-apathy.

One day, probably in July, I began reading the book from the beginning. I made it two-thirds of the way through and although the content was wonderful, nothing struck me as particularly significant. That was until I got to one page. I remember I was standing in my kitchen. It had been a particularly hard day and I stood reading and eating. The author was speaking of the analogy of a farmer throwing seed on the land.

"With that simple act, the farmer's work is done. He watches television, washes clothes, repairs the hole in the roof, and travels to Delaware, New Mexico, and Oregon to visit his three children. Whether it is night or day, whether the farmer is asleep or awake, at home or on the road, the seed he scattered sprouts and grows. He does not have a clue how it happened. The earth does it all without his help. First the shoot, then the ear, then the full grain in the ear.

One sunlit morning, he has six buttermilk pancakes and four slices of Canadian bacon for breakfast, walks out the door, scratches his head at the ripened grain, and reaps his harvest.

That is the way it is with trust. Over the years it ripens into confidence. Based on the solid, irrefutable evidence of God's relentless faithfulness, a certainty in the trustworthiness of the tremendous Lover evolves without the least sweat and strain on our part. After the farmer casts the seed on the ground, he sleeps unperturbed, and the earth 'of itself'—in the Greek text, 'automatically'—brings forth fruit. The growth of trust into confidence is likewise 'of itself…'"

But it was this next part that made me weep, for as I began reading it for the first time, it was as if it had been inscribed on the page just for me:

"When the farmer arises in the morning, unreconciled to getting out of bed, he feels no anxiety that he has wasted time through his sleep; au contraire, he is confident that the seed has continued to grow during the night. So, too, the spiritual woman does not fret and flap over opportunities missed, does not hammer herself for not working hard enough, and does not have a panic attack wondering whether she has received grace in vain. She lives in quiet confidence that God is working in her by day and by night. Like the farmer, she is not totally passive or presumptuous. The woman knows that she has her full measure of work to do, but she realizes that the outcome rests with God and that the decisive factor is unearned grace. Thus, she works as if everything depends on God and prays as if everything depends on her."[198]

I stood in the kitchen speechless. It wasn't the last day I had a panic attack. A few weeks later I would begin seeing a counselor; a few months later I would discover essential oils; now, years later, I'm a completely different woman. But I'll never forget that day, because it was the day seeds of trust were planted. Seeds that are still being cultivated daily.

We've talked at length about the nature of trust and worth. If the soil of our lives as healthy individuals is the combination of the elements trust and worth—trust that your basic needs will be met in a timely and consistent manner and an understanding that you are worthy of giving and receiving affirmation and affection—it is sure to be a vibrant life.

Walter Burghardt writes, "When I trust you, I wed faith and hope. I rely on you to be faithful, to be trust to your promises, true to yourself. It is not quite the same as confidence. Trust, Webster's Second Unabridged tells us, 'is often instinctive, less reasoned than confidence, which is apt to suggest somewhat definite grounds of assurance.'"[199]

Over the years, I've discovered that often when we fight hopelessness, it's because we're believing a lie that nothing is going to change. As a result, we either white knuckle our way through with frustration and sheer grit *or* we resign ourselves to living life the way that it is now because we're too exhausted to do anything else. Neither of those options have to be in the cards for you.

**I'm here to tell you that freedom is available. I'm here to say that you are one who is destined to thrive. What you've known in the past doesn't have to be what the future holds. Sometimes healing is instantaneous and sometimes it's a process over time, but healing *does***

**come. I've experienced it and I've seen it in countless others and I know that it can be reality for you. In fact, it _is_ reality for you. The healing may not have manifested yet in your life, but you are going to thrive and it can start today.**

Healing is available for you, but it's not just for you. The beautiful thing about plants is that when they're next to each other in a field, one single plant effects everything around it. The nutrients emitted by one plant affect the entire ecosystem. From the bees that come to drink from the nectar of a flower and then pollinate the surrounding area, to the nutrients that come from a life as it's planted and fertilizes the soil and creates an atmosphere for others to thrive. Maybe it's the fresh air and oxygen that you begin to give off as your healing manifests that allows someone else to breathe deeply and receive nourishment from the life you're living. My healing isn't just for me; my healing is available for you. Likewise, your healing as you obtain it isn't just for you. It's meant to be shared with the world as a beacon of hope to others that life can be new and is possible, in greater measure than ever before, in fresh ways, with vibrancy.

**As you embark on each new day, fresh with possibilities and brimming with hope, may you know that you are worthy of receiving and all that you have need of will be provided. That is the nature of grace: it's the enabling power that causes you to thrive; it's living in the light and loving the freedom within. We are plants who can't earn it; it's freely given. We open ourselves to receive it and sometimes, when we're desperate and broken and unaware of our need, grace meets us somewhere pro-found (or somewhere like your kitchen, in the middle of reading a book after a panic attack). Because every breath is grace.**

"...but equally amazing to me is the steadfast grace that allows us to remain relentlessly faithful through the disasters and disappointments, the struggles and the heartaches of the human adventure. Our graced track record instills a modest confidence that, although we often stumble and fall, we will keep getting up; that we will not be numbered among the superficial... or the defeated who fight long and struggle honorably for their faith but eventually yield to despair; that the grace for the next step and the courage to receive it will be given."

-B. Manning[200]

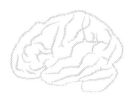

# A Note

When I began writing this book, I had much of the information and the roadmap of where I wanted to go and what I wanted to communicate. What I didn't know was how the book was going to change me. This process didn't start when I pulled the first research study or wrote the first word. Rather, this process began for me years ago when I started becoming free in my mind and heart. I thought I was in a good space when I started putting pen to paper, but I had no way of knowing how profoundly I would be changed during the course of this project.

For probably my entire life, I had (inadvertently) allowed myself to be more comfortable with my intellect (all of the functions I could do) than understanding who I was inherently. Before I began writing, I knew very clearly who I was writing for and how it would impact people. That, even now, excites and motivates me and I pray many people are changed. But I realize now, at the end point of writing, that this book wasn't ever actually to be written for you... this book came about because I needed to learn about the value of my own heart from the process.

*"Heart work is what we're going to be doing and it's my favorite work. It's beyond just emotions—it's beyond will or intellect or understanding. It's a quiet inner working that sometimes you won't have words for. A flower doesn't have to serve a purpose except to be delighted in. Words don't have to be exchanged. I just like looking at it."*

I journaled the above toward the beginning of this process one night in Sydney, Australia after drawing a map of my heart. It stands to be seen if there is a day when I will fully understand that my life exists only to be delighted in. It's my own journey of minding my brain and heart. But I can assure you that I'm not where I used to be and I'm learning to just *be*—planted in trust and worth.

My prayer for you is that you too understand that though your brain is incredible, it's your human heart that is the most valuable real estate in the universe. May Love be rooted in your heart as it was, has been, and is being continually in mine.

# A GUIDE TO NEUROTRANSMITTERS

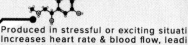

## ADRENALINE
### (epinephrine)
*fight or flight neurotransmitter*

Produced in stressful or exciting situati
Increases heart rate & blood flow, leadi
to a physical boost & heightened awarene

Deficit: Low energy, depression
Surplus: Linked with cardiac arrest, man
behaviors, paranoia, ADHD

## NORADRENALINE
### (norepinephrine)
*concentration neurotransmitter*

Affects attention & responding actions
in the brain, & involved in fight or flight response.
Contracts blood vessels, increasing blood flow.

Deficit: Mental disorders, especially depression
Surplus: Anxiety

## DOPAMINE
*pleasure neurotransmitter*

Feelings of pleasure and also addiction
movement, and motivation. People repe
behaviors that lead to dopamine releas

Deficit: Parkinson's Disease
Surplus: Schizophrenia, Drug addiction

Contributes to well-being & happiness;
helps sleep cycle & digestive system regulation.
Affected by exercise & light exposure.

Deficit: Depression, mood disorders
Surplus: Autism

## SEROTONIN
*mood neurotransmitter*

## GABA
*calming neurotransmitter*

Calms firing nerves in CNS. High levels
improves focus; low levels cause anxiet
Also contributes to motor control & visi

Deficit: Anxiety, seizures, tremors, & insom
Surplus: Sleep and eating disorders

Involved in thought, learning, & memory.
Activates muscle action in the body. Also
associated with attention and awakening.

Deficit: Alzheimer's Disease
Surplus: Severe Muscle Spasms

## ACETYLCHOLINE
*learning neurotransmitter*

## GLUTAMATE
*memory neurotransmitter*

Most common brain neurotransmitter.
Involved in learning & memory, regulate
development & creation of nerve contac

Surplus: Too much glutamate (and too li
GABA) associated with epilept
seizures.

Released during exercise, excitement, & sex,
producing well-being & euphoria, reducing
pain. Biologically active section shown.

Deficit: Body experiences pain.
Surplus: Body may not give adequate
warning about pain. Artificial highs.

## ENDORPHINS
*euphoria neurotransmitters*

# APPENDIX B –
# A GUIDE TO AMINO ACIDS

(*Note: Essential Amino Acids are marked with an asterisk below.)

**Alanine:** A nonessential amino acid that helps to build protein. It plays a major role in the transfer of nitrogen from peripheral tissues to the liver, aids in the metabolism of glucose, and guards against the buildup of toxic substances that are released in the muscle cells when muscle protein is broken down to meet energy needs quickly (such as what happens with aerobic exercise).

**Note: Research has shown that for people with insulin-dependent diabetes, taking an oral dose of L-alanine can be more effective than a conventional bedtime snack in preventing nighttime hypoglycemia.

**Arginine:** One of the better-studied amino acids that has been shown to be helpful for several conditions. It retards the growth of tumors and cancer by enhancing immune function. It increases the size and activity of the thymus gland, which manufactures T lymphocytes (T cells), crucial components of the immune system. It can help people with angina, congestive heart failure, high blood pressure, HIV, impotence, infertility, interstitial cystitis, surgical recovery, and wound healing.

Arginine can be produced in the body, however in newborn infants, production may not occur quickly enough to keep up requirements. It is therefore deemed essential early in life.

Foods high in arginine include: carob, chocolate, coconut, dairy products, gelatin, meat, oats, peanuts, soybeans, walnuts, white flour, wheat, wheat germ, and watermelon.

**Note: People with viral infections such as herpes should NOT take supplemental arginine and should avoid foods rich in arginine and low in the amino acid lysine. Pregnant and lactating women should avoid L-arginine supplements. Persons with schizophrenia should avoid amounts over 30mg daily. Long-term use, especially of high doses, is not recommended.

***Aspartic Acid (Asparagine):*** Asparagine is created from another amino acid, aspartic acid, and is needed to maintain balance in the central nervous system. It is useful for preventing either overly nervous feelings or overly calm. As it is converted back into aspartic acid, asparagine releases energy that brain and nervous system cells use for metabolism.

Because aspartic acid increases stamina, it is good for fatigue and depression, and it plays a vital role in metabolism. In proper balance, aspartic acid is beneficial for neural and brain disorders. It has been found in increased levels in persons with epilepsy and in decreased levels in people with some types of depression. Plant protein, especially that found in sprouting seeds, contains an abundance of aspartic acid.

**Note: The artificial sweetener aspartame is made from aspartic acid and phenylalanine, another amino acid.

***Carnitine:*** Carnitine is not an amino acid in the strictest sense, but rather an amino-like substance that is related to the B vitamins. However, because it has a chemical structure similar to that of amino acids, it is usually considered together with them. Its main function in the body is to help transport long-chain fatty acids, which are burned within the cells, mainly in the mitochondria, to provide energy. This is a major source of energy for the muscles. Carnitine thus increases the use of fat as an energy source. This prevents fatty buildup, especially in the heart, liver, and skeletal muscles. Carnitine has been shown to have several benefits for cardiovascular problems, such as congestive heart failure and high triglycerides. It may be useful in treating Alzheimer's disease.

The synthesis of carnitine depends on the presence of adequate amounts of vitamin C, iron, vitamin B1 (thiamine), vitamin B6 (pyridoxine) and the amino acids lysine and methionine. Carnitine can also be obtained from food, primarily meats and other foods of animal origin.

Acetyl-L-carnitine (ALC), a carnitine derivative produced naturally in the body, is involved in carbohydrate and protein metabolism and in the transport of fats into mitochondria. ALC is being studied in regard to degeneration of the brain and nervous system, including Alzheimer's and depression.

**Note: No toxic or serious side effects have been reported. However, it should NOT be taken along with the drug pentylenetetrazol.

**Citrulline:** The body makes citrulline from another amino acid, ornithine. Citrulline promotes energy, stimulates the immune system, is metabolized to form L-arginine, and detoxifies ammonia, which damages living cells. Citrulline is found primarily in the liver. It is helpful for treating fatigue.

**Cysteine (and Cystine):** These two amino acids are closely related. Cysteine is very unstable and is easily converted to L-cystine; however, each form is capable of converting the other as needed. Both aid in the formation of skin and are important for detoxification and antioxidant support. Cystine or the N-acetyl form of cysteine (N-acetylcysteine, or NAC) may be used in place of L-cysteine. NAC aids in preventing side effects from chemotherapy and radiation therapy. It has an antiaging effect on the body.

**Note: Do not use if prone to developing cystine kidney stones (a rare genetic condition called cystinuria). People who have diabetes should be cautious because it is capable of inactivating insulin.

***GABA (Gamma-aminobutyric Acid):*** GABA is an amino acid that acts as neurotransmitter in the central nervous system. It is essential for brain metabolism, aiding in proper brain function. GABA is formed in the body from another amino acid, glutamic acid. Its function is to decrease neuron activity and inhibit nerve cells from over-firing. Together with niacinamide and inositol, it prevents anxiety- and stress-related messages from reaching the motor centers of the brain by occupying their receptor sites.

GABA can be taken to calm the body in the same way as diazepam (Valium), chlordiazepoxide (Librium), and other tranquilizers, but without the fear of addiction. It has been used to in the treatment of epilepsy and hypertension. It is often helpful with ADHD and muscle tightness.

**Note: GABA should NOT be combined with pharmaceutical psychiatric or anticonvulsant medications. Too much GABA can cause increased anxiety, shortness of breath, numbness around the mouth, and tingling in the extremities. Abnormal levels of GABA unbalance the brain's message-delivery system and may cause seizures.

***Glutamic Acid:*** Glutamic acid is an excitatory neurotransmitter that increases the firing of neurons in the central nervous system. It is a major excitatory neurotransmitter in the brain and spinal cord. It is converted into either glutamine or GABA. The brain can use glutamic acid as fuel. It can detoxify ammonia. The conversion of glutamic acid into glutamine is the only means by which ammonia in the brain can be detoxified.

Glutamic acid helps to correct personality disorders and is useful in treating childhood behavioral disorders. It is used in the treatment of epilepsy, mental retardation, muscular dystrophy, ulcers, and hypoglycemic coma. It is component of folate (folic acid), a B vitamin that helps the body break down amino acids.

**Note: Because one of its salts is monosodium glutamate (MSG), glutamic acid should be avoided by anyone allergic to MSG.

**Glutamine:** Glutamine is the most abundant free amino acid found in the muscles of the body. Because it can readily pass the blood-brain barrier, it is known as brain fuel. In the brain, glutamine is converted into glutamic acid, which is essential for cerebral function, and vice versa. It also increases the amount of GABA, which is needed to sustain proper brain function and mental activity. Glutamine helps to clear ammonia from the tissues, especially brain tissue.

It is found in large amounts in the muscles and helps to build and maintain muscles. It helps to prevent muscle wasting due to illness or prolonged bed rest. It is often used to assist with alcohol withdrawal, athletic performance, gastritis, HIV, surgical recovery, and ulcers. Many plant and animal substances contain glutamine, but cooking easily destroys it. If eaten raw, spinach and parsley are good sources.

**Note: Supplemental glutamine must be kept absolutely dry or the powder will degrade into ammonia and pyroglutamic acid. Do not take supplemental glutamine with cirrhosis of the liver, kidney problems, Reye's syndrome, or any type of disorder that can result in the accumulation of ammonia in the blood.

**Glycine:** Glycine retards muscle degeneration by supplying additional creatine, a compound present in muscle tissue and is utilized in the construction of DNA and RNA. It improves glycogen storage, thus freeing up glucose for energy needs. It is essential for the synthesis of nucleic acids, bile acids, and other nonessential amino acids in the body. It is necessary for central nervous system function and a healthy prostate. It can help with epileptic seizures, manic (bipolar) depression, and hyperactivity.

Caution: Too much glycine can cause fatigue, but the right amount produces more energy.

**Histidine\*:** Histidine is an essential amino acid that is significant in the growth and repair of tissues. It greatly aids the maintenance of the myelin sheaths, which protect nerve cells, and is needed for the production of both red and white cells. It protects the body against radiation damage, helps lower blood pressure, aids in removing heavy metals from the body, and may help in the prevention of AIDS.

Too high levels of histidine may lead to stress and even psychological disorders such as anxiety and schizophrenia. Not enough histidine may contribute to rheumatoid arthritis and nerve deafness.

Histamine, an important immune system chemical, is derived from histidine. Histamine aids in sexual arousal and indigestion resulting from a lack of stomach acid. Histidine is naturally found in rice, wheat, and rye.

\*\*Note: Persons with manic (bipolar) depression should not take supplemental histidine unless a deficiency has been identified.

**Isoleucine\*:** Isoleucine is an essential amino acid that is needed for hemoglobin formation and also it stabilizes and regulates blood sugar and energy levels. It is metabolized in muscle tissue.

It has been found to be deficient in people suffering from many different mental and physical disorders. A deficiency of this amino acid can lead to symptoms similar to hypoglycemia. Food sources of isoleucine include: almonds, cashews, chicken, chickpeas, eggs, fish, lentils, liver, meat, rye, most seeds, and soy protein.

**Note: Isoleucine can be taken in a supplemental form, also, but always with the correct balance of the other two branched-chain amino acids, L-leucine and L-valine.

**Leucine\*:** Leucine, is an essential amino acid and one of the branched-chain amino acids (along with isoleucine and valine). The three work together to protect muscle and act as fuel. Leucine, plus other dietary proteins, encourages muscle growth even without the other two branched-chain amino acids. They promote the healing of bones, skin, and muscle tissue, and aid in recovery after surgery. Leucine also lowers elevated sugar levels and aids in increasing growth hormone production. Leucine can be found naturally in brown rice, beans, meat, nuts, soy flour, and whole wheat.

**Note: Supplemental leucine must be taken in balance with L-isoleucine and L-valine, or symptoms of hypoglycemia may result. Too high of an intake of leucine may contribute to pellagra, and may increase the amount of ammonia present in the body.

**Lysine\*:** Lysine is an essential amino acid that is a necessary building block for all protein. It is needed for proper growth and bone development in children. It also helps calcium absorption and maintains a proper nitrogen balance in adults. Lysine helps in the production of antibodies, hormones, and enzymes, and helps collagen formation and tissue repair. In doing these actions, it is very valuable for those recovering from surgery and sports injuries. It is also very useful for fighting cold sores and herpes viruses, including shingles. Taking supplemental L-lysine, together with Vitamin C with bioflavonoids, can effectively fight and/or prevent herpes outbreaks, especially if foods containing the amino acid arginine are avoided.

Because it is an essential amino acid and cannot be manufactured by the body, it is vital that adequate amounts of it are found in the diet. Deficiencies of lysine can lead to anemia, blood-shot eyes, enzyme disorders, hair loss, poor concentration, irritability, lack of energy, poor appetite, reproductive disorders, retarded growth, and weight loss. Good food sources of lysine are cheese, eggs, fish, lima beans, milk, cottage cheese, avocadoes, potatoes, red meat, soy products, wheat germ, and yeast.

**Methionine\*:** Methionine is an essential amino acid that assists in the breakdown of fats, thus helping to prevent a buildup of fat in the liver and arteries that might obstruct blood flow to the brain, heart, and kidneys. It helps the digestive system and helps to detoxify harmful agents such as lead and other heavy metals. It also helps to diminish muscle weakness, prevent brittle hair, and protects against radiation.

Methionine is a powerful antioxidant and detoxification agent. It is a good source of sulfur, which inactivates free radicals and helps to prevent skin and nail problems. It is used for conditions like HIV, pancreatitis, and Parkinson's disease.

Although it is an essential amino acid, methionine is not synthesized in the body and so must be obtained from food sources or dietary supplements. Good food sources are beans, eggs, fish, garlic, lentils, meat, onions, soybeans, seeds, and yogurt. Because the body uses methionine to derive a brain food called choline, it is wise to supplement the diet with choline or lecithin (which is high in choline) to ensure that the supply of methionine is not depleted.

**Note: B vitamins, especially B6, folic acid, and B12, should be supplemented along with methionine to prevent the build-up of homocysteine, a risk factor for cardiovascular disease.

***Ornithine*:** Ornithine helps to prompt the release of growth hormone, which promotes the metabolism of excess body fat. This effect is enhanced if ornithine is combined with arginine and carnitine. Ornithine is necessary for proper immune system and liver function. It detoxifies ammonia and aids in liver regeneration. It is found in large amounts in the skin and connective tissue, and helps promote the healing and repairing of damaged tissues.

**Note: Children, pregnant women, nursing mothers, or anyone with a history of schizophrenia should not take supplemental L-ornithine, unless they are specifically directed to do so by a physician. High doses, above 10g, may cause digestive upset.

***D-Phenylalanine*\*:** Phenylalanine is an essential amino acid that can cross the blood-brain barrier. It can have a direct effect on brain chemistry. It is available in three different forms: designated as L-, D-, or DL. This amino acid serves to build protein and acts as precursor to L-tyrosine, L-dopa, norepinephrine, and epinephrine.

D-phenylalanine acts as a painkiller. It is used also for depression, lower back pain, osteoarthritis, Parkinson's disease, and rheumatoid arthritis. It is not naturally occurring in the body, but can be converted into phenylethylamine to elevate mood and decrease pain.

**Note: Supplemental phenylalanine, as well as products containing aspartame (an artificial sweetener made from phenylalanine and another amino acid, aspartic acid), should not be taken by pregnant women or by people who suffer from anxiety attacks, diabetes, high blood pressure, phenylketonuria

(PKU), or preexisting pigmented melanoma, a type of skin cancer.

**L-Phenylalanine*:** L-phenylalanine is the most common type of phenylalanine and is the form in which phenylalanine is incorporated into the body's proteins. It functions as a building block for proteins, increases mental alertness, suppresses the appetite, and helps people with Parkinson's disease. It has been used to alleviate the symptoms of premenstrual syndrome (PMS) and various types of chronic pain. L-phenylalanine occurs naturally in foods.

**Note: Supplemental phenylalanine, as well as products containing aspartame (an artificial sweetener made from phenylalanine and another amino acid, aspartic acid), should not be taken by pregnant women or by other people who suffer from anxiety attacks, diabetes, high blood pressure, phenylketonuria (PKU), or preexisting pigmented melanoma, a type of skin cancer.

**Proline:** Proline improves skin texture by aiding in the production of collagen and reducing the loss of collagen through the aging process. It is needed to repair tissue after a major sunburn or severe burn. It also helps in the healing of cartilage and the strengthening of joints, tendons, and heart muscle. Proline works with Vitamin C to promoted healthy connective tissue. Proline can be found mainly from meat sources, dairy products, and eggs.

**Serine:** Serine is needed for the proper metabolism of fats and fatty acids, the growth of muscle, and the maintenance of a healthy immune system. Serine is found in brain proteins and the protective myelin sheaths that cover nerve fibers. It is important in the functioning of both RNA and DNA cell membrane formation and creatine synthesis. If the levels are not overly high, serine contributes to a strong immune system. Serine can be made from glycine in the body, but this process requires the presence of adequate levels of vitamins B3 and B6 and folic acid. Good food sources of serine are meat, soy foods, dairy products, wheat gluten, and peanuts.

**Taurine:** Taurine is a building block of all the other amino acids as well as a component of bile, which is needed for the digestion of fats, absorption of fat-soluble vitamins, and the control of serum cholesterol levels. The heart muscle, white blood cells, skeletal muscle, and central nervous system all have high concentrations of taurine in them. As a result, taurine is useful for people with atherosclerosis, edema, heart disorders, hypertension, or hypoglycemia. It is vital for the proper use of sodium, potassium, calcium, and magnesium in the body. This helps to prevent the development of potentially dangerous cardiac arrhythmias.

Taurine has a protective effect on the brain, especially if the brain is dehydrated. It is used to treat anxiety, epilepsy, hyperactivity, poor brain function, and seizures. Taurine is found in concentrations up to four times greater in the brains of children than in those of adults. It may be that a deficiency of taurine in the developing brain is involved with seizures. Taurine supplementation may reduce symptoms of alcohol withdrawal. And for diabetics, supplementation with taurine may decrease the need for insulin. Taurine is found in eggs, fish, meat, and milk, but not in vegetable proteins. It can be synthesized from cysteine in the liver and from methionine elsewhere in the body, as long as sufficient quantities of vitamin B6 are present.

**Threonine*:** Threonine is an essential amino acid that helps to maintain the proper protein balance in the body. It is important for the formation of collagen, elastin, and tooth enamel. Threonine aids the liver and lipotropic function when it is combined with aspartic acid and methionine. Threonine is found in the heart, central nervous system, and skeletal muscle. It helps to prevent fatty buildup in the liver and enhances the immune system by aiding the production of antibodies. It may be helpful in treating some kinds of depression.

**Note: Vegetarians are more likely than others to have threonine deficiencies, as the threonine content of grains is low.

**Tryptophan***: Tryptophan is an essential amino acid that is necessary for the production of vitamin B3 (niacin). It used by the brain to produce serotonin. Serotonin is a necessary neurotransmitter that transfers nerve impulses from one cell to another and is responsible for normal sleep. As a result of this, tryptophan helps to combat depression and insomnia and to stabilize moods. More commonly, it is used to treat sleep problems. In children, tryptophan helps to control hyperactivity, alleviates stress, is good for the heart, assists weight control by reducing the appetite, and it enhances the release of growth hormone. The best dietary sources of tryptophan are found in brown rice, cottage cheese, meat, peanuts, and soy protein.

**Tyrosine**: Tyrosine is important for overall metabolism. It is a precursor of adrenaline and the neurotransmitters norepinephrine and dopamine, both of which regulate mood, stimulate metabolism, and the nervous system. One of the ways that Tyrosine acts is as a mood elevator. A lack of tyrosine can result in depression. Other ways it acts is as a mild antioxidant, suppresses the appetite, and helps to reduce body fat. Because tyrosine attaches to iodine atoms to form active thyroid levels, low plasma levels of tyrosine have been associated with hypothyroidism. Tyrosine deficiency can manifest with low blood pressure, low body temperature (such as cold hands and feet) and restless leg syndrome. Supplemental L-tyrosine has been used for stress reduction and it may be helpful against chronic fatigue and narcolepsy. It has been used to help people suffering from anxiety, depression, low sex drive, allergies, headaches, withdrawal from drugs, and Parkinson's disease. Tyrosine can be found naturally in almonds, avocadoes, bananas, dairy products, lima beans, pumpkin seeds, and sesame seeds. Supplements of L-tyrosine should be taken at bedtime or with a high-carbohydrate meal so that it does not have to compete for absorption with other amino acids.

Caution: Persons taking monoamine oxidase (MAO) inhibitors, commonly prescribed for depression, must strictly limit their intake of foods containing tyrosine and should NOT take any supplements containing L-tyrosine, as it may lead to a sudden and dangerous rise in blood pressure. Anyone who takes prescription medications for depression should discuss necessary dietary restrictions with their physician.

***Valine*\***: Valine is an essential amino acid that has a stimulant effect. It is needed for muscle metabolism, tissue repair, and the maintenance of a proper nitrogen balance in the body. It is found in high concentrations in muscle tissue. It may be helpful in treating liver and gallbladder disease. It also good for correcting the type of severe amino acid deficiencies that can be caused by drug addiction. If valine levels in the body get too high, symptoms such as a crawling sensation on the skin and even hallucinations can occur. Valine can be gotten by eating dairy products, grains, meat, mushrooms, peanuts, and soy protein.

**Note: Since it is one of the three branched-chain amino acids, supplemental L-valine should always be taken in balance with the other two branched-chain amino acids, L-isoleucine and L-leucine.

# APPENDIX C –
# A GUIDE TO VITAMINS

***Vitamin A (palmitate, beta-carotene)***: (also known as retinol, retinal) - Vitamin A's functions include assisting vision, growth and development, strengthening the immune system–most notably, the respiratory tract and mucous membranes, and it is a good antioxidant. Good food sources include liver, chili peppers, carrots, vitamin A-fortified milk, butter, sweet potatoes, parsley, kale, spinach, mangoes, broccoli, and squash.

> Recommended Daily Allowance:
>> Infants under 1 year: 1875 IU
>> 1-3 years: 2000 IU
>> 4-6 years: 2500 IU
>> 7-10 years: 3500 IU
>> 11 years to adult:
>> Men: 5000 IU
>> Women: 4000 IU

> Optimal intake:
>> Adult men: 5000 IU
>> Adult women: 2500 IU

Toxicity: Overdoses of Vitamin A can produce symptoms of vomiting, joint pain, abdominal pain, bone abnormalities, cracking, dry skin, headache, irritability, and fatigue. Symptoms disappear after supplementation has been discontinued.

*Note: Pregnant women or those with liver disease should avoid vitamin A supplementation dosages above 2500 IU.

***Vitamin B1 (thiamine)***: Vitamin B1's function is for energy metabolism (carbohydrate metabolism), neurological activity, and brain and heart function. Good sources include: pork, beef, liver, brewer's yeast, whole grains, brown rice, and legumes.

Optimal intake: 5 to 10 mg.

Toxicity: None reported.

**Vitamin B2 (riboflavin)**: Vitamin B2 helps with energy production, as well as fatty acid and amino acid synthesis. Organ meats such as liver, milk products, whole grains, green leafy vegetables, eggs, mushrooms, broccoli, asparagus, and fish are great food sources of Vitamin B2.

Optimal intake: 10 to 15 mg. for adults

Toxicity: None reported.

**Vitamin B3 (niacin)**: Vitamin B3 helps with energy production, formation of steroid compounds, red blood cell formation, cognitive function, and mood. It is found in organ meats, peanuts, fish, yeast, poultry, legumes, milk, eggs, whole grains, and orange juice.

Optimal intake: 50 to 100 mg.

Toxicity: Large doses of niacin can cause dilation of the blood vessels and flushing of the skin. Use a non-flushing form (inositol hexaniacinate) if you are sensitive to regular niacin. Time-released niacin products may result in liver damage.

**Vitamin B5 (pantothenic acid)**: Vitamin B5 helps with metabolism of carbohydrates, pro-teins, and fats for energy production, and the production of adrenal hormones and red blood cells. It is easily found in organ meats, fish, chicken, eggs, cheese, whole grains, avocados, cauliflower, sweet potatoes, oranges, strawberries, yeast, and legumes.

Optimal intake: 50 to 100 mg.
Toxicity: None reported.

**Vitamin B6 (pyridoxine)**: Vitamin B6 helps with the formation of body proteins, neurotransmitters, red blood cells, and immunity. Meats, poultry, egg yolk, soy, peanuts, bananas, potatoes, whole grains, and cauliflower are all great sources of Vitamin B6.

Optimal intake: 10 to 25 mg.

Toxicity: Very high dosages can cause nerve symptoms – numbness and tingling.

**Vitamin B12 (cobalamin)**: Vitamin B12 assists with the synthesis of DNA, red blood cells, and nerve development. It is found in gut bacteria synthesis, organ meats, clams, oysters, soy, milk products, cheese, chlorella, and spirulina.
Optimal intake: 50 to 200 micrograms (mcg.)

Toxicity: None reported.

**Vitamin C (ascorbic acid)**: Vitamin C is a great antioxidant, assists with immunity, collagen formation, bone development, cancer prevention and treatment, gum health, hormone and amino acid synthesis, adrenal gland hormones, and wound healing. Great sources of Vitamin C are citrus fruits, tomatoes, green peppers, dark-green leafy vegetables, broccoli, cantaloupe, strawberries, brussel sprouts, potatoes, and asparagus.

Optimal intake: 500 to 1500 mg.

Toxicity: The first symptom of too much Vitamin C is generally diarrhea, which disappears when the dosage is reduced.

**Vitamin D (Vitamin D2 – ergocalciferol, Vitamin D3 - cholecalciferol:**
Vitamin D2 is derived from plant sources. Vitmin D3 is derived from animal sources. Vitamin D promotes calcium and phosphorous absorption from intestines, increases calcium deposition into bones, and mobilizes calcium and phosphorous from bones. It prevents certain cancers and is required for proper thyroid function. Great sources of Vitamin D are cod liver oil, cold-water fish (salmon, herring sardines, mackerel), milk (fortified with vitamin D), egg yolk, small amounts in dark-green leafy vegetables, and mushrooms. Sunlight is converted into vitamin D.
Optimal intake: 2000 to 5000 IU.

Toxicity: Nausea, anorexia, weakness, headache, digestive disturbance, kidney damage, calcification of soft tissues, and hypercalcemia.

**Vitamin E – Complex (tocopherol, tocotrienols)**: This complex includes alpha, beta, and gamma tocopherol, as well as tocotrienols. Most supplements refer to alpha tocopherol. Vitamin E is a good antioxidant and assists with immunity, wound healing, red blood cell formation, estrogen metabolism, and nerve health. Good sources of it include vegetable oils, seeds, nuts, brown rice, and whole grains.

Optimal intake: 400 IU.

**Vitamin K (phylloquinone, menaquinone)**: Vitamin K is necessary for blood clotting, bone formation, and as an antioxidant. It is found in dark-green leafy vegetables, parsley, broccoli, cabbage, spinach, soy, egg yolks, liver, legumes, and is synthesized by intestinal bacteria.

Optimal intake: 50 to 100 micrograms (mcg.)

Toxicity: Hemolytic anemia

**Folic acid (folacin, folate)**: Folic acid prevents neural tube defects (must be taken by the mother in early pregnancy, ideally prior to pregnancy). It is a methyl donor that is required for many processes in the body and it reduces homocysteine levels. It assists with cardio-vascular health, red blood cell production, and skin and nail health. Good sources of folic acid are dark green vegetables (such as spinach, kale, broccoli, and asparagus), as well as organ meats, kidney beans, beets, yeast, orange juice, and whole grains.

Optimal intake: 400 to 800 micrograms (mcg).

Interesting fact: Even though folic acid is added to many foods, folic acid deficiency is the most common vitamin deficiency in the world. The activated, natural form of folic acid is available in supplement form. It is known as L-5 methyl tetrahydrofolate.

Toxicity: None reported.

**Choline**: Choline is required to manufacture the neurotransmitter acetylcholine and to meta-bolize fats. Good sources of choline are grains, legumes, egg yolks, whole grains, and soy.

Optimal intake: 500 mg.

Toxicity: Rare, but symptoms of fishy breath, sweating, salivation, low blood pressure, and liver toxicity.

**Inositol**: Inositol's function is as a component of cell membranes. It is used for depression and to prevent complications of diabetes. Great sources of it are found in citrus fruits, whole grains, nuts, seeds, and legumes.

Optimal intake: 250 mg.

Toxicity: None reported.

**Biotin**: Biotin helps with the metabolism of fats, proteins, and carbohydrates, as well as nail and hair growth. It is found in gut bacterial synthesis, organ meats, cheese, soybeans, eggs, mushrooms, whole wheat, and peanuts.

Optimal intake: 300 micrograms (mcg.)

Toxicity: None reported.

# APPENDIX D –
# A GUIDE TO MINERALS AND TRACE ELEMENTS

**Calcium:** Calcium is needed for bone and tooth formation, muscle contraction, heartbeat, blood clotting, and nerve impulse.

Sources: Good sources of calcium include kelp, cheese, collards, kale, turnip greens, almonds, yogurt, milk, broccoli, and soy.

Optimal intake: 1000 to 1500 mg.

Deficiency signs: Lack of calcium can be evidenced by leg and feet cramps, anxiety, numbness, muscle tension, insomnia, irritability, nervousness, periodontal disease, bone deformity (rickets), growth retardation, and osteoporosis.

Toxicity: Signs of calcium toxicity can include bone and tissue calcification. Normally, there are no toxic effects with large doses. Some researchers feel that people with a tendency to develop kidney stones should avoid high doses of calcium, although this has not been proven.

**Chromium:** Chromium is extremely effective at helping with blood sugar control. Good sources of it are whole grains, meats, potatoes, liver, and brewer's yeast.

Optimal Intake: 200 micrograms (mcg.)

Deficiency signs: Elevated blood sugar levels

Toxicity: Chromium appears to be safe, with no major toxic side effects reported.

**Copper:** Copper's functions are for collagen formation, red blood cell formation, bone formation, energy production, mental function, and many other enzyme systems.

Sources: Copper can be found in whole grains, shellfish, nuts, eggs, poultry, organ meats, peas, dark-green leafy vegetables, and legumes.

Optimal intake: 2 to 3 mg.

Deficiency signs: It is rare, but could include low immune function, poor collagen and connective tissue strength, bone and joint abnormalities, and anemia.

Toxicity: Nausea, vomiting, and dizziness

**Iron:** Iron is needed for hemoglobin production to supply oxygen to cells, collagen synthesis, and normal immune function. Sources: Good sources of iron are in liver and organ meats, beef, legumes, dark-green leafy vegetables, kelp, and blackstrap molasses.

Deficiency signs: Iron deficiency is characterized by fatigue, paleness, poor memory and concentration, developmental delays and behavioral disturbances, chronic colds, and weakened immunity, as well as a craving for indigestible materials (e.g. pencils, dirt, ice, etc.)

Optimal intake:
    Men: 10 mg.
    Women (normal cycle or no cycle): 10 mg.
    Women with a heavy cycle: 20 mg.

Toxicity: Too much iron is associated with an increased risk for developing heart disease and cancer. Acute iron poisoning in children can result in damage to the intestinal tract, liver failure, nausea and vomiting, shock, and death.

**Magnesium:** Magnesium is needed for bone and teeth formation, energy production, glucose metabolism, and muscle and nerve impulses.

Sources: Whole grains, nuts, legumes, soy, and green leafy vegetables are great sources of magnesium.

Therapeutic dosage: 400 to 600 mg.

Deficiency signs: Weakness, confusion, mood changes, muscle spasms/tremors, nausea, poor coordination, heart disturbances, insomnia, susceptibility to kidney stones.

Toxicity: People with kidney disease or on heart medications should not supplement magnesium unless instructed to do so by their doctor. Diarrhea is usually the first symptom of too much magnesium.

**Manganese:** Manganese is required for enzyme systems involved with energy production, blood-sugar control, fatty acid synthesis, thyroid hormone function, connective tissue and bone formation, and sprains and strains.

Sources: It can be found in liver, kidney, whole grains, nuts, spinach, and green leafy vegetables.

Optimal intake: 5 to 10 mg.

Deficiency signs: No symptoms have been observed in humans. Animal studies show growth problems.

Toxicity: Too much manganese can interfere with iron absorption and can cause iron deficiency.

**Potassium:** Potassium's functions are for nerve transmission, water balance, acid-base balance, heart function, kidney function, and adrenal function.

Sources: Great sources of potassium include fruits and vegetables, especially apples, bananas, carrots, oranges, potatoes, tomatoes, cantaloupe, peaches, plums, strawberries, meat, milk, and fish.

Optimal intake: 2000 to 3000 mg.

Deficiency signs: Muscle wasting, weakness, spasm, fatigue, mood changes, heart disturbances, and nerve problems.

Toxicity: Impaired heart and kidney function; people with heart or kidney conditions or who are on blood pressure medication should not take potassium unless instructed to do so by a physician.

***Selenium*:** Selenium is very helpful as an antioxidant, for cancer prevention, immunity, thyroid function, and development of the fetus during pregnancy.

Sources: Foods that have plentiful amounts of selenium are liver, kidney, meats, and seafood. Grains and vegetables are good sources, but selenium content depends on the level in the soil where they are grown.

Therapeutic dosage: 200 micrograms (mcg.)

Deficiency signs: Selenium deficiency is associated with an increased risk for heart disease, cancer, and poor immune function.

Toxicity: Teeth abnormalities, depression, nausea, and vomiting

**Sodium**: Sodium is necessary for correct acid-base balance, muscle contraction, nerve impulse, and amino acid absorption.

Sources: Sodium is naturally found in meats, milk products, water, eggs, poultry, and fish. It is abundant in canned foods and other commercially processed foods.

Optimal intake: 2000 mg.

Deficiency signs: Deficiency of sodium is very uncommon, except in the case of dehydration through profuse sweating or diarrhea. Symptoms can include muscle weakness and cramping, low blood pressure, muscle twitching, mental confusion, anorexia, and fainting.

Toxicity: High blood pressure, especially when potassium intake is low.

**Zinc**: The functions of zinc include over 200 enzymatic reactions. It is required to manufacture many hormones, as well as needed for good immunity, skin healing, growth, vision, blood-sugar metabolism, antioxidant support, reproductive development, and fertility.

Sources: Good food sources of zinc are oysters, herring, shellfish, red meat, whole grains, legumes, and nuts.

Optimal intake: 15 to 30 mg.
Deficiency signs: Hair loss, poor wound healing, poor immune function, diarrhea, skin conditions (e.g. acne), mental disturbance, and white spots on the nails.

Toxicity: Rare. Very high dosage (above 150 mg.) can lead to immune system suppression, digestive upset, or anemia.

# APPENDIX E – RESOURCES FOR FURTHER STUDY

## On Essential Oils:

*Handbook of Essential Oils: Science, Technology and Applications* edited by Baser and Buchbauer

*The Chemistry of Essential Oils Made Simple* by Dr. David Stewart

*Medical Aromatherapy: Healing with Essential Oils* by Kurt Schnaubelt

*The Healing Intelligence of Essential Oils: The Science of Advanced Aromatherapy* by Kurt Schnaubelt

*Releasing Emotional Patterns with Essential Oils* by Carolyn L. Mein, D.C.

## On Inner Healing, the Mind, and the Brain:

*Switch On Your Brain: The Key to Peak Happiness, Thinking, and Health* by Dr. Caroline Leaf

*The Emotional Life of Your Brain* by Dr. Richard J. Davidson and Sharon Begley

*How Emotions Are Made: The New Science of the Mind and Brain* by Lisa Feldman Barrett

*Transforming The Inner Man: God's Powerful Principles for Inner Healing and Lasting Life Change* by John Loren and Paula Sandford

# Endnotes

1. Zimmer, C. (2004). *Soul Made Flesh: The Discovery of the Brain — and How It Changed The World.* (New York, NY: Free Press).

2. Steinberg, E. M. (2000). *The Balance Within: The Science Connecting Health And Emotions* (p. 5). (New York, NY: W. H. Freeman and Company)

3. Zimmer, C. (2004). *Soul Made Flesh: The Discovery of the Brain — and How It Changed The World* (p. 38). (New York, NY: Free Press).

4. Text used as reference material for this chapter:

Baser, K. H. C., and Buchbauer, G. (2010). *Handbook of Essential Oils: Science, Technology, and Applications.* (Boca Raton, FL: CRC Press).

Bakkali, F., Averbeck, S., Averbeck, D., Idamoar, M. (2006) Biological effects of essential oils — A review. *Food and Chemical Toxicology* 46 (2008) 446-475.

Bone, K. and Mills, S. (2013). *Principles and Practice of Phytotherapy: Modern Health Medicine* 2nd e. (Churchill Livingstone: Elsevier)

McMurry, J. (2016). *Organic Chemistry* 9e. (Boston, MA: Cengage Learning)

Rose, J. (1992) *The Aromatherapy Book: Applications & Inhalations* (Berkeley, CA: North Atlantic Books)

Sadgrove, N. and Jones, G. (2015). A Contemporary Introduction to Essential Oils: Chemistry, Bioactivity and Prospects for Australian Agriculture. *Agriculture* 5: 48-102.

Stewart, D., (2010). *The Chemistry of Essential Oils Made Simple.* (Marble Hill, MO: Care Publications).

5. Schnaubelt, K. (1999). *Medical Aromatherapy: Healing with Essential Oils* (p. vii). (Berkeley, CA: Frog Books).

6. Schnaubelt, K. (1999). *Medical Aromatherapy: Healing with Essential Oils* (p. 141). (Berkeley, CA: Frog Books).

7. Stewart, D., (2010). *The Chemistry of Essential Oils Made Simple* (pp. 75-77). (Marble Hill, MO: Care Publications).

8. Lis-Balchin, M., Deans, S. G., and Eaglesham, E. (1998). Relationship between bioactivity and chemical composition of commercial essential oils. *Flavour Fragrance J.* 13: 98–104.

9. Zellner, B. D. A., Dugo, P., Dugo, G., Mondello, L. (2010). Analysis of Essential Oils. *Handbook of Essential Oils: Science, Technology and Applications*; Bas er, K. H. C., Buchbauer, G., Eds.; (London: CRC Press, Taylor and Francis Group).

10. Adams, T. B., Taylor, S. V. (2010). Safety evaluation of essential oils: A constituent-based approach. *Handbook of Essential Oils: Science, Technology and Applications*; Bas er, K. H. C., Buchbauer, G., Eds.; (London: CRC Press, Taylor and Francis Group).

11. Schnaubelt, K. (2011). *The Healing Intelligence of Essential Oils: The Science of Advanced Aromatherapy* (p. 59). (Rochester, VT: Healing Arts Press).

12. Text used as reference material for this chapter:

Note, J. (2009). *The Human Brain: An Introduction to its Functional Anatomy.* (Philadelphia, PA: Mosby Elsevier)

13. Wolfe, J. M., Kluender, K. R., Levi, D. M. (2015). *Sensation & Perception*, 4e. (Sunderland, MA: Sinauer Associates, Inc.).

14. Rajmohan, V., & Mohandas, E. (2007). The limbic system. *Indian Journal of Psychiatry, 49*(2), 132.

15. Pert, C. B. (1997). *Molecules of Emotion* (p. 27). (New York: Scribner).

16. Pert, C. B. (1997). *Molecules of Emotion* (p. 143). (New York: Scribner).

17. Hebb, D. O. (1949). *The Organisation of Behavior: A Neuropsychological Theory.* (New York: Wiley and Sons).

18. Hebb, D. O. (1949). *The Organisation of Behavior: A Neuropsychological Theory.* (New York: Wiley and Sons).

19. Leaf, C. (2015). *Switch On Your Brain: The Key to Peak Happiness, Thinking, and Health* (p. 64). (Grand Rapids, MI: Baker Books).

20. Davidson, R. J. (1984). Affect, cognition, and hemispheric specialization. In S. E. Izard, J. Kagan, and R. Zajonc, (Eds.). *Emotions, Cognition, and Behavior* (pp. 320-365). (Cambridge, UK: Cambridge University Press).

21. Herz, R. (2007). *The Scent of Desire: Discovering Our Enigmatic Sense of Smell.* (New York: Morrow).

22. Schild, D., Restrepo, D. (1998). Transduction mechanism in vertebrate olfactory receptor cells. *Physical Rev* 37: 369-375.

23. Bushdid, C. M., Magnasco, O., Vosshall, L. B., Keller A. (2014). Humans can discriminate more than 1 trillion olfactory stimuli. *Science* 343: 1370-1372.

24. Holbrook, E. H., Wu, E., Curry, W. T., Lin, D. T., and Schwob, J. E. (2011). Immunohistochemical characterization of human olfactory tissue. *Laryngoscope* 121: 1687-701.

25. Krestel, D., Passe, D., Smith, J. C., and Jonsson, L. (1984). Behavioral determinants of olfactory thresholds to amyl acetate in dogs. *Neurotic Biobehav Rev* 8: 169-174.

Willis, C. M., Church, S. M., Guest, C. M., Cook, W. A., McCarthy, N., Bransbury, A. J., Church, M. R. T., and Church, J. C. T. (2004). Olfactory detection of human bladder cancer by dogs: Proof of principle study. *Br Med J* 329: 712-714.

26. Franco, M. I., Turin, L., Mershin, A., and Skoulakis, E. M. C. (2011). Molecular vibration sensing component in *Drosophila melanogaster* olfaction. *Proc Natl Acad Sci USA* 108: 3797-3802.

Turin, L. (1996). A spectroscopic mechanism for primary olfactory reception. *Chem Senses* 21: 773-791.

27. Wolfe, J. M., Kluender, K. R., Levi, D. M. (2015). *Sensation & Perception*, 4e. (p. 442). (Sunderland, MA: Sinauer Associates, Inc.).

28. Boesveldt, S., Lindau, S. T., McClintock, M. K., Hummel, T., and Lundstrom, J. N. (2011). Gustatory and olfactory dysfunction in older adults: A national probability study. *Rhinology*, 49:324-330.

Doty, R. L. and Cameron, E. L. (2009). Sex differences and reproductive hormone influences on human odor perception. *Physiol Behav 97: 213-228.*

29. Dalton, P. (2002). Olfaction. In H. Paschler, S. Yantis, D. Medin, R. Galistel, and J. Wixted (Eds.), *Stevens' Handbook of Experimental Psychology* (3rd ed.), Vol. 1: *Sensation and Perception* (pp. 691-746). (New York: Wiley).

30. Pierce, J. D., Jr., Wysocki, C. J., Aronov, E.V., Webb, J. B., and Boden, R. M. (1996). The role of perceptual and structural similarity in cross-adaptation. *Chem Senses* 21: 223-237.

31. Kadohisa, M. and Wilson, D. A. (2006). Olfactory cortical adaption facilitates detection of odors against background. *J Neurophysiol* 95: 1888-1896.

32. Wolfe, J. M., Kluender, K. R., Levi, D. M. (2015). *Sensation & Perception*, 4e. (p. 445). (Sunderland, MA: Sinauer Associates, Inc.).

33. Stewart, D., (2010). *The Chemistry of Essential Oils Made Simple* (pp. 447-448). (Marble Hill, MO: Care Publications).

34. Dhopeshwarkar, G. A. (1983). *Nutrition and Brain Development* (p. 23). (New York: Plenum).

35. Berg, J.M., Tymoczko, J.L., Stryer, L. (2002). *Biochemistry,* 5e. (Section 30.2). (New York: W H Freeman).

36. Payne, R. K. (1996). *A Framework for Understanding Poverty* (pp. 42-43). (Highlands, Texas: aha! Process, Inc.).

37. Pereira, A. C., Huddleston, D. E., Brickman, A. M., Sosunov, A. A., Hen, R., McKhann, G. M., Sloan, R., Gage, F.H., Brown, T.R., Small, S. A. (2007). An in vivo correlate of exercise-induced neurogenesis in the adult dentate gyrus. *Proc Natl Acad Sci* (USA). 104: 5638–5643.

38. Nokia, M. S., Lensu, S., Ahtiainen, J. P., Johansson, P. P., Koch, L. G., Britton, S. L. and Kainulainen, H. (2016). Physical exercise increases adult hippocampal neurogenesis in male rats provided it is aerobic and sustained. *J Physiol*, 594: 1855–1873.

39. Hillman, C. H., et al. (2014). Effects of the FITKids Randomized Controlled Trial on Executive Control and Brain Function. *Pediatrics*, 134 (4).

40. Meamarbashi, A., and Rajabi, A. (2013). The effects of peppermint on exercise on performance. *Journal of the International Society of Sports Nutrition*. 10 (15).

41. Larson, Joan Mathews. (1999). *Seven Weeks to Emotional Healing: Proven Natural Formulas for Eliminating Anxiety, Depression, Anger, and Fatigue from Your Life* (p. 109). (New York, NY: The Ballantine Publishing Group).

42. Pfeiffer, Carl. (1975). *Mental and Elemental Nutrients: A Physical Guide to Nutrition and Health Care* (pp. 402-408). (New Canaan, Conn: Keats Publishing).

43. Gropper, Sareen S., et al. (2018). *Advanced Nutrition and Human Metabolism*, 7e. (p. 178). (Boston, MA: Cengage Learning).

44. Bourre, J. M., Bonneil, M., et al. (1993). Function of Dietary Polyunsaturated Fatty Acids in the Nervous System. *Prostaglandins Leukotrienes & Essential Fatty Acids* 48, no. 1, 5-15.

45. Larson, Joan Mathews. (1999). *Seven Weeks to Emotional Healing: Proven Natural Formulas for Eliminating Anxiety, Depression, Anger, and Fatigue from Your Life* (p. 53). (New York, NY: The Ballantine Publishing Group)

46. Lipton, B. H. (2008). *The Biology of Belief* (p. 97). (Carlsbad, CA: Hay House).

47. Davidson, R. J., and Begley, S. (2012). *The Emotional Life of Your Brain* (p. 10). (London: The Penguin Group).

48. Pert, C. B. (1997). *Molecules of Emotion* (p. 144). (New York: Scribner).

49. Gerrig, R. J. and Zimbardo, P. G. (2002). *Psychology And Life,* 16e. (Boston, MA: Allyn and Bacon). http://www.apa.org/research/action/glossary.aspx?tab=18.

50. Cohen, S., Janicki Deverts, D., Miller, G. E. (2007). Psychological Stress and Disease. *JAMA*, 298 (14), 1685.

51. Leaf, C. (2015). *Switch On Your Brain: The Key to Peak Happiness, Thinking, and Health* (p. 37). (Grand Rapids, MI: Baker Books).

52. Davidson, R. J., and Begley, S. (2012). *The Emotional Life of Your Brain* (pp. 92-93). (London: The Penguin Group).

53. Ecole Polytechnique Fédérale de Lausanne. (2012, September 17). 'Blue Brain' project accurately predicts connections between neurons. *ScienceDaily*. Retrieved October 5, 2017 from www.sciencedaily.com/releases/2012/09/120917152043.htm

54. Chanes, L., & Barrett, L. F. (2016). Redefining the role of limbic areas in cortical processing. *Trends Cogn Sci., 20* (2), 96-106.

55. Pert, C. B. (1997). *Molecules of Emotion* (p. 143). (New York: Scribner).

56. Brown, B. (2015). *Daring Greatly: How the Courage to be Vulnerable Transforms the Way We Live, Love, Parent, and Lead* (pp. 33, 35). (New York, NY: Avery).

57. Babbel, S. (2010, April 08). The Connections Between Emotional Stress, Trauma and Physical Pain. Retrieved October 15, 2017, from https://www.psychologytoday.com/blog/somatic-psychology/201004/the-connections-between-emotional-stress-trauma-and-physical-pain

58. A Treatment Improvement Protocol: Trauma-Informed Care in Behavioral Health Services, *U.S. Department of Heath and Human Services*. (Rockville, MD). 2014. xvii

59. Davidson, R. J., and Begley, S. (2012). *The Emotional Life of Your Brain* (p. 39). (London: The Penguin Group).

60. Barrett, L. F. (2017). *How Emotions Are Made: The New Science of the Mind and Brain* (p. 124). (New York, NY: Houghton Mifflin Harcourt).

61. Gross, J. J., & Barrett, L. F. (2011). Emotion Generation and Emotion Regulation: One or Two Depends on Your Point of View. *Emot Rev., 3* (1), 8-16.

Oschner, K. N., & Gross, J. J. (2005). The cognitive control of emotion. *TRENDS in Cognitive Sciences., 9* (5), 242-249.

62. Bremner, J. D. (2006). Traumatic stress: effects on the brain. *Dialogues in Clinical Neuroscience., 8* (4), 445-461.

63. Davidson, R. J., and Begley, S. (2012). *The Emotional Life of Your Brain* (p. 39). (London: The Penguin Group).

64. Kim, J. M., & Whalen, P. J. (2009). The structural integrity of an amygdala-prefrontal pathway predicts trait anxiety. *J Neurosci., 29* (37), 11614-11618.

Goldstein, L. E., Rasmusson, A. M., Bunney, B. S., Roth, R. H. (1996). Role of the Amygdala in the Coordination of Behavioral, Neuroendocrine, and Prefrontal Cortical Monoamine Responses to Psychological Stress in the Rat. *The Journal of Neuroscience, 16* (15), 4787-4798.

65. Zhang, L. X., Levine, S., Dent, G., Zhan, G., Xing, G., Okimoto, D., Gordon, M. K., Post, R. M., Smith, M. A. (2002). Maternal deprivation increases cell death in the infant rat brain. *Developmental Brain Research.* 133:1-11.

66. Hanson, J. L., Chung, M. K., Avants, B. B., Rudolph, K. D., Shirtcliff, E. A., Gee, J. C., Davidson, R. J., Pollak, S. D. (2012). Structural variations in prefrontal cortex mediate the relationship between early childhood stress and spatial working memory. *J Neurosci.* 32 (23): 7917-7925.

67. Gould, E., Tanapat, P., McEwen, B. S., et al. (1998). Proliferation of granule cell pre- cursors in the dentate gyrus of adult monkeys is diminished by stress. *Proc Natl Acad Sci U S A.* 95: 3168-3171.
Magarinos, A. M., McEwen, B. S., Flugge, G., et al. (1996).

Chronic psychosocial stress causes apical dendritic atrophy of hippocampal CA3 pyramidal neurons in subordinate tree shrews. *J Neurosci.* 16: 3534-3540.

McEwen, B. S., Angulo, J., Cameron, H., et al. (1992). Paradoxical effects of adrenal steroids on the brain: Protection versus degeneration. *Biol Psychiatry.* 31: 177-199.

Nibuya, M., Morinobu, S., Duman, R. S. (1995). Regulation of BDNF and trkB mRNA in rat brain by chronic electroconvulsive seizure and antidepressant drug treatments. *J Neurosci.* 15: 7539-7547.

Sapolsky, R. M., Uno, H., Rebert, C. S., et al. (1990). Hippocampal damage associated with prolonged glucocorticoid exposure in primates. *J Neurosci.* 10: 2897-2902.

Sapolsky, R. M. (1996). Why stress is bad for your brain. *Science.* 273: 749-750.

68. Luine, V., Villages, M., Martinex, C., et al. (1994). Repeated stress causes reversible impairments of spatial memory performance. *Brain Res.* 639: 167-170.

Diamond, D. M., Fleshner, M., Ingersoll, N., et al. (1996). Psychological stress impairs spatial working memory: Relevance to electrophysiological studies of hippocampal function. *Behav Neurosci.* 110: 661-672.

70. Nibuya, M., Morinobu, S., Duman, R. S. (1995). Regulation of BDNF and trkB mRNA in rat brain by chronic electroconvulsive seizure and antidepressant drug treatments. *J Neurosci.* 15: 7539-7547.

Malberg, J. E., Eisch, A. J., Nestler, E. J., et al. (2000). Chronic antidepressant treatment increases neurogenesis in adult rat hippocampus. *J Neurosci.* 20: 9104-9110.

Czeh, B., Michaelis, T., Watanabe, T., et al. (2001). Stress-induced changes in cerebral metabolites, hippocampal volume, and cell proliferation are prevented by antidepressant treatment with tianeptine. *Proc Natl Acad sci U S A.* 98: 12796-12801.

Santarelli, L., Saxe, M., Gross, C., et al. (2003). Requirement of hippocampal neurogenesis for the behavioral effects of antidepressants. *Science.* 301: 805-809.

Lucassen, P. J., Fuchs, E., Czeh, B. (2004). Antidepressant treatment with tianeptine reduces apoptosis in the hippocampal dentate gyrus and temporal cortex. *Eur J Neurosci.* 14:161-166.

71. Moussaieff, A., Gross, M., Nesher, E., Tikhonov, T., Yadid, G. & Pinhasov, A. (2012). Incesole acetate reduces depressive-like behavior and modulates hippocampal BDNF and CRF expression of submissive animals. *Journal of Psychopharmacology.* 26 (12): 1584-1593.

72. Linck, V. M., da Silva, A. L., Figueiro, M., Caramao, E. B., Moreno, P. R. H., & Elisabetsky, E. (2010). Effects of inhaled Linalool in anxiety, social interaction and aggressive behavior in mice. *Phytomedicine.* 17: 679-683.

73. Atsumi, T., & Tonosaki, K. (2007). Smelling lavender and rosemary increases free radical scavenging activity and decreases cortisol level in saliva. *Psychiatry Research.* 150: 89-96.

74. Henikoff, S. and Matzke, M. A. (1997). Exploring and explaining epigenetic effects, *Trends Genet* 13 (8), 293-5.

75. Oh, G. & Petronis, A. *Etiology of Major Psychosis: Why Do We Need Epigenetics?* in *Epigenetics in Biology and Medicine*, edited by Esteller, M. (2009). (Boca Raton, FL: CRC Press).

76. Kellerman, N. P. F. (2013). Epigenetic Transmission of Holocaust Trauma: Can Nightmares Be Inherited? *Isr J Psychiatry Relat Sci* 50:1, 33-39.

77. Kellermann, N. P. F. (2009). *Holocaust trauma: Psychological effects and treatment.* (New York, NY: iUniverse).

78. Meaney, M. J., & Szyf, M. (2005). Environmental programming of stress responses through DNA methylation: Life at the interface between a dynamic environment and a fixed genome. *Dialogues Clin Neuroscience.* 7: 103-123.

79. Van der Kolk, B. (1994). The body keeps the score: Memory and the evolving psychobiology of post traumatic stress. *Harv Rev Psychiatry.* 1:253-265.

80. Kellerman, N. P. F. (2013). Epigenetic Transmission of Holocaust Trauma: Can Nightmares Be Inherited? *Isr J Psychiatry Relat Sci.* 50: 1, 35.

81. Davidson, R. J., and Begley, S. (2012). *The Emotional Life of Your Brain* (p. 101). (London: The Penguin Group).

82. Fargo, M. F., Ballestar, E., Paz, M. F., Ropero, S., Setien, F., Ballestar, M. L., Heine-Suñer, D., et al. (2005). Epigenetic Differences Arise During the Lifetime Of Monozygotic Twins. *Proceedings of the National Academy of Sciences* 102: 10604-9.

83. Leaf, C. (2015). *Switch On Your Brain: The Key to Peak Happiness, Thinking, and Health* (p. 32). (Grand Rapids, MI: Baker Books).
Kandel, E. R. (2006). *In Search of Memory: The Emergence of a New Science of Mind* (New York: Norton).

84. Leaf, C. (2015). *Switch On Your Brain: The Key to Peak Happiness, Thinking, and Health* (p. 35). (Grand Rapids, MI: Baker Books).

85. Truman, K. K. (2003). *Feelings Buried Alive Never Die...* (pp. 23-27). (St. George, Utah: Olympus Distributing).

86. Weaver, I. C. G., Champagne, F. A., Brown, S. E., Dymov, S., Sharma, S., Meaney, M. J., Szyf, M. (2005). Reversal of Maternal Programming of Stress Responses in Adult Offspring through Methyl Supplementation: Altering Epigenetic Marking Later in Life. *The Journal of Neuroscience* 25 (47): 11045-11054.

87. Rowan, Alison. "Undoing Epigenetics." *Nature Reviews Genetics*, vol. 6, Jan. 2006, p. 1.

88. Truman, K. K. (2003). *Feelings Buried Alive Never Die...* (p. 30). (St. George, Utah: Olympus Distributing).

Chopra, D. (1998). *Quantum Healing: Exploring the Frontiers of Mind/Body* (New York: Bantam Books).

89. Sandford, J. L. & Sandford, P. (2007). *Transforming the Inner Man* (pp. 93, 104). (Lake Mary, FL: Charisma House).

90. Text used as reference material for this chapter:

*Essential Oils Desk Reference: Sixth Edition* 2014. (United States: Life Science Publishing)

Baser, K. H. C., & Buchbauer, G. (2010). *Handbook of Essential Oils: Science, Technology, and Applications* (Boca Raton, FL: CRC Press)

91. Wolfe, J. M., Kluender, K. R., Levi, D. M. (2015). *Sensation & Perception*, 4e. (p. 462). (Sunderland, MA: Sinauer Associates, Inc.).

92. Schnaubelt, K. (2011). *The Healing Intelligence of Essential Oils: The Science of Advanced Aromatherapy* (p. 36). (Rochester, VT: Healing Arts Press).

93. Schnaubelt, K. (2011). *The Healing Intelligence of Essential Oils: The Science of Advanced Aromatherapy* (p. 39). (Rochester, VT: Healing Arts Press).

94. Schnaubelt, K. (2011). *The Healing Intelligence of Essential Oils: The Science of Advanced Aromatherapy* (pp. 39-41). (Rochester, VT: Healing Arts Press).

95. Stewart, D., (2010). *The Chemistry of Essential Oils Made Simple* (p. 292). (Marble Hill, MO: Care Publications).

96. Grunwald, M., Weiss, T., Krause, W. et al. (1999). Power of theta waves in the EEG of human subjects increases during recall of haptic information. *Neurosci. Lett.*, 260 (3): 189–192.

Hoedlmoser, K., Schabus, M., Stadler, W., et al. (2007). EEG Theta-Aktivität während deklarativem Lernen und anschließendem REM-Schlaf im Zusammenhang mit allgemeiner Gedächtnisleistung. *Klinische Neurophysiol.* 38: 976432.

97. Razumnikova, O.M. (2007). Creativity related cortex activity in the remote associates task. *Brain Res. Bull.*, 73 (1–3): 96–102.

98. Lorig, T.S. & Schwartz, G.E. (1988). Brain and odor: I. Alteration of human EEG by odor administration. *Psychobiology*, 16 (3): 281–284.

99. Kepecs, A., N. Uchida, & Mainen, Z. F. (2006). The sniff as a unit of Olfactory processing. *Chem. Senses* 31 (2): 167–179.

100. Schandry, R. (1989). *Lehrbuch der Psychophysiologie.* 2. Au age. (Weinheim, Germany: Psychologie Verlags Union).

101. Kaetsu, I., Tonoike, T., Uchida, K., et al. (1994). Effect of controlled release of odorants on electroencephalogram during mental activity. *Proc. Int. Symp. on Controlled Release of Bioactive Materials* 21ST: 589–590.

102. Ali, B., Al-Wabel, N. A., Shams, S., Ahamad, A., Khan, S. A., & Anwar, F. (2015). Essential oils used in aromatherapy: A systematic review. *Asian Pac J Trop Biomed* 5(8): 601-611.

103. Babita, S. (2001). Aromatherapy: The best way to relax using essential oils, *Agric Watch* 1 (4): 50-62.

104. Watanabe, E., Kuchta, K., Kimura, M., Rauwald, H. W., Kamei, T., Imanishi, J. (2015). Effects of bergamot (*Citrus bergamia* (Risso) Wright & Arn.) essential oil aromatherapy on mood states, para-sympathetic nervous system activity, and salivary cortisol levels in 41 healthy females. *Forsch Komplementmed* 22 (1): 43-9.

105. Watanabe, E., Kuchta, K., Kimura, M., Rauwald, H. W., Kamei, T., Imanishi, J. (2005). Effects of bergamot (*Citrus bergamia* (Risso) Wright & Arn.) essential oil aromatherapy on mood states, parasympathetic nervous system activity,

and salivary cortisol levels in 41 healthy females. *Complementary Medicine Research* 22: 43-49.

106. Kumar, N., Dhayabaran, D., Nampoothiri, M., Nandakumar, K., Puratchikody, A., Lalani, N., Dawood, K., & Ghosh, A. (2014). Atypical Antidepressant Activity of 3,4-Bis(3,4-Dimethoxyphenyl) Furan-2,5-Dione Isolated from Heart Wood of *Cedrus deodara*, in Rodents. *Korean J Physiol Pharmacol* 18: 365-369.

107. Viswanatha, G. L., Nandakumar, K., Shylaja, H., Ramesh, C., Rajesh, S., Srinath, R. (2009). Anxiolytic and Anticonvulsant Activity of Alcoholic Extract of Heart Wood of *Cedrus deodara roxb* in rodents. *JPRHC*. 1 (2): 217-239.

108. Moretti, M. D. L., Peana, A. T., Satta, M. (1997). A study on anti-inflammatory and peripheral analgesic action of *Salvia sclarea* oil and its main components. *J. Essent. Oil Res.* 9, 199–204.

Peana, A. T., Moretti, M. D. L. (2002). Pharmacological activities and applications of *Salvia sclarea* and *Salvia desoleana* essential oils. In: Ur- Rahman, A. (Ed.), *Studies in Natural Product Chemistry*, vol. 26, part G. Elsevier, UK, pp. 391–425.

109. Lee, K. B., Cho, E., Kang, Y.S. (2014). Changes in 5-hydroxytryptamine and cortisol plasma levels in menopausal women after inhalation of clary sage oil. *Phytother Res* 28 (11): 1599-605.

110. Burns, E., Blamey, C., Ersser, S. J., et al. (2000). *Complement Ther Nurs Midwifery*. 6 (1): 33–34.

111. Ludvigson, H. W., Rottman, T. R. (1989). Effects of ambient odors of lavender and cloves on cognition, memory, affect and mood. *Chemical Senses* 14:4, 525-536.

112. Siddique, Y. H., et al. (2013). GC-MS analysis of *Eucalyptus citriodora* leaf extract and its role on the dietary supplementation in transgenic Drosophila model of Parkinson's disease. *Food Chem Toxicol*. 55: 29-35.

113. Moussaieff, A., Gross, M., Nesher, E., Tikhonov, T., Yadid, G. & Pinhasov, A. (2012). Incesole acetate reduces depressive-like behavior and modulates hippocampal BDNF and CRF expression of submissive animals. *Journal of Psychopharmacology*. 26 (12): 1584-1593.

114. Moussaieff, A., Rimmerman, N., Bregman, T., Straiker, A., Felder, C. C., Shoham, S., Kashman, Y., Huang, S. M., Lee, H., Shohami, E., Mackie, K., Caterina, M. J., Walker, J. M., Fride, E., & Mechoulam, R. (2008). Incesole acetate, an incense component, elicits psychoactivity by activating TRPV3 channels in the brain. *The FASEB Journal.* 22: 3024-3034.

115. Moussaieff, A., Yu, J., Zhu, H., Gattoni-Celli, S., Shohami, E., & Kindy, M. S. (2012). Positive effects of incesole acetate on cerebral ischemic injury. *Brain Research* 1443: 89-97.

116. Bishnoi, M., Patil, C. S., Kumar, A., et al. (2005). *Methods Find Exp Clin Pharmacol.* 27 (7): 465–470.

117. Janssen, G., Bode, U., Breu, H., et al. (2000). *Klin Padiatr.* 212 (4): 189–195.

Streffer, J. R., Bitzer, M., Schabet, M., et al. (2001). *Neurology.* 56 (9): 1219–1221.

Kirste, S., Treier, M., Wehrle, S. J., et al. (2001). *Cancer.* 117 (16): 3788–3795.

118. Winking, M., Boeker, D. K., Simmet, T. H. (1996). *J Neurooncol.* 30 (2): P39.

119. Reising, K., Meins, J., Bastian, B., et al. (2005). *Anal Chem.* 77 (20): 6640–6645.

120. Morris, N., Birtwistle, S., Toms, M. (1995). Anxiety reduction by aromatherapy: Anxiolytic effects of inhalation of geranium and rosemary. *Int. J. Aromather. 7*, 33–39.

121. Lis, B. M. (1997). A chemotaxonomic study of *Pelargonium* (Geraniaceae) species and their modern cultivars, *J Hort Sci*, 72: 791-795.

Asgarpanah, J. & Ramezanloo, F. (2015). An overview on phytopharmacology of *Pelargonium graveolens* L. *Indian Journal of Traditional Knowledge* 14 (4): 558-563.

122. Perry, N., & Perry, E. (2006). Aromatherapy in the Management of Psychiatric Disorders: Clinical and Neuropharmacological Perspectives. *CNS Drugs* 20 (4): 257-280.

123. Diego, M. A., Jones, N. A., Field, T., Hernandez-Reif, M., Schanberg, S., Kuhn, C., McAdam, V., Galamaga, R., & Galamaga, M. (1998). Aromatherapy positively affects

mood, EEG patterns of alertness and math computations. *Int. J. Neurosci. 96*, 217–224.

124. Kawakami, M., Aoki, S., Ohkubo, T. (1999). A study of "fragrance" on working environment characteristics in VDT work activities. *Int. J. Prod. Econ. 60–61*, 575–581.

125. Sayorwan, W., Siripornpanich, V., Piriyapunyaporn, T., Hongratanaworakit, T., Kotchabhakdi, N., & Ruangrungsi, N. (2012). The effects of lavender oil inhalation on emotional states, autonomic nervous system, and brain electrical activity. *J. Med. Assoc. Thai. 95*, 598–606.

126. Masago, R., Matsuda, T., Kikuchi, Y., Miyazaki, Y., Iwanaga, K., Harada, H., & Katsuura, T. (2000). Effects of inhalation of essential oils on EEG activity and sensory evaluation. *J. Physiol. Anthropol. 19*, 35–42.

127. Lee, I. (2016). Effects of inhalation of relaxing essential oils on electroencephalogram activity. *Int. J. New Technol. Res. 2*, 37–43.

128. Goel, N., Kim, H., Lau, R. P. (2005). An olfactory stimulus modifies nighttime sleep in young men and women. *Chronobiol. Int. 22*, 889–904.

129. Diego, M. A., Jones, N. A., Field, T., Hernandez-Reif, M., Schanberg, S., Kuhn, C., McAdam, V., Galamaga, R., & Galamaga, M. (1998). Aromatherapy positively affects mood, EEG patterns of alertness and math computations. *Int. J. Neurosci. 96*, 217–224.

130. Motomura, N., Sakurai, A., Yotsuya, Y. (2001). Reduction of mental stress with lavender odorant. *Percept. Motor Skill. 93*, 713–718.

131. Akhondzadeh, S., Kashani, L., Fotouhi, A. et al. (2003). Comparison of Lavandula angustifolia Mill. tincture and imipramine in the treatment of mild to moderate depression: a double-blind, randomized trial. *Progress in Neuro-Psychopharmacology and Biological Psychiatry* 27 (1): 123–127.

See also:
Kasper, S., Gastpar, M., Muller, W. E., et al. (2010). Efficacy and safety of silexan, a new, orally administered lavender oil preparation, in subthreshold anxiety disorder—evidence from clinical trials. *Wiener Medizinische Wochenschrift* 160 (21-22): 547– 556.

Kasper, S., Gastpar, M., Muller, W. E. et al. (2010). Silexan, an orally administered Lavandula oil preparation, is effective in the treatment of 'subsyndromal' anxiety disorder: a randomized, double-blind, placebo controlled trial. *International Clinical Psychopharmacology* 25 (5): 277–287.

132. Nagai, M., Wada, M., Usui, N., Tanaka, A., Hasebe, Y. (2000). Pleasant odors attenuate the blood pressure increase during rhythmic handgrip in humans. *Neurosci. Lett. 289*, 227–229.

133. Campenni, C. E., Crawley, E. J., Meier, M. E. (2004). Role of suggestion in odor induced mood change. *Psychol. Rep. 94*, 1127–1136.

134. Rho, K.H., Han, S. H., Kim, K. S., Lee, M.S. (2006). Effects of aromatherapy massage on anxiety and self-esteem in korean elderly women: A pilot study. *Int. J. Neurosci. 116*, 1447–1455.

135. Re, L., Barocci, S., Sonnino, S. et al. (2000). Linalool modifies the nicotinic receptor-ion channel kinetics at the mouse neuromuscular junction *Pharmacological Research* 42 (2): 177–181.

136. Wang, D., Yuan, X., Liu, T. et al. (2012). Neuroprotective activity of lavender oil on transient focal cerebral ischemia in mice *Molecules* 17 (8): 9803–9817.

137. Ching, M. (1999). Contemporary therapy: aromatherapy in the management of acute pain? *Contemporary Nurse* 8 (4): 146–151.

138. Sasannejad, P., Saeedi, M., Shoeibi, A. et al. (2012). Lavender essential oil in the treatment of migraine headache: a placebo-controlled clinical trial *European Journal of Neurology* 67 (5): 288–291.

139. Hirokawa, K., Nishimoto, T., & Taniguchi, T. (2012). Effects of lavender aroma on sleep quality in healthy Japanese students *Perceptual & Motor Skills* 114 (1): 111–122.

140. Moeini, M., Khadibi, M., Bekhradi, R. et al. (2010). Effect of aromatherapy on the quality of sleep in ischemic heart disease patients hospitalized in intensive care units of heart hospitals of the Isfahan University of Medical Sciences. *Iranian Journal of Nursing and Midwifery Research* 15 (4): 234–239.

141. Chien, L. W., Cheng, S. L., & Liu, C. F. (2012). The effect of lavender aromatherapy on autonomic nervous system in midlife women with insomnia. *Evidence-Based Complementary and Alternative Medicine*, Article ID 740813, 8 pages.

142. Lewith, G. T., Godfrey, A. D., & Prescott, P. (2005). A single-blinded, randomized pilot study evaluating the aroma of Lavandula augustifolia as a treatment for mild insomnia. *Journal of Alternative and Complementary Medicine* 11 (4): 631– 637.

143. Kawakami, M., Aoki, S., Ohkubo, T. (1999). A study of "fragrance" on working environment characteristics in VDT work activities. *Int. J. Prod. Econ. 60–61*, 575–581.

144. Rho, K.H., Han, S. H., Kim, K. S., Lee, M.S. (2006). Effects of aromatherapy massage on anxiety and self-esteem in korean elderly women: A pilot study. *Int. J. Neurosci. 116*, 1447–1455.

145. Ogeturk, M., Kose, E., Sarsilmaz, M., Akpinar, B., Kus, I., Meydan, S. (2010). Effects of lemon essential oil aroma on the learning behaviors of rats. *Neurosciences* 15 (4): 292-293.

146. Komiya, M., Takeuchi, T., Harada, E. (2006). Lemon oil vapor causes an anti-stress effect via modulating the 5-HT and DA activities in mice. *Behavioural Brain Research* 172: 240-249.

147. Campêlo, L. M., et al. (2011). Antioxidant activity of *Citrus limon* essential oil in mouse hippocampus, *Pharmaceutical Biology* 49 (7): 709–715.

148. Abuhamdah, S., Chazot, P. L. (2008). Lemon Balm and Lavender herbal essential oils: old and new ways to treat emotional disorders? *Current Anaethesia & Critical Care* 19, 221-226.

149. Perry, N., & Perry, E. (2006). Aromatherapy in the Management of Psychiatric Disorders: Clinical and Neuropharmacological Perspectives. *CNS Drugs* 20 (4): 257-280.

150. Ballard, C., et al. (2002). Aromatherapy as a safe and effective treatment for the management of agitation in severe dementia: A double-blind, placebo-controlled trial with Melissa. *J. Clin. Psychiatry* 63: 553–558.

151. Afarineshe, K. M. R., et al. (2013). Antinociceptive Effect of Aqueous Extract of *Origanum vulgare* L. in male Rates: Possible Involvement of the GABAergic System. *Iran J Pharm Res.* 12 (2): 407-13.

152. Force, M., Sparks, W. S., Ronzio, R. A. (2000). Inhibition of enteric parasites by emulsified oil of oregano in vivo. *Phytother Res.* 14 (3): 213-214.

153. Barker, S., et al. (2003). Improved performance on clerical tasks associated with administration of peppermint odor. *Percept Mot Skills.* 97 (3 pt. 1): 1007-1010.

154. Kawakami, M., Aoki, S., Ohkubo, T. (1999). A study of "fragrance" on working environment characteristics in VDT work activities. *Int. J. Prod. Econ. 60–61*, 575–581.

Moss, M., Hewitt, S., Moss, L., Wesnes, K. (2008). Modulation of cognitive performance and mood by aromas of peppermint and ylang-ylang. *Int. J. Neurosci. 118*, 59–77.

155. Goel, N., Lau, R. P. (2006). Sleep changes vary by odor perception in young adults. *Biol. Psychol. 71*, 341–349.

156. Moss, M., Hewitt, S., Moss, L., Wesnes, K. (2008). Modulation of cognitive performance and mood by aromas of peppermint and ylang-ylang. *Int. J. Neurosci. 118*, 59–77.

157. Gobel, H., et al. (1994). Effect of peppermint and eucalyptus oil preparations on neurophysiological and experimental algesimetric headache parameters. *Cephalalgia.* 14 (3): 228-234.

Borhani Haghighi, A., et al. (2010). Cutaneous application of menthol 10% solution as an abortive treatment of migraine without aura: a randomised, double-blind, placebo-controlled, crossed-over study. *Int J Clin Pract.* 64 (4): 451-456.

158. Masago, R., Matsuda, T., Kikuchi, Y., Miyazaki, Y., Iwanaga, K., Harada, H., & Katsuura, T. (2000). Effects of inhalation of essential oils on EEG activity and sensory evaluation. *J. Physiol. Anthropol. 19*, 35–42.

159. Rho, K.H., Han, S. H., Kim, K. S., Lee, M.S. (2006). Effects of aromatherapy massage on anxiety and self-esteem in korean elderly women: A pilot study. *Int. J. Neurosci. 116*, 1447–1455.

160. Moss, M., Hewitt, S., Moss, L., Wesnes, K. (2008). Modulation of cognitive performance and mood by aromas of peppermint and ylang-ylang. *Int. J. Neurosci. 118*, 59–77.

161. Nyeem, M. A. B., Alam, M. A., Awal, M. A., Mostofa, M., Uddin, M., Islam, S. J. N., *et al.* (2006). CNS Depressant Effect of the Crude Ethanolic Extract of the Flowering Tops of *Rosa Damascena. Iran J Pharm Res* 5: 171-174.

162. Boskabady, M. H., Shafei, M. N., Saberi, Z., Amini, S. (2011). Pharmacological Effects of *Rosa Damascena. Iranian Journal of Basic Medical Sciences.* 14 (4): 295-307.

163. Rakhshandah, H., Hosseini, M., and Dolati, K. (2004). Hypnotic Effect of *Rosa damascena* in Mice. *Iranian Journal of Pharmaceutical Research.* 3: 181-185.

164. Awale, S., Tohda, C., Tezuka, Y., Miyazaki, M., and Kadota, S. (2011). Protective Effects of *Rosa damascena* and Its Active Constituent on $A\beta(25-35)$-Induced Neuritic Atrophy. *Evidence-Based Complementary and Alternative Medicine* 1-8.

165. Diego, M. A., Jones, N. A., Field, T., Hernandez-Reif, M., Schanberg, S., Kuhn, C., McAdam, V., Galamaga, R., & Galamaga, M. (1998). Aromatherapy positively affects mood, EEG patterns of alertness and math computations. *Int. J. Neurosci. 96*, 217–224.

166. Moss, M., Hewitt, S., Moss, L., Wesnes, K. (2008). Modulation of cognitive performance and mood by aromas of peppermint and ylang-ylang. *Int. J. Neurosci. 118*, 59–77.

167. Rho, K.H., Han, S. H., Kim, K. S., Lee, M.S. (2006). Effects of aromatherapy massage on anxiety and self-esteem in korean elderly women: A pilot study. *Int. J. Neurosci. 116*, 1447–1455.

168. Sayorwan, W., et al. (2013). Effects of inhaled rosemary oil on subjective feelings and activities of the nervous system. *Sci Pharm.* 81 (2): 531-42.

169. Morris, N., Birtwistle, S., Toms, M. (1995). Anxiety reduction by aromatherapy: Anxiolytic effects of inhalation of geranium and rosemary. *Int. J. Aromather. 7*, 33–39.

170. Machado, D. G., et al. (2013). Antidepressant-like effects of fractions, essential oils, carnosol and betulinic acid isolated from *Rosmarinus officials* L. 136 (2): 999-1005.

171. Perry, N. S. L., Bollen, C., Perry, E.K., et al. (2003). Salvia for dementia therapy: review of pharmacological activity and pilot tolerability clinical trial. *Pharmacol Biochem Behav* 75: 651-9

Perry, N. S., Houghton, P. J., Jenner, P., et al. (2002). *Salvia lavandulaefolia* essential oil inhibits cholinesterase in vivo. *Phytomedicine* 9 (1): 48-51.

Wake, G., Court, J., Pickering, A., et al. (2000). CNS acetylcholine receptor activity in European medicinal plants traditionally used to improve failing memory. *J Ethnopharmacol* 69: 105-14.

Perry, N.S., Houghton, P.J., Theobald, A., et al. (2000). In-vitro inhibition of human erythrocyte acetylcholinesterase by *Salvia lavandulaefolia* essential oil and constituent terpenes. *J Pharm Pharmacol* 52: 895-902.

172. Azmathulla, M., Bilal, S., Baidya, M., & Satish Kumar, B. N. (2010). Effect of *santalum album linn* on memory enhancing activity on mice. *Journal of Chemical and Pharmaceutical Sciences*. 3. 172-177.

173. Masago, R., Matsuda, T., Kikuchi, Y., Miyazaki, Y., Iwanaga, K., Harada, H., & Katsuura, T. (2000). Effects of inhalation of essential oils on EEG activity and sensory evaluation. *J. Physiol. Anthropol. 19*, 35–42.

174. Kawakami, M., Aoki, S., Ohkubo, T. (1999). A study of "fragrance" on working environment characteristics in VDT work activities. *Int. J. Prod. Econ. 60–61*, 575–581.

175. Satou, T., Miyagawa, M., Seimiya, H., Yamada, H., Hasegawa, T., Koike, K. (2014). Prolonged anxiolytic-like activity of sandalwood (*Santalum album* L.) oil in stress-loaded mice. *Flavour and Fragrance Journal*. 29 (1): 35-38.

176. Murphy, K., Kubin, Z. J., Shepherd, J. N., Ettinger, R. H. (2010). *Valeriana officialis* root extracts have potent anxiolytic effects in laboratory rats. *Phytomedicine*. 17(8-9): 674-678.

177. Maroo, N., Hazra, A., Das, T. (2013). Efficacy and safety of polyherbal sedative-hypnotic formulation NSF-3 in primary insomnia in comparison to zolpidem: a randomized controlled trial. *Indian J Pharmacol*. 45 (1): 34-9.

Modabbernia, A., Akhondzadeh, S. (2013). Saffron, passionflower, valerian and sage for mental health. *Psychiatr Clin North Am*. 36 (1): 85-91.

178. Saiyudthong, S., Pongmayteegul, S., Marsden, C. A., & Phansuwan-Pujito, P. (2015). Anxiety-like behaviour and c-fos expression in rats that inhaled vetiver essential oil. *Natural Product Research*, 29 (22), 2141-2144.

179. Velmurugan, C., Shajahan, S. K., Ashok Kumar, B. S., Kumar, S. V., Priyadharshini, R. A., Thomas, S. (2014). Memory and learning enhancing activity of different extracts of roots of *Vetiveria zizanioides*. *International Journal of Novel Trends in Pharmaceutical Sciences* 4 (6): 174-182.

180. Sagawara Y, et al. (2013). Relationship between mood change, odour, and its physiological effects in humans while inhaling the fragrances of essential oils as well as linalool and its enantiomers. *Molecules*. 18 (3): 3312-38.

181. Kawakami, M., Aoki, S., Ohkubo, T. (1999). A study of "fragrance" on working environment characteristics in VDT work activities. *Int. J. Prod. Econ. 60–61*, 575–581.

182. Hongratanaworakit, T., Buchbauer, G. (2006). Relaxing effect of ylang-ylang oil on humans after transdermal absorption. *Phytother. Res. 20*, 758–763.

183. Moss, M., Hewitt, S., Moss, L., Wesnes, K. (2008). Modulation of cognitive performance and mood by aromas of peppermint and ylang-ylang. *Int. J. Neurosci. 118*, 59–77.

184. Text used as reference material for chapter:

Phillips, A. C. (2003). *Introduction to Quantum Mechanics* (Sussex, England: John Wiley & Sons Ltd.)

Shlain, L. (1991). *Art & Physics: Parallel Visions in Space, Time, and Light* (New York, NY: HarperCollins).

185. Einstein, A. and Infeld, L. (1938). *The Evolution of Physics* (p. 31). (New York, NY: Simon and Schuster).

186. Schwartz, J. M. & Begley, S. (2002). *The Mind and the Brain: Neuroplasticity and the Power of Mental Force*. (New York, NY: Harper Collins).

187. Murphy, J., revised by McMahan, I. (2000). *The Power of Your Subconscious Mind* (p. 55). (United States: Reward Books).

188. For a full explanation, visit http://MindYourBrain.online/Downloads for a PDF.

189. Schwartz, J. M. & Begley, S. (2002). *The Mind and the Brain: Neuroplasticity and the Power of Mental Force.* (New York, NY: Harper Collins).

Spence, S. S. & Frith, C. (1999). *Towards a functional anatomy of volition. The volitional brain: towards a neuroscience of free will* (ed. B. Libet, A. Freeman & K. Sutherland), (pp. 11–29). (Thorverton, UK: Imprint Academic).

190. Schwartz, J. M., Stapp, H. P., Beauregard, M. (2005). Quantum physics in neuroscience and psychology: a neurophysical model of mind-brain interaction. *Phil. Trans. R. Soc. B.* 360: 1309-1327.

191. Ochsner, K. N., Bunge, S. A., Gross, J. J. & Gabrieli, J. D. E. (2002). Rethinking feelings: an fMRI study of the cognitive regulation of emotion. *J. Cogn. Neurosci.* 14, 1215–1229.

192. Oschman, J. L. (2000). Chapter 9: Vibrational Medicine. *Energy Medicine: The Scientific Basis* (pp. 121-137). (Edinburgh: Harcourt Publishers).

193. Lipton, B. H. (2008). *The Biology of Belief* (pp. 87-88). (Carlsbad, CA: Hay House).

194. Stewart, D., (2010). *The Chemistry of Essential Oils Made Simple* (p. 716). (Marble Hill, MO: Care Publications).

195. Brezinka, V. (2008). Treasure Hunt – a Serious Game to Support Psychotherapeutic Treatment of Children. *EHealth Beyond the Horizon – Get IT There* (*OS Press).*

196. Truman, K. K. (2003). *Feelings Buried Alive Never Die...* (pp. 281-282). (St. George, Utah: Olympus Distributing).

197. Pert, C. B. (1997). *Molecules of Emotion* (pp. 310-311). (New York: Scribner).

198. Manning, B. (2000). *Ruthless Trust: The Ragamuffin's Path To God* (pp. 128-130). (New York, NY: HarperCollins).

199. Burghardt, W. J. (1980). *Tell the Next Generation* (p. 41). (New York, NY: Paulist Press).

200. Manning, B. (2000). *Ruthless Trust: The Ragamuffin's Path To God* (pp. 131-132). (New York, NY: HarperCollins).

All graphics are original or have been licensed with the exception of:

Fig. 3.2: This work is a derivative of "Brain human sagittal section.svg" by Patrick J. Lynch, used under CC BY 2.0.

Fig. 3.7: This work is a derivative of "Chemical_synapse.jpg" by Vtvu, used under CC Attribution-Share Alike 3.0 Unported license.

Fig. 3.8: This work is a derivative of "Head olfactory nerve – olfactory bulb_en" by Patrick J Lynch, used under CC BY 2.5.

ARE YOU READY FOR PUR
ESSENTIAL OILS?

DISCOVER MORE

MINDYOURBRAIN.ONLINE/ESSENTIALOIL

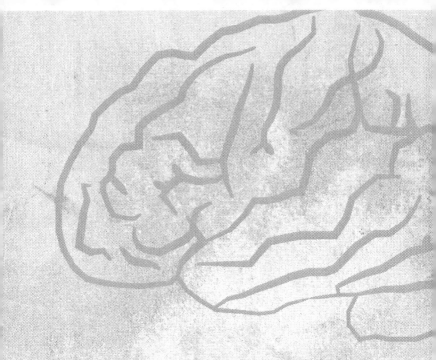

# EVER STOP MINDING YOUR BRAIN

## CONTINUE THE JOURNEY

### www.MindYourBrain.online